THE BULL

THE BULL

My Story

JOHN HAYES

with Tommy Conlon

SIMON &
SCHUSTER

London · New York · Sydney · Toronto · New Delhi

A CBS COMPANY

First published in Great Britain by Simon & Schuster UK Ltd, 2012
A CBS COMPANY

Copyright © 2012 by John Hayes

1 3 5 7 9 10 8 6 4 2

Simon & Schuster UK Ltd
1st Floor
222 Gray's Inn Road
London WC1X 8HB

www.simonandschuster.co.uk

Simon & Schuster Australia, Sydney
Simon & Schuster India, New Delhi

A CIP catalogue for this book is available from the British Library.

Hardback ISBN 978-1-47110-092-5
Trade Paperback ISBN 978-1-47111-428-1

Typeset by M Rules
Printed and bound by CPI Group (UK) Ltd, Croydon, CR0 4YY

For Fiona. And for Sally, Róisín and Bill.

Foreword

by Brian O'Driscoll

I usually stood beside John Hayes for the anthems. I can remember one of the first games we played after he retired, standing in the line-up and thinking it was weird that he wasn't there beside me.

It was part of the ritual. An Ireland game, the national anthems, and Hayes standing beside you with a big brawny arm across your shoulder. I mean, he was always there. I made my international debut in 1999, he made his in 2000. There were very few Test matches I played that he wasn't there.

I still can't get my head around the fact that he played 54 consecutive games in the Six Nations. To play five international matches in a seven, eight-week period, for eleven successive seasons? That's a remarkable feat in the modern game. The hits and bangs and knocks mean you're always going to miss games along the way. You're bound to. But he didn't. And as a prop forward he took all the punishment that was going. That sort of durability was phenomenal.

And during that time he was the cornerstone of our scrum. It's a massively important position, tight-head, and if he wasn't ever-present we might have struggled badly. Hayes's longevity doesn't just make for a great statistic; it was crucial to our stability as a team and to our successes in those years.

He'll probably be squirming in his seat reading all this praise. That was the other thing about him. I never played with anyone else who cared so little for plaudits or pats on the back. He was the ultimate team man. He'd get embarrassed if he was singled out for special attention. It's probably why he made very few media appearances over the years. He didn't like that aspect of modern sport. He loved playing the game, he enjoyed the company of his team mates and he liked winning. The other stuff, the trappings that went with it, didn't appeal to him at all.

Very few of us who are in that position can give up all the trappings of celebrity and fame. It'd be very hard to, anyway, even if you tried. But when you saw someone who was all about doing his job, and doing it well, and just living a decent, regular life after that, I think it helped to keep us all grounded.

And I'm sure it's one reason why people came to see him as a kind of folk hero. His personality never changed, no matter what he achieved or how popular he became. People saw that quality and responded to it. I think perhaps they saw him as representing them, the average person on the street. They were able to identify with him.

And it's why he was so popular among his team mates too. I was at home injured, watching on television when Hayes scored his one international try, against Scotland in 2005. I burst out laughing when he scored. I was just delighted for him. The whole team went over to congratulate him. You don't get that unless you're liked by everyone.

Now, Hayes wouldn't want me pretending he's a complete angel either. For starters, he could give as good as he got when the slagging started. He wasn't one bit shy or quiet when it came to the verbals. In fact he was very funny and fairly lethal too.

And in fairness, he didn't hold back on the pitch either. He was never into cheap shots or trash talking or any of that nonsense. But, put it this way, if you were lying on the wrong side of the ball he wouldn't think twice about getting you off it with the boot. I can recall a shoeing or two! But I think it was more, not for the laugh, exactly, but to have one over on you. So as he could slag you about it afterwards. He got a fair few shoeings himself in the line of duty too.

There's a photo of the two of us holding the Grand Slam trophy that day in the Millennium Stadium. And it stands out for me especially because Hayes is in it. Normally he'd be on the edge of the picture; he wouldn't want to be seen milking the moment in any way. But that day, I think the sheer joy of the occasion caught him off guard. I'm holding one side of the trophy, he's holding the other.

It's a serious rarity, a photo like that. I'm glad I have it. I'm glad that someone as honest and genuine got his moment in the limelight. John Hayes deserved it; he deserved the great career that he had; he deserved all the good things that came his way.

I wish him every happiness in his retirement.

Prologue

It was my last match for Munster, my last ever game of professional rugby. About two minutes in I got a perfect pass from Ian Keatley. A child would've caught it. But wouldn't you know it, I dropped the ball. I was cursing before it even hit the ground. The ref blew his whistle for a knock-on. All of a sudden I was annoyed and frustrated. But then I heard the crowd laughing. There were even a few cheers. Fellas were shouting good-humoured remarks at me. The whole place was roaring laughing. You normally didn't get this kind of reaction when you made a cock-up like that in Thomond Park. You'd hear the groans and the moans a mile away. But I suppose they were always going to be kind to me on the night that was in it. It was St Stephen's night, 2011. We were playing Connacht in a league game. I think there were over 15,000 people there that night. They could've been lots of other places the same night but a fair few of them turned up, I suppose, to see me off. It was a lovely gesture which meant a lot to me.

I didn't want to milk the occasion. I hadn't expected it to end like this. I wasn't even a member of the official Munster squad at the start of the season. My last IRFU contract was due to end on 31 October. It coincided with the end of the Rugby World Cup in New Zealand. If I'd travelled to New Zealand with the Ireland squad, my Munster career would already have been over the previous May. But I wasn't selected, I was asked to remain on standby.

So I rang the Munster coach Tony McGahan in August looking to train with them and keep my fitness up. He couldn't promise me any game time, but I was more than welcome to join them for training. Then BJ Botha got injured in a pre-season friendly and suddenly I was starting or substituting in a lot of matches through September and October. I figured I'd slip away quietly after the game against Aironi in Musgrave Park a few days before the 31 October deadline. But Tony then asked me to sign an extension until the end of December.

I had a lot of luck throughout my career and this was one last blessing I suppose. Because that was how I ended up getting my 100th cap in the Heineken Cup, against Northampton in November. That match will always be remembered for Ronan O'Gara's drop goal deep into injury time after forty-one phases of play. It was great to be part of another moment of incredible drama like that. There'd been a lot of them over the previous twelve and more years. I hope it wasn't just a blast from the past. I hope there'll be many more moments like it in the years to come. But for me it was a thrill to experience that kind of pressure and excitement one more time.

The contract extension was also why I ended up in Thomond Park the day after Christmas. It was the first time I could ever remember being totally relaxed the day of a game. Normally I was nervous, and I always wanted to be nervous. It was the sign that you were ready. But there wasn't a bother on me. Our eldest daughter Sally was five and a half. I told her this was going to be my last match, I wouldn't be playing any more games. 'Does this mean that you won't be going away anymore?' Yeah, I suppose it does.

I went in early, hours before kick-off, and sat in the stand. The stadium was empty. I just wanted to take it all in while the place was still quiet and peaceful. Come kick-off time the lads sent me out of the dressing room first and onto the field on my own. The crowd gave me a fantastic reception. I was delighted to get it and a bit awkward about it at the same time. I was hoping the rest of the players would follow me onto the field fairly lively.

Then the match started and Ian threw me that pass and I fumbled it. What could I do but laugh; everyone else was. The lads took care of the result. I was doing my bit but I wasn't stressed about it. In fact, I was loving every minute of it. Absolutely loving being out there one last time. I was tearing around the field like a young buck. At one stage Ian was lining up a penalty and the usual hush descended around the ground. Then this voice piped up from the crowd: 'Let the Bull take it!' I burst out laughing – again – and so did a few of the lads around me too.

They took me off with about twenty minutes still to play. At the final whistle my wife Fiona came down to the dugout with Sally and her baby sister Róisín. All the Connacht lads made a point of coming over and wishing me well. I went out into the middle of the field with the family and got another huge ovation. It was heartfelt and genuine. I wanted to thank them too for their magnificent support over the years.

After that it was down the tunnel and into the dressing room. I walked into another round of applause from all my teammates. They wouldn't let me go without saying a few words. A lot of young Munster players were in the dressing room that night. I just told them that it all passes too quickly. I told them to try to enjoy it because it'll be over before they know it. I thanked everyone, packed my bag and headed for the car park.

Not many players, I suppose, get to say their goodbyes on their own terms. Injuries dictate it a lot of the time, or their place is taken by a younger player and they just fade to the margins. I was very fortunate to be able to retire on my own terms. I was luckier still to get one last hurrah in the special ground that is Thomond Park. It was the cherry on top of a long career and a marvellous life experience. It was the perfect way to close the door and take my leave.

1

The game of rugby has given me so much. I can say with hand on heart that it changed my life.

But the very first thing it gave me was the fine set of cauli-flower ears I have to this day. I was eighteen going on nineteen, I was only a few weeks with Bruff RFC and suddenly it looked like I'd been in the wars all my life. But I was a GAA player from Cappamore. I knew nothing about the game. I knew that you passed the ball backwards rather than forward and that was about it.

I was tall and skinny: 6 ft 4 in and about 15½ stone. Bruff was a small club in rural Limerick and they were always stuck for num-bers. It's about sixteen miles from Cappamore. A neighbour of ours at home, John O'Dea, had been playing with them for years. That's his proper name but everyone calls him Jack Day. He'd mentioned it to me a few times in previous years about trying the rugby, but I wasn't really bothered one way or another. Then I met him at the Cappamore Agricultural Show in August '92 and he mentioned it again; I was kind of interested but still not sure about it.

A few weeks later, I happened to meet him on the road outside our house one evening. I was closing a set of gates and had the tractor parked on the road and he was passing in his car. It was a chance meeting but the timing was perfect. I'd never have gone into a completely new environment on my own. But he said he was going training that night and he'd be back down to collect me in half an hour. And that made my mind up for me. I didn't even have a pair of boots, but Jack had a spare pair that fitted. And over we went to Bruff rugby club that evening.

We trained that Tuesday night, again on the Thursday night and played Newcastle West in a pre-season friendly the following Sunday. This was with the first XV. There was a second team, but they decided to throw me in at the deep end. I wasn't to know it at the time, but getting thrown in at the deep end became a kind of pattern throughout my career.

The Bruff coach at the time was Noel Ryan, a former player with Shannon. He decided to try me in the back row that day in Newcastle West, number six. I didn't know the rules, even basics like the offside laws. I was making it up as I went along. If Newcastle West knew how raw I was, they'd have been running every back row move down my side of the scrum because I didn't have a clue about tackling. I didn't really have a clue what was going on. The game finished 0–0. You couldn't say it was a feast of running rugby.

But I do remember the lineouts. There was no lifting allowed at that stage, but I was jumping in the middle of the lineout and got my hands to a few throws. People who knew me only as a 20 stone prop forward might be surprised to know there was a time when I could get off the ground and was fairly mobile around the field.

What I remember most about that first game is that I loved every minute of it. I'll never forget the feeling of enjoying it so much. I think it was the contact, the physicality; I felt you could get stuck into fellas, you could flatten them and no one would pass any remarks. When you played hurling or Gaelic football, any bit of a shoulder and it was a free against you. Here you could get stuck in as hard as you wanted and it was all legal, more or less. There was a freedom about it.

I knew pretty much there and then that I'd found my game. It suited me. I didn't know if I suited it, but I was mad to learn. I was mad for more. And I can remember, having played my first game, feeling part of something. I was a lackadaisical GAA player, but straightaway I had a whole different attitude now: I wanted to train, I wanted to play, I wanted to be involved. I don't think I missed a training session for the rest of that season.

Within a week or so of that first match they decided to try me in the second row. It was a bit safer tactically from a defence and attack point of view, and I had the height. Anyway, I started to learn the ropes of second row scrummaging at training one night. You had to stick your head between the hips of the prop and the hooker. Jack was a prop and I was pushing behind him. I had two big floppy ears and they were ate off me that night. The abrasion was something fierce. I came home that night and I could feel the throbbing and the pulsing in them. I'd obviously burst a few blood vessels and the ears started to swell up. That was the start of the cauliflowers. If I'd known they were going to turn into the yokes I have now, I might have done something about it. But I didn't tape them up that first night and when the swelling went down, didn't bother, or didn't remember, to bring any tape the following nights. They'd swell up every night after another scrummaging session and within a few weeks they were mutilated for good. The lads had a great laugh about it. Some of them were there the guts of twenty years and hadn't done the damage I'd done in two weeks.

When I knew better I'd bring the tape in my kit bag, but I never got into the habit of using it because, until the last day of my career, I hated taping up my ears. I just hated the feeling of the thing around my head. My hearing was never affected – even if my wife Fiona reckons I have 'selective hearing' from time to time! Róisín used to find Daddy's lumpy lugs very amusing. When she was teething she used to gnaw on them for comfort, which meant they were good for something.

Bruff as a rugby club has come on in leaps and bounds during the twenty years since. The facilities there are brilliant now; the under-age structure is well-organised and playing numbers have multiplied. Nowadays they play in the second division of the All-Ireland senior league. Back then we were playing in the second tier of the Munster junior league, which was pretty much the basement of the game in the province. It'd be fair to say I started at the bottom.

There was also the Munster Junior Cup which was played off in the springtime and which had real prestige as a competition. But the bread-and-butter stuff was your weekly league game, and for me that first season was a bit of a voyage of discovery around the clubs of Munster. The team bus would strike off on a Sunday morning for places like Cobh, Clonakilty, Skibbereen, Tralee or Waterford. You had the Clare clubs, Kilrush and Ennis. In Tipperary it was Clonmel, Clanwilliam and Kilfeacle, and then you had some of the Limerick clubs like Richmond, Thomond and St Mary's.

I was a late starter. I was literally learning from match to match how to play the game, and in fairness it was a hard enough school. The rugby was rough and ready. It was basically the two forward packs going at it hammer and tongs. I was totally naïve; luckily for me, the rest of the Bruff pack was anything but. They were all in their thirties and some of them were pushing forty. The front row would be the pick of Timmy Quirke, Jack Day, Micheál Leahy and Liam Doherty; second row was myself and Ger Malone, whose son Peter is now in the Munster rugby academy; back row would've been Jed Moynihan, Mickey Cahill and Kynan McGregor from New Zealand. They were a bunch of hard old nuts and they knew what they were doing.

Looking back, I know that they protected me, but I didn't really know it at the time. Especially at lineouts. I was a bit of a sitting duck for opposing teams. The lineout was still a jungle in those days. There was no proper gap so they'd be crawling all over you, trying to put you off your jump; there'd be fists and elbows flying when the ball was coming in. And I was innocent enough to be concentrating on the ball, trying to win it clean. I got my share of digs but I'd say I'd have got a lot more if it weren't for the lads around me. Jed Moynihan would probably have been behind me in most lineouts and Jack Day in front of me. I reckon they spent a lot of their time clattering fellas who were about to clatter me, or just clearing bodies out of the way so I could get a clean jump. The referee would be doing his best, but there was no way he could police everything. The touch judges were usually from either team so they turned a blind eye whenever they needed to – which was plenty often. So if I'd been part of a young pack in those early days, I'd say I'd have got some harsh lessons. Even with our own lads, if they knew an opposing pack had two or three young fellas on it, the attitude would've been, 'Right, we're going to fuckin' clobber those young fellas'. No one complained either, on any team, as far as I can remember. The unspoken rule was that this was what you signed up for when you played Munster junior rugby. So everyone just got on with it and took their medicine if it came their way.

Those days out on a Sunday were great crack. The bus always left from Bruff and came back to Bruff that night. I didn't drink much, and I was fairly quiet by nature anyway, but the other lads would be drinking their cans and joking and slagging all the way home – especially if we'd won.

It took no length of time to feel comfortable in their company; in fact, they made me feel welcome from the first night I turned up. They knew I was a novice and kept encouraging me. There was plenty of help and advice, and no criticism. The big motivation I had was to try to learn this game, to improve and get better. Kynan McGregor was a great help. He had played rugby in New

Zealand and was a top player at our level. He had a lot of knowledge and was very generous in passing it on to me. Liam Doherty was the hooker and we spent a lot of time working on lineout situations, practising the throw and jump, trying to get our timing right. Gradually I started making a contribution to the team, one small increment at a time. If I did something good in a game, like a tackle or a carry or an offload, it might only be a moment, but each time it was a foothold for my confidence. I could hold onto it and use it to take another step forward. Then I scored a try one day, against the Cobh Pirates, and something like that gave me another spurt of self-belief.

But it wouldn't take long for the reality to hit home again. I was just so aware of how green I was. And actually this is something that can work for you: to know what you know, and know what you don't know. It was always in my mind, how little I knew, how far I had to go. But enjoying it made it easier to stick with it. Even when you were carrying Jack Day on your back in training, all nineteen stone of him, and your legs were buckling under the weight of him running up the hill. You were learning but you were having plenty of laughs along the way too.

In the spring of '93 our season was winding down, and Willie Conway one day suggested I should try out for the Shannon Under-20s. Willie had played with Bruff for years and was a big influence in its growth as a rugby club. He was still playing a bit, but was doing more coaching by then and reckoned a stint at playing in my own age-grade would bring me on. Bruff didn't have an Under-20 team at the time. Willie had played for Shannon in the late 1970s and had contacts there. Shannon was one of the big powerhouse clubs in Limerick rugby, and the thought of it left me a bit excited and a bit daunted. But Willie organised it and in I went one night. I made sure to arrive good and early, and the very first person I met was a lad my own age by the name of Anthony Foley. Axel, as we called him, had arrived early too, and we stood there chatting outside the clubhouse for twenty minutes before anyone else turned up.

It was actually coming to the tail-end of the season. I think I spent about five weeks there, but it was a fantastic finish to my first season. I played two or three games with their Under-20s and I noticed the difference straight away. It was faster and a lot more expansive; there wasn't half the pulling and dragging and general mullocking of junior rugby. We trained on the back pitch in Thomond Park and sometimes joined in with the Shannon seniors. I remember Mick Galwey walking onto the pitch one night. To me this was unbelievable. Only a month or so earlier I'd seen him on television scoring his famous winning try for Ireland against England at Lansdowne Road. And soon he'd be off playing with the British and Irish Lions in New Zealand.

Gaillimh was a star at the time. He didn't know me from Adam, but one night out of the blue he handed me a pair of boots and a tracksuit top. I can only imagine he took one look at the state of the gear I was wearing inside in Thomond Park and took pity on me. Or maybe it was that coming from another small club himself years earlier, Castleisland, he knew a raw recruit when he saw one. But I never forgot the gesture and I remember to this day what he gave me: a Munster team tracksuit top and a pair of the big, old-fashioned Adidas flanker boots. He gave them to me and told me to keep them. I did too: they're still to be found in a box some-where in my parents' house.

I got some buzz out of those few weeks with Shannon. It was a small glimpse of the big time and I couldn't wait to get stuck back into it with Bruff the following season. But first I spent the summer drawing silage. I got a job with a silage contractor from Hollyford, Con Morgan. They were long days and early starts, up at five or six in the morning and heading off in the back of the van to various farms around Hollyford, Rearcross, Cappamore and Doon. You'd have a tractor pulling a trailer and a harvester blowing the grass into the trailer. Once you were loaded you'd head for the silage pit in the farmyard, tip the load and head back out to the fields again. The pressure would be on to get the job done because the next farmer would be waiting his turn; there was no hanging around. But you were out in the open all day and it was very enjoyable.

The second season with Bruff I felt that bit faster and stronger, but the Shannon experience had opened my eyes. I'd seen the way the seniors trained, the effort and intensity they brought to every session, and I realised I was a long way from that level. I was still only a junior player and I knew it. Some of the veterans with Bruff were starting to wind down by now and we ended up having a fairly average season, in league and cup. I turned twenty in November '93, which meant I was eligible again for the Under-20s that season. I rejoined Shannon in about March '94 and went straight into the team. It was a seriously good team, they had been winning all round and about them, and many of them went on to play with the Shannon team that won the famous four-in-a-row of All-Ireland League (AIL) titles.

The faces in the Under-20s dressing room were pretty familiar to me now, but a new lad had also arrived while I was putting in my second season with Bruff. In fact, his face was familiar as well; it just took me a minute or two to place it on my first night back. 'That's yer man that plays for Clanwilliam,' said I to myself, 'I'm nearly sure it is.' I found out that night his name was Alan Quinlan. And apparently Quinny was thinking to himself the same night, 'That's yer man that plays with Bruff.' We often had a laugh about it afterwards. We clicked pretty quickly because both of us were in a similar situation, arriving into Shannon from two country clubs and trying to make an impression.

A few weeks later I was called into the first team squad. Niall O'Donovan was the coach. Niallo would have a big influence on my development as a player over many years, at Shannon,

Munster and Ireland, and this was the first step. But I couldn't believe I'd been called up. A couple of lads were out injured and suddenly I found myself on the bench for an AIL game against Cork Constitution. I didn't get off the bench that day, but a week later we were facing into one of the big traditional clashes of the season, Shannon vs. Garryowen at Thomond Park. It was my first taste of the legendary rivalry between two of the big city teams. The old Thomond Park was packed, and I was sitting on the bench trying to take it all in when next thing I was told to get ready. It was only about twenty minutes into the game, but one of our lads had to come off injured, and suddenly I was packing down with Gaillimh in the second row. I hadn't time to think about it, but when the first scrum happened I had time for one thought. I can remember saying to myself, 'Jesus, I'm going to have to push hard here because I don't want them thinking that Gaillimh's side of the scrum is stronger than mine.' So I pushed like a madman. I was very conscious that people might be saying the scrum got weaker when I came on.

Foley was in the back row, along with Kieran Maher and Eddie Halvey. It goes without saying that you come across a lot of tough nuts in this game. I'd say Kieran Maher was one of the hardest men I ever met. And there's a lot of fellas who played with or against him would probably back me up on that. Maher was tough out. Keith Wood was playing for Garryowen that day. They had Richard Costello in the second row, all 6 ft 7 in of him, and I was supposed to be jumping against him. But we won it anyway and I was on cloud nine afterwards: the noise, the atmosphere, the level of competition; it was all brilliant. Literally three weeks earlier, I'd been playing with Bruff in the second division of the Munster junior league. Now I was binding in the second row with Mick Galwey in front of a full house in Thomond Park. You couldn't ask for better.

I played a few more AIL games that season, in a Shannon team that just about managed to avoid relegation. I also played in the

Munster Senior Cup semi-final, where we were beaten by a good Sundays Well side.

I didn't mind; it was all new to me and I was thrilled with the progress I was making. Not that I had any goals written down, or long-term plans drawn up. I never sat down and made goals for myself in my life. I think some fellas, even when they're playing schoolboy rugby, are aiming to go all the way in the game, up to full international status. The way it worked for me was different. I played for a team and then someone asked me to play for a slightly better team. I played for that team and someone asked me to play for a better team again. I never forced it, or said anything, or went looking for the next move. For me it kind of happened organically, you could say, moving to the next level when it felt like the natural step to take. Of course, you had to be asked, you couldn't do it yourself. And if I was asked, I was happy to move on and move up. It turned out that every step up was usually well-timed, neither too early nor too late. It didn't mean I was leaving it all in the hands of others. I had my own inner drive, but it was less about the career and more about just getting better at the game.

I was training to be a welder at the time and was doing a course with FÁS in Limerick. Dad had a workshop in the yard at home where he did a lot of his own welding, and I was always tipping about in there with him. He had all his own equipment, angle grinders and drills and the like. He used to make his own gates and fix the machinery. Then I got a job with Willie Conway that summer. Willie had his own engineering works on the Dock Road in Limerick, near the cement factory. I was put making the iron crash barriers you'll see in factories, made from tubular piping. Other days I'd be out on sites with the experienced tradesmen, basically as a labourer, muling all the stuff in off the truck and muling it back onto it that evening. I was happy with my lot, learning the welding trade by day and the rugby trade by night. I suppose this could've been the life mapped out for me, and I wouldn't have complained if it was: welder, farmer, amateur rugby player.

Despite the highs with Shannon at the end of '93/94, I went back to Bruff for pre-season training later that year. Legally I could still play junior rugby even though I'd clocked up some senior games at this stage. I had dual status as a part-time senior and full-time junior. I didn't expect for a minute to stay with Shannon. I wasn't waiting on tenterhooks all that summer hoping they'd ask me to transfer. In fact, Brian Rigney joined them that summer, and he was going to be Gaillimh's new partner in the second row. Rigney was a massive man and already an Ireland international. And like a lot of people he was very helpful too when I got to train with him and play with him inside in Shannon. But those guys were in a different league to me, and I was content to go back to Bruff for another season. I knew my place was there still. It goes back to knowing what you know and knowing what you don't know. I knew I had an awful lot more to learn and that I'd learn it better with my home club. I'd still train with Shannon on the nights I wasn't training with Bruff, but I was looking at another season in the Munster junior league, and that was good enough for me.

The only other plan I had was to do a bit of travelling. The travel bug had been itching away for a while and Kynan McGregor had planted an idea with me. Kynan had spent two years with Bruff and would be going back home in the summer of '94. He was from Invercargill and had played for the Marist rugby club there. I asked him one evening about the chances of playing with them. Would I be good enough? Would it help me? Would I be able to find work there? Kynan was all for it; he said he'd follow it up. And talk about things falling into place. Kynan phoned home a few nights later only to be told that Vin Nally was in Ireland at that very time. Vin Nally has since turned out to be a great friend to me and my family. He was a big part of the Marist set-up and was actually going to be taking over as coach of their first team the following season. Vin's father was from Ireland and he had come over to trace his father's roots and home place. But this was the era before Skype and emails, and the only problem would be tracking Vin down. After a few more long-distance calls, Kynan discovered that Vin and his wife Jan were actually staying in a B&B in Limerick, of all places. I figured it was absolutely meant to happen after that. Kynan and I went into Limerick and had a long chat with Vin and Jan. He made no promises about getting a game for Marist; he hadn't a clue who I was. And it wasn't just about that for me anyway. I had a fair idea that the standard over there would be good and I wasn't sure if I'd be good enough. So I wasn't banking on that. I really just wanted to travel and see a bit of the world and fit in a bit of rugby too. But he said if I was interested in playing it'd be better to come out in the new year. They were in the middle of their season back home and there wouldn't be much point arriving when it was nearly over. From that day on I started making plans. I wanted to get as fit as I could to give myself a chance when I did arrive in New Zealand.

In February '95 I packed my bags and headed off. I knew that New Zealand was going to be a crash course in rugby for me. But I was twenty-one now and as fit and as strong as I'd ever been. So deep down I had a core of confidence that I could make a go of it. I felt good about the decision to leave; it felt like the right thing to do, at the right time. And looking back now, I don't think there were many decisions I made that were the wrong ones. This was definitely a right one. A few years earlier and I'd have been killed in New Zealand club rugby. A skinny white young fella – you'd have been murdered!

If I never played rugby I'm sure I'd have gone travelling anyway. I had uncles in Australia and more than likely I'd have spent at least a year working there and enjoying the lifestyle. But rugby was already opening doors for me. There was a job waiting for me in Invercargill and a rugby club that was going to take me in; I had contacts there and a place to stay. None of this would've happened if I hadn't taken that first step with Bruff rugby club. That's why I owe them so much, and that's what I think is so important about the small rural clubs. They have so much to offer young country lads who might be too intimidated to walk into a big city club if they don't have any family history or any connections there.

I might have plucked up the courage to go into Bruff some day on my own, but it might've been a few years later and, who knows, it might've been a few years too late. I definitely would never have gone into Shannon on my own, knowing absolutely no one there. It's not that they wouldn't have made me feel made welcome. They couldn't have been nicer to me. Shannon stalwarts like Niall O'Donovan or Brian O'Brien or Eddie Price would welcome any fella like he was one of their own. But it's hard to break the ice on your own. Jack Day broke the ice for me at Bruff, Willie Conway broke the ice for me at Shannon. And now Kynan McGregor had broken the ice for me at a club that was on the other side of the world.

2

It was snowing the day I left from Shannon Airport. Forty hours later I stepped off the plane into the New Zealand summer. I'd never been on a plane before. I had to change terminals at Heathrow, and it was a miracle I managed to do it without getting lost. I had no idea how long or how draining the flight was going to be: Shannon-Heathrow, Heathrow-Los Angeles, Los Angeles-Auckland, Auckland-Christchurch, Christchurch-Invercargill. I didn't know which end of me was up by the time I arrived.

Vin Nally and his son Brendan met me at the airport. Invercargill is a small city of about 50,000 people at the bottom of the South Island. It is the main town in the region known as Southland. All around it is farming country: flat, fertile land and millions of sheep grazing on it. Vin had fixed me up with a job in a tannery out the road from Invercargill. It was owned by a former international prop forward, Jack Hazlett, who'd played for the All Blacks in the 1960s. Sheep skins were processed and tanned there in their thousands. I was part of the maintenance crew working on the machines. Vin's other son Pat had a spare room in his house, and that was my accommodation sorted.

I had my first training session with Marist a few nights after I arrived. Kynan and Vin were there to make the introductions, but no one was thinking that they'd brought over a big star from Ireland. Naturally enough, they were wondering if I was any good, and waiting to see if I could prove myself. New Zealand is the powerhouse of rugby and I was anxious to prove that an Irish fella could cut it in their company. It helped that I arrived straight off a season back home. Shannon had really raised the standard of training after the previous year, so I was physically fit and match fit. I was ready to play straightaway.

The one thing I wasn't ready for was the weather. Invercargill had five or six rugby clubs, and Marist was one of the stronger ones. They had three senior teams. Our first outing would be a couple of pre-season friendlies against Alexandra up in Central Otago. The plan was to play two games using two Marist teams that were a mixture of firsts and seconds. I hit the ground running, played fairly well and scored a try. But they took me off halfway through the second half, for fear I'd end up with sunstroke. I was turning pinker by the minute. I had gone from snow back in Ireland to playing in thirty-five degrees heat about nine days later. Central Otago gets the hottest summers in New Zealand and it was scorching that afternoon. The other players were laughing at the state of me in the dressing room, but I'd scored a try on my debut and it was a good start, even if I wasn't right for days afterwards.

The Marist first team played in division one of the Southland league. It was club rugby, similar in standard to the AIL back home. AIL teams still had their international players turning out for them in those days, but it was different in New Zealand. The top players would be playing for their provincial sides and they didn't really turn out for their clubs anymore. Irish rugby went down that road too a few years later. The big difference for me was the weather. The pitches were hard and fast. A few weeks before I'd left Ireland Shannon played a match against Blackrock in Stradbrook. The pitch was a mud bath; you couldn't tell the difference between the team jerseys in the end. As usual, it was a matter of mullocking your way through it. The hard grounds in New Zealand made for faster rugby. But at that level the players weren't really any better than back home. We were all amateurs, training twice a week and playing a game at the weekend.

The teams were generally made up of local lads. A lot of them in Invercargill worked in the big meat processing plants. They were known as 'freezing workers'. The rugby scene would be fairly tight-knit at that level, and it didn't take long for word to get out among other clubs that Marist had an Irish lad playing for them in the second row. I got the impression early on that a few teams were trying to intimidate me to see how I'd react. I definitely got some fair shoeings in the first couple of weeks. I never got stamped or kicked or gouged or anything like that, but if you ended up lying on the wrong side of the ball, they were quick to take their chance. And the referee wouldn't have any sympathy for you either. I got the togs and jersey shredded a few times. Most of the time they'd be shoeing you purely to get the ball released. But there were a few fellas who did it just because they could. They'd take pleasure in it. They'd be looking at you while they were doing it. I didn't mind; most fellas who play the game don't mind getting a shoeing. There's even an element of pride about it, having the scars of battle on you. And if you had the chance to do the same to someone else, and you didn't take it, he'd be wondering if there was something wrong with you. I remember in the 2002 Heineken Cup final against Leicester, at one stage Martin Johnson tried to pull down a maul of ours. He ended up on the floor and I absolutely booted him while he was down there. And the fact that it was Johnson, their leader, the captain of England, gave me even more encouragement (not that I needed it). In those days, most forwards would have torn strips off him if they could. As soon as he got up, he just jogged back to his side of the field. Never said a word to me or anyone. He knew he'd tried to pull down a maul, and I did what he expected me to do. In fact, I think he'd have been disappointed if he hadn't been booted like he was. If he'd got away with it, he'd probably be thinking these fellas are a bunch of softies, they wouldn't even shoe you when you were on the ground.

It was the exact same mentality in New Zealand. I remember in the showers after one game, the Marist lads were slagging me because the train tracks I had went down my back and down the arse and legs too. In any rugby dressing room, it was a sign that you were doing what you were supposed to be doing, which was slowing the ball and generally getting stuck in at the breakdown. And if you hadn't a scratch on you after a match, then what were you doing for the last eighty minutes? There was a big aluminium smelter outside Invercargill; we wore aluminium studs on our boots. The lads would be roaring in the dressing room before a match, 'Don't fucking spare the studs today, aluminium's not scarce around here.'

My first season with Marist coincided with their seventy-fifth anniversary. Originally founded as a Catholic club, it had built up a proud heritage in the years since, and they wanted the seventy-fifth to be a good season. There was a great buzz around the club, and a lot of celebrations were planned. The players obviously wanted to do their bit on the field too. The big club competition in Southland is the Galbraith Shield, which is run on a league basis through the season, with the top four playing off in semi-finals and final. Our first game happened to be a local derby against Marist's biggest rivals, the Invercargill Blues. Normally you'd play every team in the division home and away, but this game was fixed for the main stadium in Southland, Rugby Park, which is also in Invercargill. It was a cracking match played in front of about 5,000 people, and I ended up scoring the winning try. They'd run away with it in the first half and led by twenty points at one stage. We stormed back into it in the second half and pulled level. Then they scored again, and right at the end I managed to get the try that won it. I can't say it was a mazy break from forty metres. It was just a pick-and-jam off the side of a ruck from about a metre out – I fell over the line. But it made for a great night that night and it meant I was really accepted as a Marist player from there on. The club had very much welcomed me from the moment I arrived, but at the same time I still had to earn their respect as a player and I think I did that day. I was never stuck for an invitation to dinner after that. Supporters really made an effort to make me feel welcome; I was invited into a lot of people's homes over the next two years.

The night of the Blues game there was a party back in the clubhouse, but I wasn't drinking. I didn't drink at all that first season. It was a decision I made before I went to New Zealand. I felt I had a lot to prove, so I wanted to be in the best possible shape. I wanted to give myself every chance of making the Marist first team and staying in it. Even though I was never a big drinker, I did enjoy a few pints, but that season I abstained completely. My new teammates were a bit taken aback the first time we went for a drink and I ordered a mineral. They couldn't understand a rugby player not having a beer, even more so an Irish rugby player not having a beer. But in fairness it wasn't hard staying on the dry because Invercargill wasn't a party town anyway. It's a very nice sort of rural town with low buildings and huge wide streets. You'd have four lanes of traffic on either side with a car parking space in the middle and broad footpaths too. So if you saw someone you knew on the other side of the street you'd have a hard job trying to catch their attention. The South Island in general is sparsely populated; there's loads of space, and everything is spread out far and wide. People are more into the outdoor life, and there just isn't the pub culture that we have in Ireland. And that suited me grand. It was a relaxed, easygoing sort of place, and I liked living there from the start.

My first year there was the first year I started putting on a few kilos. And it obviously wasn't the booze that was doing it. It was just happening to me naturally as I got older, I suppose. Brendan Nally played number eight on our team and he used to do some weight training, so I started going along with him to the gym. But I didn't do it consistently; you didn't have the sort of concentrated weight training programmes that are part and parcel of the game today. I was 100 kilos when I arrived and within three or four months I was up to 105. I was still light for my height, and I was flying fit, so I was getting around the field fairly lively as a second row.

At the end of the season I got selected for the Southland Colts, the regional Under-21 team. I was twenty-one going on twenty-two, but apparently I was still underage. Mind you, no one checked my passport. They asked me what age I was, I told them I was twenty-one, and that was good enough for them. It was my first taste of representative rugby and getting selected gave me a nice boost of confidence. I wasn't a native of the area, I'd been in the country for only about seven months, so it must've meant that I'd had a decent season. We played the provincial sides Canterbury and Otago. We made a weekend out of the game against Canterbury in Christchurch. We had no choice; the bus trip alone took seven or eight hours each way. The Southland seniors were also playing Canterbury seniors the same weekend. We played our game in a club ground on the Friday and then went to Lancaster Park on the Saturday to watch the senior game. It was a brilliant weekend. We then played Otago home and away, and that was more or less the end of a season that had turned out far better than I'd ever expected. I'd gone out to New Zealand pretty much a stranger and by the end of it felt right at home, on the pitch and off.

I played about twenty-five games in all. I was lucky with injuries, as I was throughout my career, so I didn't miss any games. Halfway through the season Marist presented me with a club blazer. They had introduced the idea at the start of that season as part of the anniversary celebrations. Once you played ten games you'd be presented with the award. The club had organised a gala night for its seventy-fifth birthday with a big marquee for all the guests, including loads of past and present players. As it happened, I was the only player who had played all ten games at that stage, and in truth I felt a bit uncomfortable going up to put on the blazer with teammates looking on who'd been there all their lives. But it was a lovely gesture, and it's another reason why I have friends at Marist, Invercargill, to this day.

The season finished in late September and I was glad of the break when it came. Between Ireland and New Zealand I'd played pretty much two seasons of rugby back-to-back and I needed to recharge the batteries. That Christmas I went up to Australia to meet the extended family. Four of my father's brothers, and a sister, had emigrated decades earlier and ended up in Melbourne and Sydney. I had cousins that I'd never met before, and it was nice to get to know them at last. I ate well and I drank well. With the rugby season over, I started drinking a few pints again, and kept going when I got to Sydney and Melbourne. Back to Invercargill then for the new year, back to the tannery, and back to Marist for the new pre-season.

Most of my clothes were wearing tight by then; the shirts were under pressure. I knew I was getting heavier. But I still got a land when I got up on the scales and saw I was nearly 120 kilos. In old money, that's the guts of 19 stone. I'd put on 3 stone in twelve months. I went running with Brendan in January before the pre-season started and reckoned I'd lose most of the weight I'd gained. As it turned out, I never lost any of it again, ever. And it was around this time, early in 1996, that the idea of putting me in the front row was floated.

Myself and Pat were over in Vin's house one night. Vin said he'd been talking to Jack Hazlett. Jack wasn't involved with the club, but he'd seen me playing and reckoned, apparently, that I was looking more like a prop forward than a second row at this stage. And having played prop for the All Blacks, he knew what he was talking about, so Vin took it on board. The other big factor was that lifting in the lineout was made legitimate in '96. It had been creeping in for years before that, fellas sneakily lifting the catcher, so they changed the rule, and now you could throw them up as high as you liked. And Vin was more or less saying to me that it wasn't going to be easy for our lads trying to lift a fella who weighed 120 kilos! The other issue for me was that at 6 ft 4 in I was starting to look a bit short for a second row player. You had monsters who were 6 ft 6 in and 6 ft 7 in coming into the game more and more, and it'd be getting harder to compete in the air. At the same time, I wasn't cut out for the back row either; I didn't have the pace or the instincts to play that position. 'So,' said Vin after all this, 'what would you think about a move to the front row?' I told him I didn't think a lot of it. My first reaction was no way. I wouldn't have a clue how to play it, and I'd get destroyed if I even tried.

I continued on in the second row for a few weeks. But Vin had planted the idea in my head. Then one night in training Doc Cournane had a chat with me. He and Vin had been talking about it too. Doc was our scrum coach and head coach, himself a former Marist player. He brought it up again, and I was more open to it this time. I said I'd try it so. And that was the first night I started learning about the front row trade. And I remember the first thing Doc told me about it. He said scrums would knock the wind out of me and that I'd struggle to get around the field after them. Second rows had tried it before, but you were using a different body position in the front row and not everyone was able to adapt. It would take a lot of getting used to. He asked me which side would I prefer but I had no idea. So he said I'd probably be better off starting at loose-head, it'd be a bit easier than the other side. The scrummaging machine was there, and Doc got me to crouch and bend a few times, explaining the body position I'd need to learn. I was starting to get curious about it now, wanting to find out a bit more. The next few training sessions I'd stay on and practise on the machine, with a hooker and prop and a few forwards pushing from behind. But it was just bits and pieces really. I was still playing second row in the games, and I was in no hurry to play anywhere else either.

But a few weeks later again someone got injured, and Vin told me I'd be playing loose-head the following Sunday. The game was against Woodlands; their tight-head was a lad named Aaron Dempsey. He wasn't much older than me, but he was good, strong and a lot more experienced than I was. And he absolutely mangled me. He was grinding away with his neck and his head, and I'd say he must've felt like he was pushing against a rag doll. I didn't know what he was doing, I had no control against him at all. He was cutting inside of me. He was splitting us right down the middle, me and our hooker, so I was actually getting left outside the scrum. I was supposed to put enough pressure on him to stop him from tunnelling in there. I was supposed to keep him straight, try and get in under him with my head and put the pressure on his shoulder and chest. But I couldn't keep him out because I didn't know how, and the muscles in my neck weren't strong enough anyway. I was gone out, he was gone in, so now they had a three-on-two in the front row when it should have been a three-on-three. And that has a domino effect on the rest of the scrum.

That was the night my real education in the front row began. But I'd say there were easier ways to learn. I was thrown in at the deep end that night and nearly sank without trace. And Doc Cournane was right about another thing too. The difference between front row and second row was night and day. There was no comparison. After every scrum I'd be panting for a couple of minutes, trying to get my wind back. I wasn't able to keep up with the play. It was just taking so much out of me I couldn't do anything else. It was one of the most horrible games I ever played in in my life. In fact, I could nearly say I hated that match, because I couldn't do anything right. And the irony is that there weren't that many scrums in the whole eighty minutes anyway. But a few more of them and they'd have been sending in the oxygen tank.

They put me back in the second row anyway for a finish. I staggered off the field with my chin on my chest because I literally wasn't able to lift my head. The muscles in the back of my neck were killing me. I can remember being back in the bar afterwards talking to people, but I wasn't able to look at them. I was looking down at the floor because the neck muscles weren't able to support my head. They were stretched like weak elastic. And I actually think that Aaron had even shown a bit of mercy to me in the scrums. I'd say he could've drilled me even worse if he'd wanted to. I happened to know him a little bit because his brother Mark was living across the road from where I was staying. And the funny thing about it is that nine years later I ended up meeting him again in another front row. Aaron was playing for Southland and I was playing for the British and Irish Lions on the 2005 tour of New Zealand. We weren't in direct opposition, because I'd long since moved over to the tight-head side. But we swapped jerseys after that game and had a bit of a reunion. A good player and a very nice fella who I'm pretty sure eased off on me that day in '96.

The one good thing, the only good thing, to come out of that experience was that it didn't spook me. I never ended up in a position where I thought my neck was going to get injured. I never got frightened at any stage. And that was important, obviously, because there was no way you'd have a future in that position if you felt any fear for your own safety. It didn't cross my mind that night. It never really crossed my mind in all the years I played there. I might've been lucky. There were other front row players who had close shaves, just a split second in a scrum when they felt vulnerable and got a fright. But that never happened to me. Mind you, there was a scary moment later that season. A scrum collapsed and our hooker, Steve Fotheringham, got a neck injury. I was playing second row that day. Fozzy broke a bone in his neck and had to be taken away in an ambulance. He was in traction in the hospital for weeks. Thankfully, he wasn't paralysed or anything like that, but I don't think he ever played again.

I spent the rest of the season alternating in games between second row and prop forward. They were picking and choosing when to put me in the front row, depending on the opposition and the players we had available. But I was working on this new position the whole time now. I was on the scrummaging machine at every session. I was basically starting from scratch again. This was my fifth season in rugby, and it bothered me a bit that I still hadn't settled in one position. It felt as if I was always having to start learning something new all over again. But at the same time it wasn't a chore or a hassle. In fact, I had a whole new focus. When I moved to New Zealand I had no notion of ever becoming a prop forward, but it was starting to happen and a lot of people seemed to be thinking that it was the natural place for me. I think they spotted more potential for me in that position than I ever did. And the more people said it, the more I thought about it.

Still, I was very surprised when Vin said to me one night that if I learned the position properly I could one day play for Ireland. And he was sober when he said it. But Vin Nally was the first person who ever said I could play for Ireland. And when you were hearing words of encouragement like that, it couldn't but spur you on.

And it did spur me on. The team wasn't playing as well this season, but on a personal level I had set myself a new goal. Any time I played prop forward I had a game within the game; I wanted to be able to break even with my opposite number; I wanted to scrummage a bit better than I had the previous game.

I never got another doing like the one I got that first night against Aaron but, Jesus, I found it a tough slog. Years ago someone asked me how I learned to play prop forward. 'The fuckin' hard way,' I replied. Everyone I came up against had played the position for years. They were toughened and seasoned. They'd be grinding away at you and my neck and shoulders would be killing me. Coming out from the pressure of a scrum, I'd be struggling to run. I found that the pressure just sapped me. Basically, in a scrum the two opposing forces are meeting in the front row. All that pressure is coming through your neck and chest and back. There's the second row and the back row behind you, and eight men on the other side driving into you. And it's all coming to a head in the front rows. If you've been doing it from underage, your body should be fairly well adapted to it. But it took me a long time to get used to it. If you had a quick scrum, it wasn't too bad. But if the ball got held up in there for seven or eight seconds, I'd be blowing a gasket. And if you had two or three resets, it was just totally knocking the shit out of me. I was way out of my comfort zone; it was a hard season to put down.

But I was still loving the game and enjoying the life in Invercargill. In fact, I was enjoying it all so much I gave serious consideration in that second year to applying for residency. I'd come out on a one-year visa and had it renewed for another year. But all this time I'd been getting calls from Ireland. Shannon were keeping in touch. The phone would ring at two o'clock in the morning and it'd be Brian O'Brien on the line. 'Hello?' 'How's it going? What time is it there?' 'It's two in the morning, Briano.' 'Oh fuck it, sorry, sorry.' He was never sorry enough not to do it the next time. Briano rang me one night, it must've been about April '96, wondering if I could join Shannon on their summer tour of Canada. They wanted me to fly from New Zealand and hook up with them in Canada. I was in the middle of the season with Marist and there was no way I could drop everything and head off. But it was good to know they hadn't forgotten me. Every so often I'd get a call from Brian or Niallo asking me how I was doing and wondering if I was thinking about coming home. I wasn't really, but Shannon had won two AILs back-to-back by the summer of '96 and the club was on a high. Brian Rigney was leaving then too, and they were letting me know there was a vacancy there. I was still reluctant to leave Invercargill. I'd made a lot of friends, played a lot of good rugby and was happy out. At the same time I had some unfinished business with Shannon. I'd only been a bit-part player in the first team when I left two years earlier. They were a serious outfit now, they were the best team in the country, and a voice in my head was telling me I should go back and stake a claim.

By September, the season with Marist was nearly over, and I was still humming and hawing about what to do. I was finding it hard, the thoughts of leaving. But the season back in Ireland was already up and running, and in the end I just bit the bullet. In October I booked a flight and packed my bags. Well, one bag anyway. I had nothing to sell up; it was just a case of saying my goodbyes, and before I knew it I was home.

3

I was about a month back in Ireland when Shannon had a Munster league game against Richmond at their place, Canal Bank. We were down numbers, players were injured, and the pack would have to be reshuffled. I was still very much a part-time prop forward. Niall O'Donovan had put me straight into the first team when I got back from New Zealand, but it was in the second row. We were missing a tight-head prop this day but with my limited front row experience they decided to keep me at loose-head, which meant that our regular loose-head, Donal 'Yogi' Costello, would have to move over to the other side. About twenty minutes into it, Yogi asked me would I switch. He wasn't enjoying it at all; he wanted to get back to his regular position. So without thinking about it too much, without thinking about it at all, I found myself playing tight-head prop for the first time in my career.

And as soon as I switched it clicked. I liked it straightaway. It felt natural; I felt comfortable. I was still trying to get used to playing loose-head after seven or eight months, but the first scrum at tight-head I felt at home. I didn't really know why I couldn't settle at loose-head until I moved to the other side. It was because at loose-head I used to feel half in and half out of the scrum. Your left side would be on the outside, so you weren't using the left side of your body as much; your neck and head had to do most of the work. You were always operating sort of sideways, trying to angle your way in. But at tight-head the whole lot of you is in; you're jammed in there between their hooker and prop; your two shoulders are in, your head is in. I found I could use my shoulders and my chest more to exert the pressure. I preferred being in the thick of it like that.

A lot of people will tell you that tight-head is physically harder to play, and I'd probably agree with that. You are under more pressure in there. But the pressure is coming at you more square on, and for some reason that suited me. I actually found it easier than playing loose-head. I don't know why one position clicks with one player and the other position clicks with another. Some fellas can play both sides and they are very valuable players to have in a squad. But I knew immediately that day which I preferred. I just found it way more enjoyable. I finished out that match feeling way better about myself. That night I more or less decided that if I was going to continue with this propping business, it'd be tight-head I'd be doing.

But that didn't mean I was ready to step up to the front row in Shannon's first team. They were the All-Ireland League champions, and the AIL was a very tough, competitive environment. Niallo had a squad to manage and games to win and a title to defend. And here was a player turning twenty-three years of age who'd never played in the front row until he was twenty-two. And who'd never played tight-head until that day in Canal Bank. So he could've told me that it was too risky to try me in the firsts, that I'd have to go off and learn my trade with the seconds or thirds. My situation was very unusual, and I'm sure there were people telling him he was wasting his time with me; that I was too old to learn and hadn't a hope of making it. But Niallo took a chance on me, and I'm very grateful that he did. He kept me in the first team, and I started most games at lock forward. But with twenty minutes or so to go he'd make a tactical substitution, bringing on another lock, or maybe a back row, and moving me to tight-head. And that's how I learned the position that season: incrementally, against quality opponents in competitive match environments. Niallo didn't throw me in for eighty minutes and tell me to sink or swim. He rationed out my minutes in the front row, and it gave me a chance to bed down in the position over the course of the season. Of course I was learning loads at training too. Shannon's sessions usually had a hard edge, with lots of fellas fighting for their places, including the prop forwards. I was a latecomer and no one was going to hand it over easy.

It was important to stay injury-free that season as well. If I'd hurt my back or neck or shoulder, people would've been saying my body wasn't able for the front row, that I was too long in the back or physically not suited and I'd be better off in the second row. But I kept playing there and kept learning a little bit more with every week that passed. And I wasn't getting screwed either; I was holding my own against most opponents and gradually I started to have a few good games too. I was getting used to the aerobic demands of it as well; I wasn't burning oil going round the pitch after a couple of scrums. By the end of the season I was starting games at tight-head.

We had some great trips on the road in those days, especially when we headed north to play the likes of Dungannon, Ballymena and Instonians. Those were the dying days of the amateur era and fellas still drank like amateurs, which isn't to say they were amateurs when it came to drinking. It's just there was no talk of rehydration and recovery sessions in swimming pools and the like. Strictly speaking, the amateur era had been over since the 1995 Rugby World Cup. There was some talk of money in the dressing room, but not a lot. Various players had part-time or full-time deals, and the likes of Foley would get a slagging on the bus home from somewhere because he could have a lie-in Monday morning while the rest of us had to do a day's work. But I wasn't tuned into the financial side of it at all, because it hadn't even crossed my mind that I might be able to make a living from the game. I had got a welding job with a company in Sixmilebridge, Shannon Precision Engineering, making brackets for fridges, refrigerated trucks and cold storage units. It fitted in well with the rugby; I was able to combine it with the team training schedule and get time off when I needed.

Shannon won their third AIL title in a row that '96/97 season, and I was delighted to win my first. Near the end of that season a letter was sent out to a large group of players to meet the new Munster coach, John Bevan. They were casting the net far and wide, and I was included in the round-up. There must've been forty to fifty players in Thomond Park that day. Bevan had played for Wales and the Lions. This was a getting-to-know-you meeting, but we didn't get to know him very well because that was the last we saw of him. But that was my first contact with the Munster senior squad. I was on the fringe of the fringes, but I was there, and it was a sign of progress. Then, in early June, it was announced that Andy Leslie, the former All Black, had been appointed Munster's director of rugby. And that didn't work out either. So for a finish they put together a coaching ticket of Niall O'Donovan and Declan Kidney, a teacher who'd coached one of the top schools teams in Munster, Presentation Brothers Cork. Jerry Holland would be the manager. We got more letters to come in one Sunday and meet the new coaching team in the University of Limerick. I'd never met Kidney before; in fact, I don't think I'd even heard of him. But he introduced himself to us in a way that we would discover later was typical of the man – kind of modest and humble. He said something like: 'I don't have a Welsh accent, I don't have a New Zealand accent, I only have an ordinary old Cork accent. But we'll have to get used to each other and see how we get along.'

In August '97 we had a short pre-season tour in Scotland. I was surprised and excited to be selected. A tour! It didn't matter that it was only going to be for a week. It turned into a week of firsts for me: I'd never been away on rugby camp before, I'd never trained full time before, and I played my first game for Munster. That was against Edinburgh in the mid-week match. I had taken the week off work and being a full-time sportsman felt like a life of luxury to me, even though we were training three times a day. It wouldn't have bothered me if we were training all day every day, but three times a day was probably a bit on the enthusiastic side. We'd have a weights session in the hotel gym first thing in the morning, but most of us were just basically arsing around there, because we didn't know how to do weights properly. It was back to bed for an hour or two after breakfast, then a pitch session at lunch time, followed by another sleep, followed by another squad session that afternoon. Loads of sleep, loads of grub, and your days spent playing sport: as far as I was concerned it was the life of Riley. It was a brilliant week and I got to know a few of the lads who would be around for years to come, including David Wallace, who I roomed with for the week.

Things were looking up, and they got even better when Munster offered me a part-time contract. The established internationals were on full-time contracts, but there was a slew of lads on part-time deals. There wasn't much ceremony in signing it. Jerry Holland called me over one night at training in UL and told me there was a contract there if I wanted one. The terms and conditions were all laid down on an official form, but I just turned it over to see what the bottom line was: £7,500. There was no such thing as playing hardball over the figures. I know the hardball I'd have got from Holland – a boot up the hole and a 'Take it or leave it' from him in his big, deep voice.

I was contracted purely as a prop forward, so all my training with Munster from there to the end of the season was in the front row. But I was still well down the pecking order. Peter Clohessy had rejoined after his stint down in Australia with the Queensland Reds. Claw was a seasoned Ireland international and the automatic choice at tight-head for Munster. I played for Munster As in the interprovincials and took my place in the queue for the senior side. But I was learning loads in training from the likes of Claw and Ian Murray, who was Munster's loose-head at the time. This was still the era before serious video analysis; there was no specialist scrum-coach filming your scrums at training sessions and giving you technical feedback; you weren't getting game footage to review either. But Claw was very good at saying what needed to be done and I was picking up information all the time. Claw was also very good at not getting injured, and Munster usually had a prop on the bench who could do both sides of the scrum if needed. So I never made the bench and basically didn't get a look-in during the 1997 Heineken Cup campaign. It was over by the middle of October anyway. These days we'd only be getting going in October, but it was in its infancy as a tournament back then – and Munster still had a long way to go too.

It was back to the new '97/98 AIL campaign after that. This was a golden era for Shannon, and it was crowned when they completed the four-in-a-row of All-Ireland League titles that season. It was an outstanding achievement for the club, and that team deserves its place in the history books. I was there for only the last two years but felt privileged to be part of it. The AIL that season had introduced semi-finals for the top four teams, with a winner-takes-all final. We beat Garryowen in what was a tense final at Lansdowne Road. Andrew Thompson was a points machine for Shannon for many years and landed the kicks that got us over the line that day. It was a special day out for the family because my younger brother Tom played for the Bruff Under-18s team in their AIL final in the curtain-raiser at Lansdowne. Pat Murray had retired from playing with Shannon and had taken over from Niallo as coach at the start of '97/98, although Niallo was still involved. Between them they continued managing my game time, picking and choosing their moments to put me in the front row. I was playing better there all the time, but I still didn't have the experience clocked up to put in a full season at tight-head.

I was in Mary Powell's physiotherapy clinic a few days after the Garryowen game, waiting for treatment on an injured elbow. Mary was the Shannon physio at the time. Next thing, Anthony Foley walked in, and before I could even say hello he blurted out the news. 'Congrats,' he said. 'On what?' said I. 'You're on the tour for South Africa. Did you not hear?' I hadn't heard. I was completely taken aback. It couldn't be true. I had played one game for Munster at this stage, a pre-season friendly, and that was it. And now I'd been called up to the international squad for a tour of South Africa? No, it couldn't be true. Axel was taking the mick with me. 'Fuck off,' were my first words back to him. But he swore it was true. He'd just seen it on Teletext. He had been recalled to the Ireland squad and I'd been picked as one of the prop forwards. This was still the time before emails and text messaging. I didn't have a mobile phone. There'd been no mention of me in newspapers or radio or anywhere as a possible contender. So I rang home from Mary's office and asked my mother to turn on the television and check the Teletext. She told me J Hayes was there in the list all right, but I still wouldn't believe it; I was wondering was it another J Hayes that played in Dublin or Belfast or somewhere. I went into training with Shannon that evening and everyone was coming up, shaking my hand and congratulating me. I got home that night and the Bruff lads were ringing the house with their congratulations too. It only started to sink in at that point. I had been selected completely and totally out of the blue. A few days later the official letter arrived from the IRFU.

Looking back on it, that was a life-changing week for me, because in the space of a couple of days I was also offered a full-time contract with Munster. Declan Kidney rang me with the news. Deccie was taking a grip on things and planning ahead for the new season. The whole Munster thing was moving up a gear

now. A lot more players were being offered full-time contracts. I
didn't think twice. I was twenty-four and this was my chance. I'd
been on a part-time contract; I'd got a taste of the professional life
the previous August in Scotland and loved it. Suddenly it was all
happening for me, without ever having planned any of it.

But before any of that kicked in there was still the Munster
Senior Cup to negotiate with Shannon. We reached the final and
in May '98, three weeks after winning the All-Ireland League,
clinched the double. We just about got over the line against
Young Munster in front of a packed house in Thomond Park.
The match was a cliffhanger played in glorious sunshine; it was a
great way to bring the curtain down on the domestic season. A
few days later I joined up with the international squad in the
Glenview Hotel in Wicklow. I can remember sitting in my room
that evening, sorting through the pile of Ireland playing gear I'd
been handed for the tour. I was like a child at Christmas, pulling
out all these jerseys and polo shirts and track suits and togs and
socks from this big kit bag. And all of it in the green and white of
Ireland; I got a huge buzz out of it. And it's still a big thing for
any young fella called into his first national squad, opening up all
this gear and looking at it and trying it on. It's one of those little
moments that every player lucky enough to get capped for his
country enjoys.

Warren Gatland had taken over as Ireland coach in February
'98. It was a new era, and he'd picked an extended thirty-four-man
squad for South Africa to start the rebuilding process. I was one of
seven uncapped players selected, along with Trevor Brennan,
Bernard Jackman, Justin Fitzpatrick, Dion O'Cuinneagain, David
Wallace and Derek Hegarty. Paddy Johns was captain, Donal
Lenihan was tour manager and Philip Danaher was assistant
coach. Gatty was a very quiet, low-key sort of man. We had our
first full squad meeting in Lansdowne Road. Gatty didn't wear us
out with talk that day, or any other day, which suited me fine.

We flew out to Cape Town a few days later and on 30 May

played our first match of the tour, against Boland in Wellington. I was the only prop forward named on the bench and just a minute before half-time Reggie Corrigan went down injured. Next thing I was running onto the field; Reggie had done his back and couldn't continue. Next thing I was running off the field and into the dressing room for half-time. Now, Reggie was playing loose-head and it hadn't dawned on me what would happen if he got injured. I'd played all season at tight-head and had been training with Ireland as a tight-head. It was only when I was on the field that I realised I'd be at loose-head in the scrum. I wasn't mad about the idea. I figured it'd be far better all round if Claw moved over and I took over at tight-head. I sat down beside him in the dressing room at half-time and told him he'd have to go over. Claw looked at me. 'Why can't you fuckin' do it?' said he. ''Cos I've no fuckin' experience and you have,' said I. 'Ah, you'll be grand.' 'I fuckin' won't be grand.' And there we were having an argument under our breath while Gatty was giving the half-time talk. Anyway, Claw, in fairness to him, compromised in the end. Which wouldn't always be like him; but I was glad he did that day. We won the match, the tour was up and running, and I had made my first appearance in a green jersey. And some jersey it was too, compared to the modern-day skintight jobs. This thing was massive, the size of a dinner table; it went down to your knees. It had the real old-fashioned, heavy, thick cloth and I was sweating so much in it that day, and taking on so much water, I'd say it was several kilos heavier by the time I took it off. It's buried somewhere in a press at home and hasn't seen the light of day since.

Results-wise, it was a fairly woeful tour. I was on the bench for the midweek games and got some minutes towards the end of those games. We were annihilated by Griqualand West in Kimberley. The team was getting decimated by injuries and I came on in the second row. Gaillimh was calling the lineouts and I remember him saying afterwards that there was one lineout, he was going to call four in the middle; then he looked round and saw just me standing there. So many fellas had gone at that stage he didn't know what to do or which way to turn. I don't think Gatland ever had any notion of playing me in the Test games or against the major provincial sides; he had the likes of Claw and Paul Wallace to call on. But I didn't mind. I was enjoying the whole experience anyway, getting to know a load of new fellas and training every day in fine weather.

Reggie went home injured, and Claw's younger brother Des was shipped out. Myself and Des ended up as water boys for the Test matches, running on and off with the drinks. The first Test was in Bloemfontein and the supporters there amused themselves by pelting me and Des with wet lumps of oranges. I only found out afterwards that they'd inject vodka into the oranges beforehand and suck the juice out of them during the game. So you had dozens of half-pissed South Africans in their seats firing them in at us for the crack. There were oranges whizzing past my head all day that day. Out on the field our lads hung tough for an hour before being overrun in the end. South Africa won 37–13, but got so much stick from the media over their performance that they went to town on us in the second Test in Pretoria. There were punch-ups and rows breaking out all over the place, but the frightening sight was the power and pace of the South Africans. They were world champions and they were in a different league at the time.

Gatland had brought in Craig White as a strength and conditioning coach and that was the first time I'd ever worked with a specialist in that field. We were in the gym working on a weights programme pretty much every day and seeing the South Africans made me realise how far I had to go. I thought I was strong and I was, I suppose; I had a fair amount of natural strength. But I needed far more explosive power for top-level rugby and I was going to get that by building up muscle in the gym. I had to get my head around the fact that this was my job now. I was a full-time professional rugby player. And being on the tour brought that home to me.

It also hit me when I got home and had no work to go to the next day. We were given a few weeks off before the pre-season and I was on my holidays. I had signed the full-time contract with Munster in the Glenview Hotel before we flew out to South Africa. Just the week before that I was still working as a welder. But I'd handed in my notice as soon as Deccie told me about the contract. Tom Coleman was my boss in the company and is still a good friend. On my last day there I asked him could I come back if the rugby didn't work out. 'Course you can,' he said. 'But I think your welding days are over.'

4

I got my first competitive start for Munster on 12 September 1998. It was against Connacht in an interprovincial match in front of a couple of hundred spectators at Dooradoyle.

There was a lot of chopping and changing going on with the team at that time. Management had options; they were trying to find the right balance in the side. In the front row you had four props looking for two places: the Clohessy brothers, Peter and Des, Ian Murray and myself. Well, it was three really, because Claw was nailed down at tight-head, or so I thought. I still hadn't got a look-in, bar a start against Morocco in a friendly at Thomond Park three weeks earlier. For the Connacht game, Deccie and Niallo decided to try a new combination: Claw at loose-head and me at number three. The game went well. A week later we had our first Heineken Cup match of the new campaign, against Padova at Thomond, and they went with most of the team that had started against Connacht. A lot of young, hungry players who would go on to have long careers were knocking on the door that season or had just recently broken through. Ronan O'Gara, Frankie Sheahan, Mick O'Driscoll, Donncha O'Callaghan, Anthony Horgan and David Wallace were there or thereabouts, and Peter Stringer was about to put his hand up too. Dominic Crotty and

John Kelly were younger than me but were already playing a couple of seasons. Actually, they were all younger than me, but that game against Connacht in Dooradoyle, as it turned out, was the day I nailed my place in the team. I didn't know it at the time, obviously, and if someone had said it to me there and then, I'd have thought they were mad; but that was the first of the 212 competitive games I would play for Munster over the next thirteen years.

No one surely would've predicted it after the doing I got against Perpignan in the south of France three weeks later. Perpignan play their home matches in the Stade Aimé Giral, but for some reason this one was played in the local rugby league ground, Stade Gilbert Brutus. It was the right name for it too because their pack was one brutal outfit. And I was brutal in the other sense of the word. There's no other way of saying it, I got fuckin' pulverised in the scrum. We were sent back-pedalling at a rate of knots, and unfortunately it was coming through me. They had a loose-head by the name of Renaud Peillard. He never played for France, but that doesn't mean a lot. He mightn't have been good enough at some other facet of the game, I don't know, but at scrummaging he was an animal. I don't mean in a dirty sense. But he just relished the confrontation. This is Catalan country, and they have this macho sort of pride in their scrummaging down there. Perpignan are famous for it. Peillard wasn't massive, but he was very strong and elusive; you couldn't pin him down. And he wasn't the only problem I had, because Raphael Ibanez was their hooker and he was gunning for me too. Ibanez was a great player; he would go on to play ninety-eight times for France. Between the two of them milled me that night good and proper. Peillard was tucking in under Ibanez and they were basically coming at me as one, kind of like an arrowhead. When it worked the first time in an early scrum they went after me lock, stock and barrel. I couldn't cope with it at all. They were twisting and turning me this way and that. It was a mixture of power and intent and technique. It was a shock to the system, the ferocity that was coming through. I'd never encountered it before. This was the first time I'd played in France and the first time I'd met a real French scrummaging unit. I wasn't expecting the intent and didn't understand the importance of the psychological edge they tried to achieve through scrums. Before I knew it, it was too late. They were piling on the scrums in that first half and we kept getting shunted back.

I got the shepherd's hook after twenty-eight minutes. Ian Murray came on, and Claw moved back to tight-head. The stadium was a bear pit that day. It was a real hostile, passionate crowd of roaring Catalans. They went delirious when they saw our scrum getting mangled. And when they saw an opposing prop forward getting taken off after twenty-eight minutes it was like all their Christmases had come at once. I was jeered and barracked all the way to the dugout. Talk about getting a lesson! It hit home that day, in a big way, how important the tight-head position is to a team. If the tight-head is getting battered in a scrum, it has a domino effect right the whole way through a team. We went in at half-time 29–3 down. Munster rallied in the second half but still lost by seventeen points. Personally, I was embarrassed. I couldn't look the other players in the eye. I went home to Cappamore and put in a long week, moping about the place and wondering where I was at. The lads were fine about it. Gaillimh just said 'Look, it happened; put it down to experience and move on.' It was good to have experienced fellas like that throwing an arm around you when you needed it.

A week later we were away to Neath in the next round of European games. Any sportsman who has a bad day at the office, the first thing they want to do is get back out and try to put it right. I badly wanted to get back out there, I'd have played the very next day if I could. But Deccie and Niall were picking the team for the Neath game and they had a big decision to make. I'm sure they were seriously doubting now whether I was ready for this level at all. They couldn't but be thinking that, after what they'd

seen. But in their wisdom they decided to throw me back in
straightaway. I played against Neath at The Gnoll and came through
without any problem. I was grateful to Deccie and Niallo for sticking with me. If they'd pulled me out of the firing line, it would have
damaged my confidence, but, as it happened, I never really suffered
from big confidence problems in the years after that. Even if I got
a right drilling, I wouldn't let it affect me too much. Any time I was
picked I took it as a vote of confidence in me: if they think I
can do the job, well then I can do the job. That was my mentality.
I didn't beat myself up too badly after a poor performance and
never got too excited after a good performance either. Mentally
and emotionally, I stayed pretty much on an even keel through
good times and bad. The main thing always for me was to get
back on the pitch the following week and keep going. Just keep
going, through thick and thin. We beat Leinster in Donnybrook
six days after Neath in the final round of the interpros. The winner
on the night would take the title, and that was the first trophy for
the young generation of Munster players. It wouldn't get a huge
mention now, but it was a nice milestone at the time. We hit the
ground running that night and played some quality rugby in the
first half. Picking up a trophy after the game was a boost to morale
and a sign that we were heading in the right direction. We also
were awarded a bonus gift on the night. Unfortunately, it wasn't
a car, or a cheque for a couple of grand a man; instead it was a
Club Tricot overcoat, a navy one with a red collar on it. My father
still wears it from time to time, and every time I see it I get a laugh
out of it.

Then came the re-match with Perpignan in Musgrave Park,
three weeks after the debacle at their place. I knew what to expect
this time, and it made all the difference. Plus, any player with an
ounce of pride in himself would be determined to make sure it
didn't happen again. Peillard was there again, but I didn't make it
a personal sort of revenge mission with him. The front row is a
position where it can get personal with opponents, because it's

literally hand-to-hand combat. It's two men wrestling; it's an individual battle within the bigger battle. But I never personalised it with any player I met over the years. And you could meet the same fellas a fair few times over the course of a career. People ask if you'd be eyeballing your opposite number when you're about to engage at a scrum, trying to psyche him out or whatever, the way boxers do. But that didn't happen. Well, I never did it anyway. There was too much else going on. I'd always be looking past them, the prop and hooker, focusing on the spot where I was going, waiting for the call and making sure I was ready for the hit. We were a lot more comfortable in the scrum this time round and got the win we needed on what was a filthy wet night. Claw had a great game; he was thriving at loose-head. I remember him telling me the move had given him a new lease of life. He found it easier, I think, and really enjoyed his rugby at loose-head during the last few years of his career.

The win over Perpignan guaranteed us a place in the quarter-finals. It was the first of twelve straight seasons in which we would qualify for the knock-out stages of the Heineken Cup. Our quarter-final would be away to Colomiers six weeks later. The autumn internationals took over in the meantime, and the squad broke up. A load of Munster players were called into the Combined Provinces team that played South Africa in Musgrave Park later that November. A week later I was up at the other end of the country playing South Africa again, this time for the Ireland As in Ravenhill. Most of us fitted in one or two AIL games with our clubs too. The Colomiers game was on 13 December. By the time we reassembled for that match, a lot of our momentum was gone. In hindsight, we probably weren't ready to go to France and win big games there anyway. On the day, we weren't good enough; we fell short in just about every department. Our season was over by Christmas.

Back with Shannon, we were hoping to turn a four-in-a-row into five. It's a rare achievement for any team in any sport at any

level, to keep it going for five straight seasons in a row. The great
Kerry team of the late 1970s couldn't quite get it done in Gaelic
football either. We were finally stopped by a good Cork Con team
in the last game of the regular league. If we'd won, it would've got
us into the semi-finals. But we ran out of road at the end of a dis-
appointing season.

During this time, and like a lot of Munster players, I was keeping an eye on the national scene and hoping they were keeping an
eye on me too. This was a World Cup year. The South African
tour the year before had raised my expectations. Ireland had a
summer tour of Australia lined up, and I was in with a shout of
making the squad. I was called into the Ireland As for the Five
Nations games in the spring of '99 and was selected for the first
match against France. A neck injury picked up in training that
week ruled me out, and I was gutted to miss that one because they
pulled off a great win over the French in Donnybrook. Mike
Ruddock was the coach and Jerry Holland the manager. We were
based in Finnstown House in Lucan, and I can remember them
calling me into one of their rooms for a chat. They knew I was disappointed and they made a point of giving me a bit of a lift. They
said I had a good future in the game and basically encouraged me
to keep working hard and improving. It was nothing earth-shat-
tering, I suppose, from their point of view, but it gave me a great
boost. That was the thing about Jerry Holland. He was Munster
manager for years afterwards, and I was only getting to know him
at the time, but he was a great manager and just had a way about
him that made you feel comfortable and good about yourself. The
Leinster prop, Angus McKeen, stepped in for the France game and
held onto the jersey for the next match against Wales. I was on the
bench that day and once again, just like against Boland the previous summer, Reggie Corrigan had to come off early with an
injury. This time there was no Claw around to negotiate with over
a change of position. I had to play loose-head; it was the first time
I'd played there since my escapades down in New Zealand and I

hated it even more this time round. Couldn't wait to get back to the other side.

I didn't play against England Saxons. I started against Scotland and came off the bench for a friendly against Italy in April. It was a bit of a mixed bag of a season, but I was still hoping that I'd done enough to make the squad for Australia. The day it was announced I was in and out of the house every twenty minutes checking the Teletext for news. I was cutting hedges that day, but didn't get a lot of work done. Then the news flashed up on the screen and there was no sign of a J Hayes in the small print. Gatty had gone with Claw, Reggie, Paul Wallace and Justin Fitzpatrick as his props. It hit me hard, that, harder than I'd have anticipated at the time. I suppose that's what you get when you raise your expectations. I'd never set myself any goals before, and as soon as I did I was disappointed. The summer before, I'd spent a month in South Africa enjoying the life of a rugby player on tour. This summer I'd be at home in Cappamore watching the games on television and bringing in the silage.

5

We were out in the Garden field one day in the summer of 1983 bringing in the hay. I was nine years old at the time and a great man to drive a tractor and trailer, or so I thought anyway. The bales of hay were piled in stacks around the field. Dad would throw the bales into the trailer and then I'd drive on to the next stack. My two cousins and my sister Rosemary were sitting in the trailer. The field has a fairly steep hill on it and we were at the top of it. I didn't put the tractor in gear. I was letting it freewheel from one stack to the next. I went to take a fairly sharp turn and next thing it took off. All of a sudden it was flying down the hill and I couldn't stop it. I don't think the brakes were working too well that day. The trailer was bouncing up and down with the speed we were going; there were bales of hay flying off it left and right. All I could do was hold onto the steering wheel and try and keep the tractor fairly straight. We were flying down towards the road, but when we got to the bottom of the hill I yanked the wheel and got the tractor turning across the field. When the ground flattened out it eventually slowed and came to a halt. My heart was thumping out of my chest. I got the fright of my young life. I was shaking like a leaf. I turned around and the sister and the two cousins were a bit shook-looking too. But at least they were still there. They were sitting on the bales and had managed to hang on.

There was no more driving that day. But an episode like that wouldn't put you off, especially when you were mad to drive the tractor, like every young country fella was and still is.

I was four or five when I first sat up on a tractor. As soon as your legs were long enough to reach the clutch and brake, you were learning to drive it. You'd be up on it every chance you got, practising steering and reversing in the yard. Since then I've always had an interest in all sorts of farm machinery and cars. Once the lads on the Munster and Ireland team found out about it, the slagging started. I got plenty of it over the years. We could be travelling on a bus somewhere and if there was a tractor in a field they'd be bringing it to my attention. 'Look, Hayes, a big blue one! Can you see it? Jaysus, that's a fine-looking tractor, in fairness.' And I'd be supposed to get all excited. It was a bit of a novelty for them, especially the city boys, having a farmer on the team.

I grew up on a farm of about 140 acres in the townland of Dromsallagh, in the parish of Cappamore, in East Limerick. Marie and Mike, our mother and father, had five children: Rosemary, myself, Carmel, Mike and Thomas, in that order. The land was half and half – one half good, the other half wet. The good land was on the hill and the upper side of the farm. And then you had the lowlands. It would officially be called 'Disadvantaged' on paper; in practice you could call it very disadvantaged. Or as Dad says, 'You'd call it land if you were shipwrecked.' On that part of the farm it was more or less a case of, close the gates in November and stay away out of it until April. The fields had different names: the Garden field, the Horses' field, the Cows' field, the Heifers' field One, the Heifers' field Two, the first meadow, the second meadow, the five-acre, Walsh's, Cunningham's, and so on.

I was born on 2 November 1973. The farm was still a dairy farm then; we gave up milking cows in 1982. We've reared suckler cows

Right: Already bringing home trophies, 4th class at Cappamore Boys' National School.

Middle: Cappamore Under-13s, East Limerick hurling and football champions, 1984. That's me in the front row on the far left.

Bottom: Hardy bucks. The Bruff team that showed me the ropes in the early years. I'm fourth from right in the back row, looking down the field for some reason.

Above: Third from the left, second row, with Marist rugby club out in New Zealand.

Left: Back with Shannon in 1997, before I started taping my ears.

Below: Munster v Pontypridd in the 1999 Heineken Cup. We made it all the way to the final, but lost to Northampton in the end.

Against Italy in my first Six Nations campaign, 2000.

Facing England in the postponed Six Nations game at Lansdowne Road, October 2001. The crowd was happy with the result, Strings and myself were pretty chuffed too. I ended up with the match ball.

Me with Anthony Foley and Malcolm O'Kelly's legs at Ireland team training.

Celebrating our 2002 Heineken Cup semi-final win against Castres. The Munster support was massive, with almost 8,000 fans following us to France that day

My final match with Shannon, against Cork Constitution, in the 2002 AIL Division One final. My brother Tom was also playing that day and we managed to scrape the win.

Fronting up with Frankie and Claw against Leicester in the 2002 Heineken Cup final.

Just about scoring a try against Ulster in the 2003 Celtic League semi-final.

Ploughing through Scotland during the 2003 Six Nations.

Getting to grips with Leicester during the 2003 Heineken Cup.

Even though we didn't win the Six Nations, we got the consolation of a Triple Crown in 2004.

Happier days still, at my wedding to Fiona in Ballinaclough. Left to right: Dad, Rosemary, myself, Carmel, Mike, Tom and Mam.

With the Lions squad on our tour of New Zealand. It was a blast from the past as we took on Southland in my old stomping ground, Invercargill.

since then, beef cattle basically which are suckled for six to eight months as calves and then fattened on grass and silage for another eighteen months or so before being sold or slaughtered. We had a herd of about thirty-five or forty milking cows back in the day. There was still a creamery in Cappamore town at the time, and Dad had a bulk tank for bringing in the milk. I can remember going with him to the creamery as a young lad during the summer holidays. It would've been a big social event at the time, all the local farmers meeting up and talking the news of the day. That's all gone now; the creamery is long closed because milk is collected at the farms these days.

You weren't long walking before you had various little jobs to do. When you got a bit older you'd be up early and sent to the field to round up the cows and bring them in for milking. Sometimes you'd do it on school days but usually it was during weekends and summer holidays. Dad had a milking machine; there was no milking by hand at that stage, thanks be to God. The milking was done morning and evening. Then, depending on the time of year, there was all sorts of other work to be done: calves to be fed, fields to be fenced, the yard cleaned, logs cut, a bit of digging with a spade, or shit to be shovelled out of cow-sheds. There was always something. Our grandmother, Dad's mother, lived with us and she kept geese and hens. At other times Dad would be fixing machinery in his workshop, and that's where I learned a bit about welding and ironwork and engines and the like. In the summer we did the silage. Like most farmers he moved from hay to silage because it was quicker and more reliable and not dependent on the weather. In later years we got a contractor in to do it, but in those times we did it ourselves. I loved doing the silage. My job as soon as I was old enough was to mow the fields. You'd hook the rotary mower onto the tractor and off you'd go across the land. Then you'd gather it in with a pick-up forage wagon. This had a pick-up reel on it that would spin up the grass and push it through to the trailer. When you had the load on you'd take it back to the silage pit in the yard and buckrake it into the pit. This was your winter feed for the cattle.

I have a memory that I was always carrying buckets. Two at a time to keep you balanced and give you muscles on both sides – that's what Dad used to say to us anyway, if we started complaining. I didn't complain much, I don't think, because I actually enjoyed doing things and being out and about. There was no 'will I or won't I' anyway, when you had a job to do. It was just do it, and no more about it. We were all roped in to do the work. There wasn't much talk about child labour laws in those days, or health and safety either, needless to say. Rosemary is a year older than me, Carmel three years younger, Mike five years and Thomas seven. One day myself and Mike and Tom were sent out to do a few jobs. I was supposed to clean the yard with the tractor and yard-scraper and I think they were supposed to bring fodder down to the cattle in the shed. Mike decided he didn't want to do it. As the older brother, I was the boss, but for some reason they didn't always see it that way. In fact, they'd have the cheek to tell me to eff off every now and then. I had to put up with a lot. Anyway Mike went on strike this day. He wanted to go back to the house but I wouldn't let him. I grabbed a hold of him and threw him into an old outhouse and locked him in. And I made him stay there until me and Tom were finished what we were doing. I was tall and strong for my age and sometimes I had to flex my authority, so to speak, with the pair of them. So they came up with a pact, a sort of a vow to get revenge. I'd say I was about eighteen or nineteen at the time. They did their calculations and reckoned that in another five years' time or so they'd be able to take me on. They came up with a date and made a note of it and all. And on this exact day they were going to bate the lard out of me. I can't honestly say I was shivering in my shoes. I'd say the pact lasted an hour. Or maybe a day.

*

I loved growing up on the farm and living in the countryside. It was an outdoors life. You had space and freedom. You could go across the fields if you wanted to clear your head and no one would bother you. I never went fishing but Dad was always out with his shotgun during the hunting season and we'd take off with him when we were old enough. Our job was to beat the bushes to rise a pheasant or whatever was in there. We used to call ourselves his hunting dogs. We shot pheasant and rabbit, but he'd give them away; they didn't end up in the pot. We used to kill our own heifers for meat. Everyone talks about food traceability these days, and it's a good idea; it's important to know where your food is coming from. A lot of people don't know where their food comes from, be it out of the ground or from an animal. I think they think it just comes from a shop. We were informed about the reality from a young age. Sometimes we'd go with Dad when he was bringing a load of cattle to the meat processing plant in Nenagh. We'd go in and see the cattle going up the line and being killed. It was no big deal; you just took it for granted. We'd keep a heifer back and it'd be butchered for our own use and kept in the freezer. The first few weeks afterwards would be great; you'd be having these lovely roasts and steaks for your dinner. Then it was onto stews and casseroles with the cheaper cuts of meat. And finally you'd arrive at the mincemeat. Mince today and mince tomorrow. Oh, Jaysus, not mince again today. I remember Mam landing home with the shopping one day and there was a bottle of tomato ketchup in the bags. It was such a treat to get that we ended up taking photographs of this magic bottle of red sauce. We fairly doused it on the mince the next time it was served up. It was all a bit of a joke. We were well fed and well looked after growing up. The farm supported the family. We were reared in the traditional rural way, I suppose, and we were blessed with the upbringing our parents gave us.

There was always a football and a few hurleys and sliotars around the house. It wasn't all work and no play. We spent plenty of time in the yard kicking a ball or having a puck-around to let off a bit of steam. We took to sport naturally and enjoyed it. Mike also went on to play for Bruff and Shannon and had a year with Connacht on a pro contract. But in the 1980s rugby was still more or less an alien sport to us. Limerick City is one of the strongholds of the game in Ireland, and we were only fifteen miles away but it hadn't spread to rural parts the way it has since. Cappamore was GAA country for generations. Gaelic football and hurling were the games handed down, and that was what we played growing up. My first competitive sporting experience was a Gaelic football match between Cappamore Boys National School and Lisnagry National School. I was ten and in fourth class. Normally the team would've been picked from the fifth and sixth classes, but numbers at the school were small, tiny by most standards. There was only eight of us in fourth class. The boys' school went from second class to sixth class. Before you joined the boys' school you went to the local convent school for the first three years of your education. In my final year at Cappamore NS there was only fifty-six pupils in the whole school. I was recruited for the football team at a young age because I was tall for my years. I played in the half-back line that day against Lisnagry. I wasn't what you'd call an attacking half back, flying up the field on solo runs. I was more of a defensive type, a man marker. Later that year I started playing with the Cappamore GAA club. The earliest underage team they had in those times was the Under-12s. In 1984 the GAA was celebrating its centenary year and we happened to have a really good Under-13 football and hurling team. We won the East Limerick championships in both codes. Hurling is a more technical game, but over the years I got a decent handle on the basic skills. I'd still be able to control a ball on the stick and hit it fairly straight if I tried it.

We had a very good Under-12 hurling team in 1985 too. We lost the Limerick county final that summer. I was eleven. It haunts me to this day. People might find it strange to hear me saying that, but that Under-12 final remains the biggest disappointment of my sporting life. The next worst is the 2000 Heineken Cup final. But this one tops the lot. I had plenty of bitter defeats with Munster and Ireland. I played for the British and Irish Lions too. It might seem trivial by comparison, an Under-12s final; you'd think that I should've forgotten about it long ago. But it cut me to the bone. I was never able to forget it. I still get a catch in my throat when I talk about it now. The complete and total emptiness I felt that day never fully left my system. There's a part of me that has never gotten over it.

I was centre half back. What really got us going was a three-game saga against Ahane in the East Limerick final. Ahane were one of the big clubs in Limerick hurling. They had the Moran brothers, Ollie and James, playing. Ollie went on to play with the Limerick senior team for years, a brilliant hurler and a fella I got to know from playing with him on an East Limerick schools team. Those three games were played in Murroe. They were massive matches for young fellas; they felt like All-Irelands to us. Winning out in the end was brilliant and the whole parish was getting behind us now. Then we beat Na Piarsaigh, the Limerick City team, in the county semi-final. The final was against Castletown-Ballyagran in Bruff. A huge crowd turned up for it, all our parents and relations and neighbours and friends. Every young fella in the club who was under twelve was allowed tog out and sit on the bench and be part of the occasion. Maybe the occasion got to us a little bit. We didn't play near as well as we did in the previous games. We lost by a goal and a point to a point. And that was the end of our little dream. We were children; it went hard on us all. The match was filmed, one man and his camera up on the back of a trailer or something. The next day we were all brought into John Hayes's pub (no relation) in Cappamore to watch it again on video. We were given crisps and minerals. We were told we'd done great, but I couldn't be consoled. I'll never forget sitting in the corner of the pub watching that game.

I went to secondary school in the CBS in Doon, four miles from Cappamore. There were only two Christian Brothers left in the school when I was there. I hardly missed a day in my five years there. It didn't mean I was a model student, mind you. I didn't get into serious trouble and was never suspended, but I was thrown out of the classroom plenty of times for messing. That was usually the offence: general messing brought on by boredom. It's a condition that affects a lot of young fellas at school, as far as I can see. There was one teacher who put the six messers in class down in a corner together, kind of like a quarantine situation. She called us 'the Contaminators'. Apparently, our behaviour was contaminating the rest of the class. I hope we didn't affect their education too badly. I don't think it affected mine too much. I was never going to end up on the academic side of things anyway. Basically I did enough to get by. I liked history and geography. I didn't mind maths but I wasn't good at it. I hated English. I couldn't understand why we had to be studying Shakespeare and trying to read *The Merchant of Venice.* And as for the poetry, I couldn't get my head around the poetry at all. You'd study a poem in class and you'd have to go home and write an essay on it. I wouldn't have the first notion how to go about it. I'd try and force something down on paper, maybe manage a paragraph or two, and then just abandon it.

Doon CBS was a hurling school. I'd say it was the influence of the Christian Brothers. There were certainly no 'foreign games' like rugby or soccer. There wasn't even Gaelic football. I remember one time Mike broke his leg in a bicycle accident. When the Brother saw him with the leg in a cast he asked what had happened. Mike told him he'd fallen off his bike. The Brother said back to him, 'If you'd been playing hurling, that wouldn't have happened.' That was the mentality at the time. But it was real hurling country anyway, being on the Tipperary border. You had fellas coming from Cappawhite, Annacarty, Clonoulty and Doon itself. We weren't big enough or good enough to compete in the

Harty Cup, which was the elite hurling competition in Munster for secondary schools. We competed in the B competition, the Corn Padraig. You had your privileges if you played on the school team. PJ McNamara was the teacher who looked after hurling. He sprung me from detention on more than one occasion. If I was kept back in school for messing, or made stay in the hall, as they used to call it, you'd get away if there was a match or a training session. PJ Mac would square it with the teacher and you'd be away on a hack. The hurling always trumped detention. It trumped pretty much everything in school, as far as I was concerned. It was a great distraction from Shakespeare and algebra.

I left Doon CBS in 1991. My school years didn't do me any harm and they probably did me a bit of good. In 2000 I was asked back to present the Student of the Year awards. A fair few of the teachers from my time were still there. I was asked to say a few words at the presentation ceremony. I said something like, 'I'm sure some of my former teachers here today will find it fairly strange seeing me up here presenting these awards, after the way I carried on when I was here.' The whole place started laughing. The irony of me being there, handing out prizes to the best students in the school, wasn't lost on them, or on me.

During my school years I was also going through the grades with Cappamore GAA club. I ended up playing football and hurling on teams three or four years ahead of my own grade. So I was usually out training or playing several times a week during the summer months in particular. In 1991 I made the Limerick county minor panel in hurling. I played two challenge games, but a couple of weeks before the championship they trimmed the panel and I was cut. But I never really had any aspirations to play for the county. Limerick didn't really have the same winning tradition as counties like Tipp or Kerry or Kilkenny. We didn't have the sporting heroes to look up to and follow. I enjoyed it, but I wasn't that committed to it. I kind of went along with it; most of my friends were involved as well, and it was an outlet to have.

I had graduated from the tractor to the car by then and we were soon discovering the delights of bars and discos. I was the designated driver a lot of the time. We stuck to the local circuit; we never went near the bright lights of Limerick. In fact, we never really had much to do with the city at all. We had our own circle of friends and we used to head for the teenage discos in Doon or Dundrum or Emly. I had a good laugh last year when I heard Paul Collins on the radio one day announcing that I was about to retire from rugby. Paul is a sports broadcaster with Today FM and he went to school in Doon CBS too; he was a few years older than me. He was on Ian Dempsey's show and he was telling Ian that we'd both gone to the same school. And Doon rang a bell for Ian too. He said he used to DJ at discos there back in the day. And I was laughing because I remember being at Ian Dempsey's discos, and there was always a big crowd in for them too.

I can't say it was the pubs or the discos that brought a premature end to my GAA career. I just drifted away from it bit by bit. In my mid-teens I started doing summer work for a silage contractor, so I wasn't turning up for as many training sessions any more. The manager of the minor hurling team was the local curate, Fr Tony Ryan, and one summer they were going fairly well. Fr Tony kept calling to our house to try and get me back playing again, but in all honesty I wasn't that interested. I was ducking and diving, saying I was too busy with work. But it so happened that one evening they were playing the East Limerick final in Pallasgreen, and the farm that I was working on actually bordered the pitch in Pallasgreen. So I had no excuse; I could hardly get into the tractor and drive home with the game about to start in the next field. They threw me in full forward. I had the height to be a target man, but I was no Joe McKenna. We won the match that night and went on to win the county B championship that year, but my heart wasn't in it anymore. I didn't want to do the training, I didn't want to be there. I still love to watch hurling; it's a great spectator sport. I went to the 2011 All-Ireland final between Tipp and

Kilkenny; it was actually my first time at an All-Ireland. There was a moment with Tommy Walsh, the Kilkenny half back, that brought home the speed and skill of the players. The ball landed in or around the square and Walsh tore onto it, flicked it with the hurl into his hand and was gone. It was all done in a split second, the ground he covered, the touch to control the ball and the clearance. To see it up close was something to behold.

I was eighteen going on nineteen when I went up to Bruff rugby club for the first time and it just transformed my attitude. The rugby overlapped with Gaelic games for the next couple of years, but I was only heading in one direction really. I played my last GAA match in 1994. It was for the Under-21 football team. We actually won the county Under-21 A championship that season, which was no small thing for a club like Cappamore. I was juggling games between Shannon and Cappamore at the time, and on the weekend of the county Under-21 semi-final I ended up playing a Munster Senior Cup match on the Saturday afternoon, the semi-final on Saturday evening and a Shannon Under-20s game on the Sunday. I was full forward on the Under-21 team. I didn't score a lot, I wasn't what you'd call a natural finisher. My job was to break the ball down for the handier forwards around me.

The county final was another three-game saga, this time against Glin. The final was set for Ballingarry on a Saturday evening, but I had an AIL game with Shannon fixed for the same afternoon. And it was away to St Mary's in Dublin. It was only my second AIL game and I didn't want to miss it. Cappamore sent two lads to collect me straight after the game in Templeville Road and bring me back to Ballingarry. We were losing the match that evening by four or five points when sadly one of our supporters in the crowd died suddenly. Phelim Carberry had been a big supporter and contributor to the GAA club for many years. He was a very popular man; everyone was shocked. The match was abandoned there and then. The replay ended in a draw, and the third instalment led to another clash of fixtures for me. This time

I was playing for the Shannon Under-20s against UCC in Musgrave Park. Again, Cappamore had a car and driver ready to collect me and ferry me home. We won the final at the third time of asking; it was a great win on the day and a big boost for the club at the time, but that was more or less the end of my playing days with the GAA. I had spent ten years playing Gaelic football, and it definitely helped me as a rugby player, specifically with ball-handling skills. Rugby has a different-shaped ball, obviously, but some of the skills transferred across. Gaelic football gave you better hands, it taught you how to catch a ball over your head and away from your body. Football and hurling would also have developed your spatial awareness on a field, and there was plenty of physical contact in both sports too. I didn't have a rugby foundation when I started playing with Bruff, but I've no doubt the years spent playing Gaelic games helped me a lot in making the transition.

By the time I got back from New Zealand I was a changed man, in more ways than one. Physically I'd put on a lot of weight and I don't think my body shape would've suited football or hurling any more. I had a lot of strength by then too, in the legs and upper body, even though I hadn't done much weight training at the time. In later years you'd hear the odd reference to me having a 'farmer's strength'. And I suppose if you're carrying buckets and dragging heavy bags of stuff and doing general labour around a farm it's bound to help some bit. But just because you're a farmer doesn't mean you'll be strong. Some farmers are as weak as water. The height and power I had was mostly genetic, I'd say. It was naturally there. I had big, strong uncles on both sides of the family and I have first cousins who are in or around 6 ft 6 in tall. Dad was a fairly powerful butt of a man; I hope he doesn't mind me putting it like that! He and his brothers had a tug-of-war team between them, which was a popular sport at one time. Dad used to throw the 56lb weight too and won loads of trophies at local sports days. One day in Reenavanna, in the parish of Doon, we all decided to have a go at the 56 lb competition. I wasn't long back from New Zealand at the time. It was basically a round lead ball, like a shot putt, with a short chain and handle attached to it. I came first, Mike came second and Dad came third. A clean sweep. I'd like to think it was all technique and timing, but Dad reckons there was 'a bit of ignorance' there as well. Anyway we still have the trophies and the photographs to prove it.

The chances of making it to the top in any professional sport are fairly slim. You can't do much about it if you haven't the right physical and mental traits to start with. I inherited the physical characteristics that would one day allow me to play international rugby as a prop forward. It was up to me to make the best use of them. I didn't get into it through the conventional route, but growing up on a farm and playing Gaelic games shaped me in all sorts of positive ways. I was a long way from the top of the sport when I first picked up a rugby ball, but I was probably better equipped for it than I realised at the time. The first eighteen years of my life had set me up well for the career that lay ahead, and I appreciate it even more with the passing of time.

6

The Ireland squad for the 1999 Rugby World Cup was announced in late August and two weeks later they played Munster in a warm-up game at Musgrave Park.

They probably couldn't foresee it at the time, but the Ireland management team were making a rod for their own back when that fixture was being planned. A lot of Munster players who didn't make the World Cup squad had their noses put out of joint. I was one of them. The likes of Foley, Quinlan, Galwey, O'Gara and David Wallace weren't happy either. A lot of us were fairly revved up that night. And if anything the crowd was worse. The famous Munster chip on the shoulder was playing its part. The atmosphere was hot and we were in no mood for holding back. At one stage there was a lineout under the stand. It was their throw and we hadn't opened the gap. It was Jeremy Davidson, I think, who pushed Gaillimh in the lineout and said something like, 'Give us the gap.' Gaillimh turned to him and said if he pushed him again, he'd lamp him. Or words to that effect. But it was that close to an all-in brawl. Then Keith Wood came on after an hour and towards the end of the game tried to do some sort of a pick-and-go around the corner of a ruck. Quinny and Axel grabbed him and fired him five yards over the touchline. The crowd roared them on. Munster won 26–19, and I suppose it was a sign of things to come for the national team. The World Cup turned into a bit of a disaster when they lost to Argentina in the quarter-final in Lens.

I didn't think about it at the time because I was fairly wound up myself that night in Musgrave Park. But when I thought about it years later, I felt it wasn't nice for an Irish crowd to be cheering against an Ireland team three weeks before a World Cup. I know it was just on the night but it wasn't right. And I suppose we the players didn't have to be as psyched-up either, but that was the mood we were in; the old Munster tribalism had taken over.

I wouldn't mind, but Keith Wood had actually joined Munster at the start of that season. Woody was our teammate! And he was one of the principal reasons why everything about us took a quantum leap forward that season. Woody was a star of world rugby at the time. He'd spent three years with Harlequins in England in a professional set-up that was a lot more advanced than ours at that stage. He was a world-class player, he had a big personality and very high standards. He brought those standards to every training session. If players started dropping balls at training, even during the warm-up, Woody'd rear up. He was liable to go off on a rant if balls started hitting the ground. Fellas who were still laughing and messing wouldn't be long getting switched on. He had that sort of presence and reputation.

Munster had made another important signing that summer, the Australian international John Langford. A completely different kind of person to Woody, he made a major impact on us too. Our first day of serious fitness work, we were doing these 800m runs. Langford took off and beat everybody. A big second row, 6 ft 7 in tall, and he was beating even the backs by fifty or sixty metres in an 800m run. We were amazed. He just blew everyone away, including the likes of Quinny and Dominic Crotty and Colm McMahon, who were among the fittest players in the squad. Langford had a big influence on my career, and we've remained good friends since. I was usually paired up with him for weights training. I was one of the strongest Munster players, and he was a long skinny lock forward, but I was still well short of what he was lifting in the gym. He started piling on the weights when I was lifting, setting new targets and pushing me harder. I hadn't actually grasped at that stage that to build muscle you have to push yourself to the absolute max lifting weights. Within a few weeks I was lifting way more than I'd ever done before. Langford led by example, and we all learned a lot from him.

The two lads made a big difference to our set piece as well. Some people had this idea that Woody couldn't be a good scrummager because he was so good around the field. From my own personal experience of playing with him I can say that Woody was a very good scrummager. He was a hard, seriously competitive fella and he brought that intensity to it. Having him there definitely raised my game, because now I was in a front row with two world-class operators in Woody and Claw. Then you had Gaillimh and Langford in the second row, so suddenly I was the only non-international in the front five.

Our lineout improved out of all recognition that season. Langford brought with him all these Australian innovations. Woody was the thrower and he had his opinions too. Niallo had a big interest in the lineout and he would soak up Langford's ideas about movement and variation and different permutations. The end result was that we spent a lot more time on the training ground practising all sorts of variations, and practising them over and over until we got them down. A lot of what we were doing that year was player-driven, and Niallo and Deccie were comfortable with that too.

This was the first season we also had a full-time fitness coach. Previous years we were given strength and conditioning programmes, but it was more or less left to ourselves to carry them out. We'd all do what was laid out for us, but it's not the same if you don't have someone there pushing you on. Fergal O'Callaghan was recruited and was there morning and evening, taking our sessions every day. We had a lot more depth on the bench that season too; Marcus Horan was coming through, and Munster had brought in two Kiwis in Mike Mullins and Jason Holland.

We were unbeaten by the time we played Pontypridd in the first round of the Heineken Cup in November '99. The game was at Thomond; we were expected to win and we did. A week later was the big one, Saracens at Vicarage Road. Saracens were a big-spending club at the time, and they had splashed the cash on several star signings. François Pienaar, their captain, was one of the most famous rugby players in the world after his exploits with South Africa at the 1995 World Cup. But their pack was full of international talent: Richard Hill, Danny Grewcock, Julian White, Scott Murray. Their out-half, Thierry Lacroix, was a star of French rugby. Their loose-head prop, Roberto Grau, was an experienced Argentina international and a serious player. Grau, George Chuter and White formed the Saracens front row and they were a rugged outfit. It made for a hard day in the scrums. Woody and Julian White knew each other from the English scene and they were doing a bit of yapping and mouthing, the usual stuff. I never really got into the verbals at any stage of my career. I'm a fairly quiet fella, anyway, at the best of times, and I never had much interest in it on the field. I didn't mind if other fellas felt like having their say. Claw would throw in the odd comment from time to time but I'd say most of them couldn't understand what he was saying anyway, the way it would come out. They'd understand Woody all right; he was able to pronounce his words better. It's not by accident he had a media career afterwards.

I was very much the rookie among those fellas. I was just trying to keep my end of the scrum up against Grau that day, and I managed to do it. I was definitely maturing and getting stronger; I could feel it. Twelve months on from the Perpignan massacre and I was feeling a lot more comfortable at this level. We beat Saracens by a point after a massive match. It was a game that swung one way, then the other, but with ten minutes to go it looked like they had it in the bag, leading 34–23. Then Axel took a quick penalty tap and we drove him over the line. We went gunning for the winner and Jeremy Staunton got over for a great try. Rog had missed the conversion off Foley's try but nailed the last one to give us the one-point victory. That was our first big win on the road. It was the first of those dramatic matches that for some reason we kept getting involved in during the years that followed. I don't know why we ended up in so many of them, but we did; we didn't make it easy for ourselves and we surely didn't make it easy for our supporters. But when we came out the right side of them it always made it sweeter.

I think that win in Vicarage Road was a landmark result for us. It gave us huge confidence. You had to win on the road in the Heineken Cup and we proved to ourselves that we could do it. Our next game would be another major test away from home, against Colomiers two weeks later. But we rolled straight into it still on a high from the Saracens match and rolled over Colomiers too, 31–15. In later years people nearly started taking it for granted that we'd go to France and win, which was an unbelievable turnaround in attitudes. Irish teams were never expected to win in France. They turned up expecting to get the shit kicked out of them, and that's usually what happened. But we were young and had a kind of youthful ignorance about us. We didn't fear them because we didn't know any better. We were missing Claw as well that day, but Marcus came in and ended up scoring a lovely try to seal it. I damaged my back and had to come off at half-time; Ian Murray replaced me and he came off injured before the end too. It left us with two hookers in the front row, Woody and Frankie, but we were in the mood that day to cope with anything.

I spent most of the next week on the flat of my back at home trying to get it right for the return match at Musgrave Park. I spent four days and four nights lying on the sitting-room floor.

Sleeping in my own bed wasn't an option if I wanted to get it sorted, and I badly wanted to get it sorted. I didn't want to miss out. We all knew at this stage that something special was starting to happen with the team. The buzz was there in the dressing room, the energy and spirit were brilliant. And it was spreading like wildfire among the supporters too. All of a sudden there was a massive demand for tickets; the hype had started and everything was on a roll. The other factor driving me on was that you couldn't take your place for granted. Marcus was making big strides and, if I wasn't around, Claw could switch back to tight-head at the drop of a hat. And I didn't want that happening. So I lay on the living-room floor at night, a fire burning in the range and me looking up at the ceiling. The back loosened up enough by the weekend and I kept my place. We beat Colomiers a week before Christmas. A week into the new year, the new millennium, we'd have Saracens to take care of in the return game.

Thomond Park was jammed to the rafters that night. A team of big-name stars was rolling into town and the crowd turned the place into a bear pit. There was a bit of the old blood lust hanging in the air. The atmosphere was hopping with electricity. It wasn't a do-or-die job for us because we still had Pontypridd to play a week later, but we knew that a win over Sarries would give us a home quarter-final. And we wanted to beat them because they were a massive scalp for us at the time. But I think people forgot that they were a seriously powerful, hard-nosed team. The likes of Pienaar, Hill and Grewcock weren't going to roll over. They weren't one bit happy getting turned over by us at Vicarage Road, and they arrived in Limerick fully intent on doing the same to us. It had the makings of a hell-for-leather game and that's exactly how it transpired. I have a scar on my head from it; Julian White clipped me with his boot going over a ruck. I got to know him on the '05 Lions tour of New Zealand. A sound fella, farmer like myself; we had plenty in common. Anyway, I got up from the ruck, the blood was flowing and it was off for a few stitches before going back to the action. And, Jesus, there was plenty of that.

Saracens played brilliant on the night. They were 17–8 up at half-time; the lead changed something like five times in the last twenty minutes. They got a try and conversion three minutes from time to lead by six. The funny thing was, we were quite calm behind the goalposts waiting for the conversion. We said we'd march straight back down the field and get over the line at their end. No one doubted that we would or we could. We had the line-out, we had the tools to do it with the new players we had in the team. Deep in injury time we kicked a penalty to the corner, Langford won the lineout and Woody was driven over the line. Rog landed the conversion and suddenly there were thousands of Munster fans streaming onto the field. They'd given us unbeliev-able energy during those last few minutes; you couldn't but be lifted by the noise and the passion that was rolling in on the field from the four sides of the ground. As it turned out, Rog didn't need to make the conversion. A one-point defeat would've been enough for us to top the pool and eliminate Saracens, but it was the sort of night that had to be crowned with a win. There was more to it than just points difference and mathematics. A game like that wouldn't have gone down in legend around Munster if it hadn't ended with a victory.

This was the season that O'Gara really made his mark. He hadn't turned into the leader and personality he would later become. He was too young for that and still had a bit of the university student about him. But he was lively, good crack, and he'd throw his tup-pence worth in during team talks. You could see the talent was there, the ball skills and ability to read a situation. He wouldn't panic in possession, he always seemed to have enough time on the ball even if he was receiving it under pressure. There wasn't a muscle on him to be seen. I'd be slagging him about his chicken legs, asking him how he could kick the ball at all with legs like those. He'd come into the gym and he'd see me smiling at him, taking the piss, and he'd laugh back knowing well what I was thinking; he was well able to take a bit of mischief.

This was the season, too, where his partnership with Peter Stringer at half-back was cemented. Strings had joined the season before but at that point there was a three-way battle for the number 9 jersey with Brian O'Meara and Tom Tierney; and he was third in line. He wasn't long about making his way to the front. The trademark pass that everyone knows about was already there. But my first memory of Strings is the day he drove into the car park for training in his father's Ford Scorpio. The Scorpio was the new version of the Granada. It was bigger than the Mondeo, a massive yoke, two foot longer than a standard car. And I remember this small little fella landing in one day with the biggest car in the car park. I burst out laughing because, I swear to God, he was looking out through the steering wheel instead of over it. Then he got out and he had this big blondie fringe on him with the hair cut tight at the back. When he picked up the ball in training it looked as big as a basketball in front of him; with the likes of Langford it looked as big as a thimble. Strings looked more like an altar boy than a rugby player, but when he started snapping out the passes and buzzing around the pitch, you could see straight-away he was a quality player.

It took us ages to get off the field in Thomond Park that night. We were absolutely mobbed. We lined up at the entrance to the tunnel to clap Saracens in and then they clapped us in. But I was one of the last Munster players to come through and as soon as they finishing clapping us I distinctly remember Pienaar turning to his team and shouting, 'Dressing room, now!' Our dressing room was on the left and theirs was on the right. He just pointed to it and barked it out like an order, like he was an army officer or something. He was not a happy man at all; none of them were. They were shocked. You could see it in their body language. We had beaten them at their place and they had come over intending to set the record straight, as they saw it. And now we had beaten them a second time. But we were still an unknown team. A lot of us hadn't made a reputation at that stage. And I got the impression their attitude was kind of like, 'These muppets are after beating us at our place and it's time to show them who's boss'; as if we had no right to beat them. They had every right to be unhappy, especially with the calibre of player they had. But when I thought about it afterwards I was nearly insulted by it. Like, why should ye be so pissed off that we beat ye? It was an attitude that followed us around for a few years after that too. A lot of the top teams in England and France, it took them a couple of years to see us as a serious force. I don't know whether they saw us just as a blood-and-guts outfit with no real class or whatever. I think it took them a while to realise that we weren't going away, but we kept beating them until eventually the penny dropped.

Pienaar was one hard man. He kept coming at us that night, and we struggled to contain him at times. You could see why he was such a great player and leader. Both teams had dinner after-wards under the old stand in Thomond Park. Quinny came in and sat down beside me, but I could see he was distracted. He was standing up and arsing around and I asked him what was wrong with him. Next thing he produced a book from under the table. It was Pienaar's autobiography, and he was waiting for the right moment to go over to him and get it signed. Now both of them played in the back row that night and Quinny wouldn't have backed away from him for a minute. But he was still a country young fella from Tipp and Pienaar was an international celebrity. Quinny anyway went up and asked him for his autograph. I was laughing my head off watching him going up 'cos there was no way I'd have done it, or even thought of doing it. We finished off a great night by going out on the beer in Schooners on Steamboat Quay. I don't know if Quinny brought his book with him, or if he still has it to this day.

*

I was lying on my bed in Room 303 of the Glenview Hotel. The Ireland squad was in camp, building up to the Six Nations game against Scotland the following weekend. The team was going to be announced the next afternoon. Ten days earlier Ireland had been hammered by thirty-two points at Twickenham. The day before that, I was on the Ireland As team that had beaten England Saxons at Franklin's Gardens. Warren Gatland named an extended squad the following week for the Scotland game. He called up a few players from the As, myself included. There was a round of AIL games scheduled for the weekend between England and Scotland. Shannon played Garryowen on the Sunday at Dooradoyle, and from there we headed to the Glenview to hook up with the rest of the squad. Gaillimh was driving. He was fairly certain that Gatty was going to shake up the team. He reckoned places were up for grabs if we made an impression. And sure enough everyone was trying to make a serious impression at training the next day. It was fairly obvious that management were looking at options, because there was a lot more fellas there than were going to make it onto the field come Saturday. I was trying to suss out their thinking too, but the way they divided up the forward packs at training, I reckoned I was down the pecking order. I wasn't in the same front row as Woody and figured that that was the formation they'd be going with.

Room 303 was Claw's room. He had a sort of honorary residency there. Every other player took whatever room he was given, but if Claw was in the Ireland squad, he got that room. I was sharing with him that week. The squad trained Tuesday morning and after lunch we went for a lie-down before a weights session that afternoon. Claw didn't do weights; he basically just did what he wanted to do. There was no sign of him when I went back to the room. The curtains were drawn and I was nodding off on the bed when the door opened and I heard someone saying, 'Is Claw there?' I knew it was Gatty by his accent, but I could barely see him. The room was dark; I was over by the window and Gatty was over by the door. So I sat up fairly lively. 'No, I think he's gone down for something.' 'OK. I'll call back later.' And out he went. I was barely lying back down when the door opened again. It was Gatty again; I still could barely make him out in the dark. He said, 'We're thinking of starting you on Saturday.' And needless to say I sat bolt upright. 'Right,' said I. 'D'you think you'd be up to it?' 'I do. Definitely. Yeah.' Then he said I'd been going pretty well with Munster and they wanted to see how I'd do on Saturday. 'Grand,' said I. Then he left without saying another word. Didn't turn on a light, or come into the room, or anything.

I lay back down on the bed and started wondering what he'd just said. They were 'thinking' of playing me. What did that mean? I was twisting and turning it over and back, not sure whether to ring my folks or not with the news. Then Claw arrived back and I was humming or hawing about mentioning it to him in case it was all confidential. I told him anyway what Gatty had said and Claw more or less shrugged his shoulders. 'You're in the team,' he said, and thought no more about it. The team was announced later that day. It would have five new caps: Shane 'Shaggy' Horgan, Simon Easterby, Stringer, O'Gara and myself. There were eight changes in all from the game in Twickenham. Gaillimh and Girvan Dempsey would start, having come off the bench against England; Denis Hickie was recalled from the As to start too. The debutants went on to have long careers with Ireland, so I suppose you could say looking back it was a changing of the guard. But none of us were to know that at the time.

Lansdowne Road on Saturday 19 February 2000 was one of the best days I've ever put down. It was just a dream of a day. I knew *Amhrán na bhFiann* from school and sang it. I knew most of *Ireland's Call* too. And *Flower of Scotland* is such a great song, you'd nearly be humming along to it as well. I wasn't used to all the preliminaries, meeting the President and everything; I was used to bursting out of a dressing room and the match starting a few

minutes later. I was unbelievably nervous, really anxious to get
started. I was going to be up against Tom Smith in the scrums and
he had a big reputation. I went really hard into the hit at every
scrum because I was expecting a big step-up in standard from the
level I'd been playing at. It was as much out of fear and adrenaline
and making sure I wouldn't be exposed at this level. And it went
well. The team played well, we won 44–22, and the eighty minutes just flew by. The level of intensity, the speed from phase to
phase, everything happened so fast that it was half-time before you
knew it. With ten minutes to go I was substituted and got a lovely
reception from the crowd. I'd enjoyed every minute of it. It was
only the second home international I'd ever been at. I'd started
playing rugby in September '92. Playing for Ireland back then, I'd
never have dreamed it or imagined it.

They plied me with drink that night in the Berkeley Court
Hotel. That was the tradition with first caps. Strings didn't drink,
fellas didn't really know Simon, so myself, Rog and Shaggy bore
the brunt of the congratulations. Every five minutes someone was
coming over with a drink. We were all called up one at a time to
get our cap from the IRFU president Billy Lavery at the dinner. I
was sitting beside Gaillimh. I went up and got my cap, and when
I came back down, Gaillimh pulled the chair out from under me
as I went to sit down. His wife Joan was there with the camera to
capture the moment. I have the photos at home to this day, me sitting on the floor with the cap on my head, looking demented.
Then the Scottish players came over with drinks for me as well.
Oh, Jesus. For some reason I can remember Doddie Weir handing
me a whisky and downing it in one go. The next thing I remember is waking up the next morning lying crossways on the bed and
wondering where the hell was I. It took me ages to realise it was
my own room. It took me longer to recover from the function
after the game than the game itself.

The win, the new players, gave Irish rugby a big lift. There'd
been an awful lot of doom and gloom after the '99 World Cup

and the defeat to England had only added to it. We put sixty points on Italy two weeks after Scotland and two weeks after that faced France in Paris. The first twenty minutes of that game, I'd never experienced anything like it in my life. The speed and intensity of the French players, the atmosphere in the crowd; it was stunning. They were coming at us in waves. All we were doing was chasing shadows and making tackles and making more tackles. It was something that became very familiar to us in the years after, with both Munster and Ireland. French teams would explode onto the field, the eyes popping out of their heads, and the pace for the first twenty would just be insane. The whole point of it is to try to knock you out early; to hit you hard enough and often enough until you've caved in; rack up enough points that you can't recover even when they've ran out of steam. But they didn't get the scores this day. They missed a few chances and we were scrambling with all our might to hang onto them. Some of our tackles were by the fingernails. But that's what you have to do against French teams in France, and we did it that day. Denis Hickie's tackle on Marc dal Maso under the posts was the best example of that; it saved a certain try. For me it epitomised the Irish attitude on the day. Everyone was giving every ounce they had.

In the scrums I was up against Christian Califano, a brilliant player, great athlete and seriously strong man. On the other side was Franck Tournaire; they had Fabien Pelous in the second row; it was an incredibly powerful unit. In one of the early scrums I got a great hit on Califano and was convinced I was in a really good position. Next thing I was going backwards. My legs weren't moving but I was sliding along the ground. Califano put the shove on, they got a huge push from the second row, and I was being driven backwards without even moving my legs. That was the sort of power they had.

But again I think the bit of youthful ignorance stood to us. Ireland hadn't won in Paris since 1972, but we didn't have that sort of baggage. A lot of us had never got beaten up badly by the

French before. And apart from all the desperate defending we had to do, we also played some fantastic running rugby too. We didn't just dog it out. We scored three tries to one. Well, Drico scored three tries to one. You could tell in training that Brian O'Driscoll was a special talent; you'd need to be blind not to see it. The pace and movement and steps and swerves he had. I had a close-up view of his third in the seventy-third minute. The ball kind of spun out of a ruck. I saw it rolling out along the ground and I was just turning when this green shirt came onto it in a blur and scooped it up and shot through the gap. He actually made it look easy but it was pure class. To see him going over was just such a pleasure. I was blowing out of my hole at that stage, but there was Drico just flying around the place. And after all that effort we still needed David Humphreys to land a long-range penalty three minutes from time to win it.

Another standout memory is a scrum about midway through the second half, maybe a bit later. Paddy Johns was in the sin bin and we were down to seven men in the pack. Andy Ward was on the field at that stage and was going into the back row on Claw's side of the scrum. But Claw told him to go over to my side. He knew they were going to be attacking the tight-head on that put-in, so he wanted to make sure I had a second row and a flanker behind me. Claw volunteered to keep his side up more or less on his own. He knew it was more important to protect the scrum first rather than worrying about the play afterwards. He was in the zone that day, Gaillimh too. It was typical of the kind of thing that fellas were doing on the day; players all over the field were going the extra mile. He more or less said to Andy, 'I don't need you, go over to Hayes.'

We did a sort of a lap of honour afterwards, maybe a half lap. It was a St Patrick's Day weekend and there was a big Irish crowd down in one corner of the Stade de France. Back inside, the dressing room was bananas. Even Gatty was showing some emotion. There was music blaring, everyone was hugging and smiling and happy. Just pure happy. It was one of those dressing rooms where you didn't want it to end. If you could bottle that sort of mood and keep it, you'd never be in bad form. Obviously after every game there's functions and travel itineraries and all that sort of stuff, but there's a half-hour or so after a win like that where the feeling is special. You don't have to do anything; you can just sit back and relax and let it all soak in. People are happy. Everything is brilliant. Everything that everyone says is funny. Everyone is content, everyone is satisfied. It's the best place in the world to be at that exact moment in time. There is nothing better. And it's the one thing I miss most in retirement.

Shaggy missed the France match through injury. The remaining four of us who'd got our first caps against Scotland, we'd now played three and won three. It was Ireland's first win in Paris in twenty-eight years. It was the first time Ireland had won three championship games in a row in eighteen years. It was the first three-in-a-row of any kind in seven years. I was on an absolute high for days after the game. Everywhere I went at home people were stopping me to talk about it. We were having a ball; this international rugby lark was a bed of roses! Needless to say, it didn't take long for the honeymoon to end. Six days after Paris, Shannon were getting their arses kicked by De La Salle Palmerston in the Dublin mountains. It was an AIL game, and we were 17–0 down after a quarter of an hour. That brought us back down to earth fairly quick. Then, after half-time, I was turning into a ruck and felt this pop in my groin. I couldn't run, I couldn't turn, I knew it was gone. I ended up sitting in the dugout with an ice pack on my groin, watching De La Salle beat us and panicking about the Six Nations game against Wales the following weekend. I got intensive treatment all week and for a finish told Gatty and Donal Lenihan that I was good to go. But I wasn't good to go. I shouldn't have played. I wasn't right, I couldn't run freely. I didn't contribute; we were beaten by four points at Lansdowne Road. But I just didn't want to not play. I'd got a taste of the international scene and couldn't stand the thought of pulling out. It was a lesson learned. If you take the field, you're supposed to be fit. You can't come out with excuses about your groin afterwards. If you're out there, you're going to be judged as if you're 100 per cent fit, and that's how it should be.

I wasn't fully 100 per cent for the Heineken Cup semi-final against Toulouse on 6 May. But I felt 110 per cent after scoring our first try. What's seldom is wonderful. It was a great feeling and I'd love to have experienced it more often, but I suppose I wasn't really cut out for the glamorous end of the game. Instead of complimenting me on it afterwards, the lads gave me an unmerciful slagging. It was their way of complimenting me, I suppose. Woody made one of his barnstorming runs, and there was a series of phases from there, the ball going over and back. I was involved in a few of the phases and was a bit slow getting off the ground after one of them. That's what the slagging was about. First I was supposed to be on the ground for about ten seconds, then it went up to twenty seconds, and these days it's about ten minutes. They reckoned I was still on my knees when Dominic Crotty happened to come back my way and that I just hopped up in time to take the pass off Dominic and fall over the line. But, like all good strikers, I was in the right place at the right time; that's my opinion, and I'm sticking to it.

The reaction from the Munster fans was loud and clear. They estimated there were about 2,500 of them in the crowd that day. It looked and sounded like an awful lot more. This was the first away game where the Munster support really turned out in big numbers. Those big away games became massive occasions, and as players we were really conscious of the bond we had with our supporters. The efforts they went to, the money they spent, the emotion they showed, I can't tell you how often it inspired us. You'd meet them at Shannon Airport on the way out, you'd meet them at the airport on the way back, and you'd meet them again in the arrivals hall back in Shannon. If we went for a stroll the evening before a game, we'd meet them in the bars and cafes. We got to know an awful lot of them. They turned those matches into occasions that lasted three or four days.

And on match days you'd run out into some stadium or other, and you'd see thousands of red jerseys splattered all over the place. Psychologically it gave us a lot of comfort to see them and hear them. Especially in France, where the home crowds would generate a seriously hostile atmosphere. The whole idea was to intimidate the visiting team. They'd go ballistic, they'd make a ferocious racket, they'd even be banging their hands on the team bus taking you into the ground. It was all to unnerve you. The funny thing was, as soon as a game was over they'd be coming up to you, patting you on the back and asking for your autograph and getting photos taken with you; they'd be the direct opposite of what they were an hour earlier. But before and during the game they'd be going berserk. They'd see it as their duty to try and scare the bejaysus out of the visiting players while galvanising their own players. That's why home advantage makes such a difference, in France in particular. And it's why the Munster support made such a difference to us. It made us feel a little bit like we were at home too. I'd go so far as to say it was *the* difference in a match as tight as the Toulouse game was. Toulouse were stacked with French internationals; they were far more experienced than we were. Our support levelled the playing field that day to some degree. Instead of hearing constant hostility and negativity, you were hearing positive noises from the crowd too.

It was boiling hot in Bordeaux that day. We had this ridiculously long walk from the dressing rooms to the pitch. Then the game started and it was just like Paris the previous March all over again. Toulouse went for the jugular straight from the off. They were tearing about the place at a hundred miles an hour, and we were hanging on by our fingertips. And no more than the game in Paris, I think they were nearly too hyped-up, because they kept making mistakes, dropping the ball and knocking it on, just when it looked like they had tries at their mercy. We rode out the storm and then hit them with two tries in the space of a couple of minutes in the second half. Rog's try was outstanding, a team try that started with a move inside our twenty-two and just flowed through several pairs of hands and finished with Crotty popping it out of the tackle underneath their posts. It showed how far we'd come in terms of confidence and ambition and skill.

Looking back, I think we broke new ground that season. We beat Colomiers down in France in December and now we'd beaten the most powerful club of them all. No one in England or France, and probably not too many anywhere, had given us a chance of going down there and beating Toulouse. They had a playing budget three times the size of ours; they had all these stars of French rugby; and they were at home. Munster had taken a right beating from Toulouse in '96; we'd lost to Bourgoin in '97, and we got a walloping from Perpignan in '98. But the more we played French teams the more familiar we became with them. We were starting to realise that these fellas had the same amount of bones in their arse as we had. The more you played them the more it took away the aura they had about themselves. It was dawning on us that we could beat them even in France. And we were a much more professional outfit now. We were training and thinking like professionals. Beating Toulouse, of all teams, was the proof of that. It was a huge stepping stone in our development, not just for that year but the years following as well.

This was still my first full season as a prop forward. It was the first season that I never played a game in the second row. I came up against Christian Califano that day in Bordeaux too. I had admired him for years before that. He'd played on the French team that won a two-Test series against New Zealand in New Zealand in '94; I'd watched him at the '95 World Cup; he was one of the strongest prop forwards I'd ever faced in a scrum. I held my own against him on the day and I won't pretend I did any more than that, but I was happy with that against a player of his calibre. Califano was the benchmark for me in those years. He speaks good English, so I've had a few chats with him over the years: a fierce nice fella and one of the best all-round players I've seen in that position.

We got a charter flight out of Bordeaux that night. The plane was loaded with supporters too and it made for a brilliant bit of crack on the way home. When we got back into Shannon there were thousands more supporters there to cheer us. People who'd watched the match at home had come out to greet us. We had three weeks to go to the Heineken Cup final but the madness was already starting. And to be honest, I don't think we handled the hype well at all. It was all new to us; we'd never experienced anything like it before. It wasn't just in Cork or Limerick; it was everywhere, from rural villages to country towns. You couldn't go anywhere without people coming up to you; everyone was talking about it; everyone was looking for tickets and planning a trip to Twickenham. There weren't enough flights out of the country to meet the demand. People were crossing on ferries by bus and car. In Cappamore our family, friends and neighbours booked a coach and filled it up. The build-up and the anticipation just got bigger and bigger as the day came nearer. It was all out of genuine, honest goodwill, but it added an awful lot of pressure on inexperienced players.

And everyone expected us to win it now too. We'd gone from being no-hopers against Toulouse to favourites against Northampton. It's a bit like a situation in GAA where a county gets to an All-Ireland final for the first time in years. The whole place goes mad for weeks before it and the players can't escape it. It all gets a bit too big for them. Whereas in Kerry or Kilkenny they're so used to these occasions that they can take it all in their stride. They know how to handle it, they know what to do. Even in Kilkenny, when they were going for the five-in-a-row in 2010, no one had

ever won five All-Irelands in a row in hurling and you wonder did
the pressure get to them a bit in the end. These were fellas who'd
seen it all and done it all, but they were trying to make history
now; they were breaking new ground too and maybe it had an
effect, I don't know. But the build-up around Munster, around the
whole country even, had an effect on us. We were holding open
days in Thomond Park and the place would be thronged with
people looking for autographs and photos and all that. It was right
and proper that we did have open days; we had open days in the
years after and they never knocked a spot off us. But this was our
first time going through all this. Did we get distracted? The answer
is probably yes. We didn't perform to our ability on the day. We
didn't play with the same freedom we did against Toulouse.

I don't know what it was like for their players walking around
the streets of Northampton in the weeks before the final, but I
think they handled the occasion better. They had a lot of experienced operators like Pat Lam and Garry Pagel and Tim Rodber
and Paul Grayson. They had their homework done on us and their
forward pack was a tough, streetwise outfit. Nothing came easy in
that game; everything was hard, everything was a scrap and a fight.
An awful lot of small things went wrong on the day. For some
reason I ended up standing straight behind Rog when he lined up
that penalty kick to win it in the eightieth minute. I was usually to
be found in the middle of the field when he was lining up his kicks
but I was standing behind him, probably because I was bollixed.
I can still see it to this day. The ball was sailing over the bar when
it left his boot. I'm certain of it. When that ball crossed the
twenty-two it was going over the bar. And between the twenty-two
and the goal post it just tailed off to the left. It must've been the
wind. There was wind blowing in various directions that day and
at the top of the goalposts it can be a lot stronger than what you're
feeling on the ground.

The silence in the dressing room afterwards, it was like a
morgue. Everyone was just gutted and empty. I went straight

home from Shannon Airport that night. Just went home and went to bed and couldn't sleep. Didn't sleep a wink that night. Complete and total emptiness. I had a lot of bad moments in the years afterwards, but few of them ever came close to this. It was the worst feeling I've ever had in rugby.

I can look back now and say that it shaped us as a team, that experience. It definitely shaped me as an individual because you find out things about yourself when you go through a sort of darkness like that. And maybe you could say it put the sort of steel in us that kept us going for years after. If we'd won the European Cup at that stage, when we were such a young and inexperienced team, it might have gone to our heads; you wouldn't know. We might've thought that this was easy. But we found out the hard way. It took us another six years to finally get there. People eventually started calling it a crusade. I don't know if that's the word I'd use, but we were driven to win it after that. We couldn't let it go. It brought us together and gave us a common goal. We'd lose a lot of players from that 1999/2000 squad along the way, including Woody, who was contracted to go back to Harlequins after that season. It's a pity that they weren't around when we finally did get over the line, but they played a big part in putting us on the road.

The day after the final there wasn't much time for moping around, no matter how sorry we felt for ourselves. Ireland had a summer tour of Argentina and America coming up and we had to be in Dublin Sunday night to join the rest of the squad. I was driving, Foley was travelling with me. Neither of us was in the mood for talking. There were a lot of long silences on the road to Dublin that day.

7

When you sign up to become a full-time rugby player you have a duty to treat every game with the same professional attitude. It's your job, it's what you're paid to do. But you don't become a robot overnight. You can't just delete a bad performance or a bad result from your mind, like it never happened.

Seven Munster players started the match against Argentina in Buenos Aires a week after the Northampton game and I don't think we were fully tuned in. We hadn't got that defeat out of our system. I certainly hadn't. It was still cutting me to the bone. We lost to Argentina, and I'm sure it had something to do with the fallout from the previous weekend.

I think it was a matter of inexperience too. I had signed my first national contract only a month or so earlier, after the Six Nations campaign. The previous contracts were one-season deals with Munster. A few days before I made my debut against Scotland I was asked to sign a temporary contract just for that game. I signed a similar contract then for each of the games against Italy, France and Wales. But the IRFU were determined at this stage to tie down their international players and keep them in Ireland. I met Philip Browne, the CEO, in the Castletroy Park Hotel. He offered me a two-year contract and I signed. I had no agent and there was no negotiating. There wasn't a line of English and French clubs queuing up for my signature, and even if there was, I wouldn't have moved anyway. I'd say the IRFU knew that too. They offered me good terms and I was happy to sign.

But getting paid to play the game doesn't insulate you from its highs and lows. It's experience and maturity that helps you cope better, whether you're amateur or professional. You learn to deal with the emotional ups and downs because you get used to them. The Northampton game was my first taste of serious disappointment and it took me longer to get over it than other setbacks in the years after.

I did my groin again in the final game of that summer tour, against Canada, and I was glad to see the back of that season in the end. It had been a pivotal season for me in many ways, making my debut with Ireland, reaching a Heineken Cup final with Munster, and signing my first national contract. But it had finished with an almighty low, and I was looking forward to a long break.

Instead, I was told I needed to do a rehab programme to get the groin sorted once and for all. It involved getting fitter, and because I couldn't run I'd have to use a bike. So I bought a bike and spent a month cycling the roads around Cappamore. Needless to say, it had to be a fairly solid machine. I was nearly twenty stone at this stage. I was keeping the tyres pumped on a fairly regular basis.

I made it back for the interpros in September, and in October we played four rounds of the Heineken Cup in quick succession. The second of them was away to Castres in the south of France. Our big theme that week was the scrum. We knew that in typical French fashion they'd be looking to mill us in the scrum on their home patch. Sure enough, they were awarded a scrum inside two minutes and straightaway Claw was barking out orders to Quinny to push like a mule behind him. Quinny was on Claw's side and Claw didn't want him half-detached when the push came on; he wanted the full drive from behind. So they put the ball in and Quinny was pushing for all he was worth. But Castres didn't go for the big shove. They got the ball in and out in a flash, and next thing their scrum half was flying down Quinny's side while Quinny was still stuck to the scrum. They tore down the field in the same move and it ended up in a try. Next thing everyone was looking at Quinny wondering why he hadn't nabbed the scrum half in the first place. We laughed about it afterwards, and it was even comical at the time, but no one saw the funny side when they were skating in for a try after only two minutes. Castres led 20–6 at one stage and 20–9 at half-time.

But we were calm in the dressing room. There was no panic; we knew at that stage how the French operated and we had a fair idea they wouldn't last the second half. They didn't, and we did. We ended up turning it around completely and coming away with a 29–32 win.

There was a lot of intelligence in that dressing room, a lot of rugby knowledge and common sense. When Foley or Gaillimh or Claw spoke you were getting solid opinions. These fellas were steeped in Munster rugby. They were well able to rev it up too, but it wasn't just all about passion and commitment. They had an awful lot of pure know-how to pass on as well. Foley was physically a very strong, very powerful man. But he was always thinking too; he was great at reading a game on the hoof; reading the opposition, reading the referee as the game was unfolding. And he'd be able to give his analysis in clear language at half-time. Someone like Killian Keane too. KK didn't play that day but he was another intelligent footballer, cool under pressure and able to make the right decisions. Gaillimh had huge presence and authority. He always had a great welcome for young fellas coming into the squad; he'd make them feel at home. And he had this kind of instinct for how fellas were feeling in the dressing room or at training. He knew how different individuals ticked, he could pick up on their mood and know what buttons to push. Rog's natural ability to manage a game was coming to the fore at this stage as well. John Kelly had a very smart rugby brain too. We had a lot of leaders in that dressing room right through this whole era, with a lot of rugby knowledge, and it was a priceless asset. It meant we could manage our way through a crisis on the field; we could think our way through it as well as battle our way through it. You were going nowhere as a team if individual players didn't have honesty and guts and heart. But I think the mental toughness we showed over the years was connected to the collective intelligence that was there as well.

The Heineken Cup game against Newport at Rodney Parade in January 2001 was a good example. That was a massive match against a team that was stacked with class and led by the South African Gary Teichmann. Newport had big ambitions that season. Munster hadn't played a competitive game in nine weeks and it showed for long stretches of the match. We were 21–10 down early in the second half. But we didn't throw the kitchen sink at them. It wasn't a helter-skelter comeback. It was gradual and methodical. We didn't blow ourselves out trying to force try-scoring moves. We played for territory and picked off penalties and drop goals. We only nudged in front, 24–25, with five minutes left. That was our first time to take the lead. We finally broke them with Mike Mullins's try in the seventy-seventh minute. We rolled on from there, beating Castres at home a week later in the final round of pool games, and Biarritz a week after that in the Heineken Cup quarter-final. We were scheduled to play Stade Français in the semi-final on 21 April in Lille.

This was the season when the relationship between international players and their clubs started to change. We were being withdrawn from more and more club games. It was one of the consequences of rugby's professional era; one of the casualties, you could say. The All-Ireland League had been a huge success over the previous ten years. The best players in the country were playing week in week out; it was generating big crowds, good sponsorship and loads of media coverage. There was great prestige in winning the title. But all of that was changing. The game at provincial level was expanding, and it would expand further the following season with the birth of the Celtic League. Players contracted to their provinces would be training and playing full time together. International players would have a full schedule between province and country. Clubs that had brought them through from under-age had to deal with the reality that they weren't available to them any more. The big Munster clubs in particular were hit hard. They had dominated the AIL from the beginning, but now their top players were tied up with country and province. It basically meant that you didn't see your club mates very much anymore.

The rot had already set in by this season. The Munster Senior Cup used to be the pinnacle of the club season, but now it was run off in October and November, and attendances had collapsed. The final was fixed for 26 November. A week later the first round of AIL games would take place, but instead of training and preparing for the season with our clubs, we had been involved with Munster all along. Then in November we were away for the autumn internationals with Ireland. We played Japan, then South Africa, and it was only after these games that we finally hooked up with the clubs. Shannon meanwhile had qualified for the Munster Senior Cup final in our absence. The club had organised a week away in Malaga for warm-weather training in the run-up to the final, and that was the first time the international players hooked up with them that season. Foley, Strings and myself flew out the day after the South Africa game. And it was some crack too, a really enjoyable week back with fellas you'd known for years. We had a few great nights out on the town; it was the old-fashioned way of bonding over pints and slagging and laughs. I still think there's a lot to be said for it as a way of bringing a team together, even with all the science and technology that goes into modern preparations.

It was even more relaxing for the international players that week because we didn't have the game to worry about – we weren't allowed play in it. The idea of a club not having its internationals for a senior cup final would've been unthinkable in previous years. But that's how it was now. Shannon beat Young Munster anyway, despite the best efforts of a young lock forward who made a big impact for Munsters when he came in off the bench, a fella by the name of Paul O'Connell.

We played a couple of AIL games in December, before turning our attention back to those Heineken Cup games against Newport, Castres and Biarritz in January. Then it was straight into the 2001 Six Nations campaign. The first game was against Italy in Rome. For a lot of us, it was our first time to visit Rome, a brilliant city that we always looked forward to seeing again. We had a private audience with the Pope in this magnificent building in the Vatican. There was probably only about a hundred people there. Pope John Paul said Mass and then we all stood in around him for a photo. He was ailing a bit at that stage, but you could feel the charisma and aura he had. We didn't get to shake hands with him or meet him individually, but he was very polite to everyone and spoke very softly. There was a bit of banter before-hand with the Ulster lads who wouldn't have been of the Catholic persuasion; David Humphreys was always good for a bit of a slag-ging. 'Lord Humphreys', we used to call him 'cos he had that sort of air about him, and in return Humps would play the part and call us 'peasants!'

We beat Italy well in the end but they gave us a rough time of it in the first half and I struggled against their loose-head, Andrea Lo Cicero. There weren't too many scrums and it didn't become a big issue, thankfully, but I didn't win my personal battle and it left me in bad humour for the week. Lo Cicero was phenomenally strong and he got to me on the day. I met him again in other games after that and got on fine; I figured him out and learned how to deal with him. The next game was against France, but it wasn't for two weeks. A gap like that leaves you stewing for a long time when all you want to do is get straight back out there and put things right. Gatty had been a hooker in his own playing days, so we spent a lot of time analysing what went wrong in the scrum and working on technical issues before the France game. It would've been stuff like not opening up my right shoulder at the hit, 'cos a tall prop like myself was always vulnerable to a shorter loose-head getting in under me. So I'd practise my movement on the engagement, making sure I was level and straight going into the hit; keeping the shoulder down; not leaving my arm up too high and giving the loose-head a gap to get under.

Any time I had a poor day at the office it was always about making sure it didn't happen the next day. Most players at that level will tell you they're their own worst critics, and I was no different. I never needed anyone to tell me when I played poorly; I knew well myself. The honest reality is that there are days, for whatever reason, when you're not at 100 per cent, as an individual or a team. I don't know why that is, I doubt it if sports psychologists know why either, but there are days where you just don't perform to your best. Sometimes it's because the other team is more motivated; they might have a cause, an emotion, that lifts their intensity above yours. And it's hard to control that. But what you try to do as an individual is set a standard every day you go out that you don't fall below; a threshold, a minimum standard that you don't drop below on good days or bad. The hardest performances to accept were the ones where you fell below that standard. If you gave your best on a given day and you were still outplayed by your opponent, it was easier to accept. Why, I don't know, because maybe you should be more worried if you gave it your best shot and it still wasn't good enough. But for me it was worse when you didn't perform to your standard. I used to imagine an opponent going home that evening thinking, 'Jesus, that fella wasn't that hard to play against.' I hated the idea of not being rated by my direct opponent. It was a respect thing. You wanted the respect of your opponent. You wanted him going home thinking, 'Christ, that was a hard day against him today.' And of course you wanted the respect of your teammates too. The last thing you wanted to be was the weak link in the chain. The respect of my peers, both teammates and opponents, was more important to me than any criticism or praise I got from anyone else over the years.

We beat France in Dublin for the first time in eighteen years. We were a lot steadier in the scrum this time round too. I had a hard hour against Sylvain Marconnet, and when they took him off, next thing I saw Christian Califano coming on to replace him. They had just scored a try, we were waiting for the re-start, and now Califano was steaming onto the field. I remember thinking to myself, 'Fuck it, this fella's going to be like a lunatic now.' It wasn't going to get any easier. It was another moment when you realised there was no easy day out in the international game.

Two wins from two, we had confidence and momentum going into the rest of the Six Nations campaign. But ten days after the France match our game against Wales was postponed. The foot and mouth crisis had erupted and pretty soon all our remaining fixtures were suspended. The squad was in the Glenview Hotel when word came through. We didn't really know what to think or what to do until somebody decided that the best thing to do would be to go on the piss. And that's exactly what we did. We piled into cars and headed into Dublin. We ended up in Copper-Face Jacks, the famous nightclub, and I was bananas by the end of the night.

We had seven weeks to the Heineken Cup semi-final and no rugby to play. Foot and mouth was a national emergency and travel restrictions were widespread; competitions across all sports ground to a halt. Eventually the AIL got the go-ahead for a round of fixtures in late March and the international players were freed up to play with their clubs. Shannon were scheduled to play Young Munster. It would be my first and only time to play against Claw. It was a strange feeling to be going up against him because we had only ever been teammates. We were all hanging around the dressing rooms before the game, and Claw came up to me. And he says, 'What're we going to do today?' 'What d'you mean?' says I. And he says, 'Do we go hard or what?' Meaning more or less do we tear into each other or do we leave the handbrake on. I told him that we'd have to go fairly hard to get a bit of benefit from the game. We were rusty, we needed a sharp battle. 'We have to get something out of it,' I said. Claw wasn't convinced. 'Ah, I dunno,' he said. I wasn't sure what way to approach the game then – until it dawned on me that maybe Claw was trying to bluff me. I was thinking to myself that if I took it easy on the first hit, the hoor would drill me! I'm not saying he would have. Just saying you couldn't rule it out! So I was taking no chances with Claw's peace offering. We ended up going hard at it and fairly belting into each other whenever we had to. There was a comment passed afterwards on the radio or somewhere that Clohessy and Hayes looked like they'd declared a truce beforehand. There was no truce, and neither of us was any the worse for it either.

With all the travel restrictions, the Munster squad had just a couple of training sessions in the build-up to Stade Français. Eight days before the game we played an Ireland selection in Thomond Park, but it was too little too late. We never really got going on the day. We hadn't played a competitive game in nearly three months, while Stade Français had been playing all along. They were match fit and we weren't. We were missing Quinny and John Kelly through injury; the spark in general was missing. And still we could've won. The game is remembered for John O'Neill's try that wasn't allowed. Johno was unlucky that day and unlucky with injuries in general too. He was one hard man, loads of pace and power, the sort of player that'd go through you for a short-cut. There was no video referee on the day, so the match referee had to make an instant decision. He disallowed the try, and in a match that we only lost by a point it could've made all the difference. We were obviously gutted about it afterwards, but I don't remember feeling particularly cheated about the decision because we hadn't played well enough anyway. The defeat didn't take near as much out of us, I don't think, than the one at Twickenham the year before.

Four days later the phone rang at home; it was seven or half-seven in the morning; Donal Lenihan was on the line. Donal was tour manager for the upcoming British & Irish Lions tour of Australia in June/July. The squad was going to be announced later that day. I was in contention and Donal rang me that morning to give me the heads-up: I wasn't picked. It was a close call, but I wasn't picked. Quinny called round to the house later that morning and the two of us watched the squad announcement as it was happening live on Sky Sports. Graham Henry was the coach and he called out the names. Then reporters starting asking him about all the players who hadn't made the cut. My name wasn't mentioned, but Henry mentioned me anyway. He said he thought I was the unluckiest player of all the ones who'd missed out. It meant a lot to me to hear that, when he hadn't even been asked about me. I always appreciated that little touch from Graham Henry. Naturally, I was badly disappointed. The lack of game time hadn't helped my cause and I hadn't scrummaged well enough against Italy either, so it was always going to be touch and go. But I was told to remain on standby in the event of injuries, and sure enough Dai Young, the Welsh prop forward, picked up a knock the week before the squad left for Australia. They were flying out on 1 June and Dai had to pass a fitness test to make the flight. I got a phone call saying that if he didn't make it, I should be ready to travel straightaway to England where the squad was based. On the day he was being tested I literally did not leave the mobile phone out of my hand. I was actually doing the silage that day; I was on the tractor up in the field, driving it with one hand and holding the phone in the other for fear I wouldn't hear it if I left it in my pocket. It rang all right, but it was the mother telling me to come in for dinner.

Instead of going to Australia I joined up with the Ireland squad for a match against Romania in Bucharest. At least it was somewhere different. It was nice going off the beaten track instead of touring the usual rugby destinations. I thought the poverty we saw in Buenos Aires was pretty bad until we got to Bucharest. Romania wasn't long out of the Communist era and you could see its legacy everywhere. We were staying in this palatial hotel, but out on the streets there were homeless people living with absolutely nothing. The contrast between the haves and the have-nots was extreme. The Communist regime had looked after the national rugby team well in its heyday. Most of their players were in the army and trained pretty much like full-time professionals. But they weren't the force they were, even though they put it up to us for the most of an hour. The one thing I remember is this massive prop forward coming trundling onto the pitch late in the game. We were waiting for a scrum when they made the change. This fella was absolutely huge, must've been 23 stone, and he had this black stubble on him that made him look even more intimidating. He was replacing their tight-head, and Claw took one look at him and said 'Jaysus Christ, look at the size of this fucker.' It was a hot day, and the last thing he wanted was a fresh battle with this lad who was the size of a gorilla. The look on Claw's face was hilarious; he was pissed off, and I was chuckling away to myself. So your man arrives over, and next thing doesn't my man move over to the other side of the scrum. And all of a sudden it's Claw that's laughing and me that's cursing. Claw was delighted, he was roaring laughing at me. I had no choice but to pack down and face the music. But it turned out this fella was an amateur. Technically he wasn't good at all, which was a bit of a relief, I can tell you.

Back in Ireland I got another phone call from the Lions telling me to stay on standby because fellas had niggling injuries, but nothing came of it in the end. We had three weeks off and then it was back to pre-season training with the national squad. Normally we'd do the pre-season work with our provinces, but this time the IRFU was taking charge of it. They came up with a different plan too. They booked us into a fitness centre in a place called Spala in Poland. That was some shock to the system. We landed in Warsaw and travelled by coach from there. Everyone was in great form on the bus, joking and messing, until we turned off the main road and drove into this place that looked a bit like an army camp. The tune changed fairly quickly once we realised where we were. It was out in the middle of nowhere. There was a forest beside it. It had a running track with a pitch in the middle of it. Apparently, it was used by Poland's Olympic athletes. It was fairly obvious to us that this was going to be no holiday camp. It was more like a boot camp. The accommodation was fairly basic. The food was healthy, but it wasn't for enjoyment. The meat was battered in something or other and you'd be asking the chef behind the counter what kind of meat it was. I'd point to something and he'd say it was pork. The fella behind me would point to the same thing, and your man would tell him it was fish. Then you'd cut it open only to find it was chicken. The food was purely for fuel; it had no taste, you just swallowed it. We did monitored weights and fitness training in the gym and long runs through the forest. There was a marker somewhere out in the forest, and it was a case of running until we reached it and turning and running back. It was good old-fashioned running and nothing more complicated than that.

Then of course there was the famous cryotherapy unit, which was the whole point of going to Spala in the first place. The theory was that a few minutes a day in cryotherapy would enable your muscles to recover faster from training sessions, so you could basically get more work done. So the first morning at training we were told how it works and handed our gear. You were given a pair of socks, gloves and shorts. You had a woolly head band to go round your ears, a mask for your face and a pair of wooden clogs for your feet. The rest of you was naked. In you'd go and it was like walking into a butcher's freezer. You did three minutes at a time, twice a day. Jesus it was bitter cold. There'd be four of us in there at a time. The first minute wouldn't be too bad. The last minute would be like an hour. We'd end up singing all sorts of stupid songs and playing silly word games just to take our minds off the cold. You'd be shivering like jelly by the end. There was no messing coming out. If some fella tried to shove us back in there for a laugh, he'd be fucked out of the way fairly lively. You'd come straight out of the cold room and onto exercise bikes, and the idea was that between the cryo and the bikes you'd be flushing the lactic acid or whatever out of your system. You'd have a quick bite to eat then and off you'd go to bed for an hour or so. To get the benefit of it you had to sleep. Then later that afternoon you'd have another training session and go through the whole process again. I honestly don't know if it worked on our bodies, but in our heads I think we felt better for doing it.

At the end of our first week Gatty let us off the leash. A bus picked us up and brought us into Warsaw a couple of hours away. Everyone dropped their bags at the hotel and piled into the fast food joints down the street. There was a KFC, a McDonald's and a Subway, and between the whole squad we cleaned the three of them out. Michael Bradley's brother had a pub in Warsaw and we watched the first Test match between the Lions and Australia there. We finished up in some night club or other, drinking and dancing like eejits. The next morning we made sure to stuff our luggage with toilet rolls. Out in Spala they had this sort of grease-proof paper in the bathrooms that wasn't fit for purpose. When the bus turned back into the camp there were groans and moans from everyone. We knew at that stage what was facing us, but it was a case of getting on with it and seeing it through. We had no choice but to get used to it because we'd be back in the years after too.

We did three weeks in Spala on that first visit. The Auschwitz concentration camp was a few hours' drive away and one day we went on an excursion to the museum there. You'd learned a small bit about the Second World War at school but this brought you face to face with the reality of what happened. I've never forgotten that visit. All I can say is that it was a very quiet bus on the way back.

It was late September before we picked up the pieces in the Six Nations. And we walked straight into a Scottish ambush at Murrayfield. Scotland played out of their skins. We were desperate. It was a woeful performance. Not that I can remember much about it because I was nearly knocked out cold in the thirty-fourth minute. I'd just tackled a player and was trying to turn him when next thing another player came flying in at a hundred miles an hour and collided with me. It was an accident. At least I hope it was, because the player was my own teammate Jeremy Davidson. I was trying to turn this Scottish player and then boom! Jeremy came steaming in and cracked me straight in the eye with the front of his big fuckin' forehead. The socket was busted good and proper. I had to get over thirty internal and external stitches; I still have the scar over my right eyebrow. I managed to walk off with a bit of help; I thought I'd get back on after it was stitched, but the doctor pulled me from the game. I was well rattled; I had concussion. I didn't feel right for days. I didn't have too many concussions, thankfully, during my career, maybe three or four. But they're not nice. You have this horrible feeling for days, groggy and all over the place and not right in yourself. It used to take me a good week to get over a concussion.

Munster were facing Castres at home in the first round of the Heineken Cup a week later. Dr Mick Molloy was medical advisor to the Irish rugby team and he was in the room as I was getting stitched up. He told me I couldn't play the next week until he saw me in person. I waited four or five days hoping it would have healed enough, but Mick took one look at the gash and ruled me out. But I got the green light for Harlequins at the Stoop a week later and was keen to measure myself against the England legend

Jason Leonard. They had Woody in the front row, too, so it was going to be a dingdong battle, and that's exactly how it turned out. The games were coming thick and fast at this stage. We notched up a great win over Harlequins, and a week later it was back with Ireland for the Six Nations game against Wales. Naturally we were hurting badly after the Scotland game and came up with the response we needed in Cardiff. The form book was gone out the window at this stage. Beaten in Edinburgh by twenty-two points, we turned round and beat Wales by thirty. A week later England came to Dublin looking for the Grand Slam. The atmosphere in Lansdowne Road that day was incredible. Their coach, Clive Woodward, said afterwards that he feared the worst after ten minutes of the match. The signs were there, I suppose; we were pumped up for it and England just couldn't match the passion we showed on the day. Woody's try off a lineout gave us huge momentum. Another big moment was Stringer's ankle-tap on Dan Luger in the second half. Luger was an out-and-out speed merchant, and it looked for all the world like he was in the clear and on his way to the line. Strings hadn't a hope in hell of catching him in a foot race but he just managed to dive and flick him on the foot and that was enough to take Luger down. It was a brilliant piece of play.

Believe it or not, I managed to tackle Jason Robinson that day too. Robinson had phenomenal feet; he could dance his way through a gap in the blink of an eye. The speed and balance he had, it was freakish. I saw him coming for me and I nearly panicked. He was stepping this way and that, hopping from one foot to the other, and he had me beaten too, except he took another sidestep that brought him back into me. I managed to grab his leg and pull him down. I couldn't believe it myself. It was like a tractor catching up with a Porsche.

Robinson was some player, and that was a great England team. They were missing Martin Johnson and Lawrence Dallaglio that day, and it showed. Johnson and Dallaglio were massive players

and powerful leaders. I admired them and I was happy for that
England team when they went on to win the Rugby World Cup in
2003. They had the mental toughness and character and class to
do it. But this was the third year in a row they'd failed to win the
Grand Slam match, and they were shattered afterwards. They still
won the championship that day and went onto this rostrum on
the field to get their medals, but you could see it meant nothing to
them. We were thrilled with beating them and our supporters were
going mental afterwards, but I don't think for us it was all about
stopping England from winning a Grand Slam. If that was the
extent of your ambition, it wouldn't say a lot for you. We wanted
to win things too, rather than just stop someone else from winning. One-off victories were great, but there had to be more to it
than that.

Jason Leonard had over ninety caps at this stage. He was as
gutted as any man could be after that defeat. But he still arrived
into our dressing room with a six-pack of Budweiser and sat down
beside us. Our place was rocking; I'd say you could've heard a pin
drop in theirs. He would've known the likes of Woody and Claw
and Gaillimh, and over he came and plonked himself down
between us. He handed out the cans and we all shared a drink
with him. There weren't many players I came across over the years
who could do something like that – a pure old-school gentleman.

You'd have thought that Warren Gatland's position as Ireland
coach was pretty secure after a momentous win like that. A month
later, in mid-November, we lost to New Zealand in Dublin, but only
after a tough battle. It was a very genuine performance against
the All Blacks – or at least we thought it was anyway. But those
performances weren't enough to save his job. Two weeks after the
New Zealand game, he was gone. It came as a shock to us. I had a
lot of time for Gatty. He'd selected me out of nowhere for the
South Africa tour in '98 and then given me my first cap in 2000.
He kept a certain amount of distance with most of the players; it
was more or less a professional working relationship and not much

more than that. If you met him in a hotel corridor, you'd say hello and keep going. I don't think I ever had a long conversation with him. We'd maybe have a chat about something technical in the scrum and that would be about it.

Munster were in the knock-out stages of the Celtic League at this stage. The quarter-finals, semis and final would be run off in December. It was a new competition created to fill out the season around the Heineken Cup. Clubs in England and France had their own championships; the Celtic League would offer a proper fixtures list for the Irish provinces and the big clubs in Wales and Scotland. There was a fair amount of scepticism as to whether it would work. It couldn't get a sponsor, and the crowds generally stayed away in the early years. But it did mean that our squad was going to be together for practically the whole season, and we definitely benefited from having those games week in week out. You wanted to win them in their own right, but coming up to Heineken Cup games they always had an extra edge about them. They were a mark of where you were at going into those European ties. You couldn't afford to take it handy in a Celtic League game, but you couldn't be psyched up for them in the same way as you would for a major Heineken game; you'd exhaust yourself mentally and physically that way. You would give 100 per cent, but it mightn't be the same as the 100 per cent you'd give, say, in France or England a week later. Some games were more important than others; it couldn't be any other way. And if the coach told you that you were being 'rested' for a Celtic League game, you could take it at face value. But if he told a player that he was being 'rested' for a Heineken Cup game, the player would take it that he'd been dropped.

I was rested for the semi-final against Ulster and the final against Leinster. I had picked up a stinger injury playing for Ireland against Samoa a month earlier, and the symptoms had come back again. A nerve in my neck was trapped, which meant

it lost its ability to send a message to the connecting muscles. I lost
an awful lot of power in my left arm at the time. I was out for six
to eight weeks and didn't make it back until the Heineken Cup
quarter-final against Stade Français in January 2002. Claw moved
over to tight-head in the meantime, and Marcus Horan came in at
loose-head. As soon as a team starts winning without you, a few
doubts creep in about your place in the scheme of things. I was
worried if I'd get back in. Claw was a world-class tight-head, and
Marcus was emerging as a future international player as well.
There was competition all over the squad. Rob Henderson had
recently arrived. John Langford had left in the summer of '01 but
another Australian arrived who would make a big contribution to
the Munster cause – Jim Williams. Paul O'Connell also broke
through this season and he was already making a big impression.
He was a hungry, aggressive twenty-two year old who wanted to
tackle everything that moved. The ability he had was plain to see,
but he had the maturity and ambition to go along with it. It was
obvious O'Connell was going to be something special.

We played Stade Français in the shadow of the famous old Parc
des Princes stadium in Paris. If people like to talk about famous
victories, this was one of them, I suppose. The second half was virtually a siege. A gale wind was blowing that day and we had it
behind us in the first half. We went in 16–3 up at half-time;
Anthony Horgan finished off a lovely move to score our only try
of the game. We knew at half-time we were in for a long forty
minutes. We didn't just want to defend; we wanted to take the
game to them too and attack whenever we could, but it was a
desperate struggle into the wind. You could spend five minutes
bursting your arse to get down into their twenty-two, and if you
turned over possession, someone like Diego Dominguez would
put you back in your own twenty-two with one kick of the ball.
And suddenly you'd be back where you started. It took serious
intent to hold out against that, and we had to do it while conceding as few penalties as possible. Dominguez could easily land them

from the halfway line with the wind behind him. I don't think too many people gave us a chance of surviving at half-time. And even fewer people gave us a chance before the game had even started. Stade Français were one of the giants of French rugby; they had the money, they had the glamour and the stars. Outside of Ireland I think we were still seen as this gutsy little Irish team. I got the impression that's how the Stade players looked at us. They were unbelievably cocky during the game, even when we were beating them. They thought they were the dog's bollocks. They were strutting around and mouthing away at us. There was a lot of provocation.

Sylvain Marconnet, my opposite number, was mouthing at me all day. He was speaking in French, so I couldn't understand him, but he even tried a few words in English too, to make sure I was getting the message. I don't know whether it was him, or the stress of the constant pressure we were under, but eventually I snapped. Most people would say I have a long fuse. It has a long, slow burn. But it blew this day. Marconnet was getting under my skin and then, with about fifteen minutes to go, I thought I saw him swinging for me coming out of a scrum. And I just let fly without thinking. It was pure instinct. I caught him flush in the mouth and flattened him. Claw and Frankie Sheahan were the only ones who saw it and they were roaring laughing. They were amazed that I'd retaliated. Claw said afterwards he thought there was going to be a fight, but it was over before it started. I lamped him and got away from the scene as fast as I could. Marconnet was on the floor. He got back to his feet, but he was taken off a few minutes later. I was like a lunatic for the rest of the game. I was still fuming with him after the match and I was waiting to have another go at him – I wasn't finished yet. And I can remember Quinny, of all people, telling me to calm down and go away into the dressing room. Talk about roles being reversed. Fiona and I were dating at this stage and she was at the game. She came down to the pitch and was trying to talk some sense into me too. Fiona had no more success than Quinny. The fuse was still blowing. I didn't find Marconnet and it was just as well. Eventually, finally, I cooled off.

As it happened, I'd thrown the punch left-handed. If nothing else, it proved I was over the stinger; the power was back in my arm.

I cut my knuckle on Marconnet's teeth. I got it stitched up afterwards and thought no more of it. The next day the Irish squad was assembling for the first Six Nations match of the season, against Wales the following weekend. We would be travelling from Limerick, but Foley had to drive my car because my arm was starting to swell. It had ballooned by the time we got to the team hotel. I showed it to Mick Griffin, the Irish team doctor, that night. Mick was a Limerick man and steeped in rugby. He got a land when he saw the state of the arm. I told him about the incident the day before and he twigged straightaway what had happened: I'd got an infection in my hand from Marconnet's mouth. I couldn't believe it. This was about the first time I'd ever stepped out of line and it was coming back to haunt me, like it was karma or something. Marconnet was having the last laugh. Mick said the human mouth was full of bacteria and that was where I'd picked up the infection. He opened the stitches to let the pus out and gave me a dose of antibiotics. I was rooming with Gary Longwell that night. I don't know how Gary put up with me, because I was awake all night holding my hand up in the air to keep the pressure off it. The next morning I was taken to the Blackrock Clinic. The consultant there, Bill Quinlan, told me I'd need an operation to clean it out. I'd have to stay in for a couple of days. But Mick Griffin, in fairness to him, knew I'd miss the match if I ended up in hospital for a day or two. He wanted to give me every chance of playing. He recommended an industrial dose of antibiotics and eventually that did the trick. I trained on the Friday, went for the captain's run Saturday, and lined out on Sunday.

It was Eddie O'Sullivan's first game in charge, and he was already putting his stamp on things. He brought in Declan Kidney as assistant coach, Niall O'Donovan as forwards coach and Mike Ford as defence coach. We got off to a flier, putting fifty-four points on Wales in Lansdowne Road. Two weeks later England put forty-five points on us at Twickenham. It was four months since we'd deprived them of the Grand Slam. Revenge was obviously the theme in their dressing room that week. They were rampant that day. They ran over us and through us. Jonny Wilkinson was something else. We all knew about his kicking game and we all knew he could tackle like a back row forward; he could burst you in a tackle. But his running with the ball that day is what I remember. They would be sweeping a move out one direction and next thing he'd get the ball and cut back the other way. He was stepping and slashing his way through gaps; he made a few massive breaks. England scored six tries. It was some shock to us after what we had done to Wales. It was 31–6 at half-time and it could've been fifty. The only thing you can do in a situation like this is try to salvage some pride. And it's important as a team that you do. It might seem a bit pointless putting your body on the line when a game is already over as a contest, but there's a lot of point in it. The final score was 45–11, which is embarrassing, but England could've put seventy points on us if we'd surrendered. And that would be humiliating, a complete disaster. So you have to go back out and try to keep the scoreline down. It's all you can do. I mean, you're not even looking at the scoreboard because you know it's so bad, and it'd be too depressing. But you have to show some pride, in the jersey, in yourself and your team.

The other thing is, you know you're going to be looking at it on video the next day. You're going to have to sit down and watch this horror show. It's up there on a big screen and we're all sitting there in this darkened room in complete silence and mortification. And if fellas see you just standing there on the pitch, not making an effort to put a tackle in, it does irreparable damage to your character, your reputation. If you bust your bollocks to make a tackle but they still recycle the ball and score anyway, at least you've kept some bit of dignity about yourself. No matter how bad it is, you have to have some personal pride in yourself. And it was bad that day. The swing in performance from Wales to England was what shocked us. It was some comedown and a fairly brutal wake-up call.

There were a few more highs and lows before that campaign was over. We put forty-three points on Scotland a fortnight later, and France put forty-four on us in early April. It was the last round of games and a Grand Slam decider for them. They weren't going to let it slip in Paris. We got another battering and limped home to lick our wounds. Three weeks later Ireland's Munster contingent would be back in France, this time for a Heineken Cup semi-final against Castres, a team we had gotten to know pretty well at this stage. As usual, we struggled in the first half, but had the measure of them in the second. O'Gara kicked six penalties and John Kelly's late try sealed the deal. By now the Munster travelling support was massive; we had something like 8,000 fans cheering us on in Béziers that day.

A week after Castres I played my last match for Shannon. It was my last club game ever. I didn't know it at the time, but that's how it turned out. At least I was able to finish on a high note. We played Cork Constitution in the AIL Division One final and managed to scrape a win in a tight finish. There were Munster teammates on both sides that day. We kept it fairly civilised. Frankie Sheahan was their hooker, and we managed to get through the scrums without doing anything stupid. Frankie was a great character in the Munster squad in those years, a funny fella and always up to some mischief. He was a sound man to have in your front row too, especially against French teams where the hooker and loose-head would be teaming up to target the tight-head. Frankie was good at taking on his own hooker; he'd even up the battle in the front row. My brother Tom played in the second row for Shannon that day, and between the two of us we managed to steal a ball at a lineout on Con's throw late in the game. Well, I lifted him and Tom stole it. The match was at Lansdowne Road and Shannon had a big crowd there on the day. We got a huge roar when we made that steal; it was a nice little moment. Tom went on to have a good career in the professional game in England and was captain of the Exeter Chiefs side that won promotion to the Aviva Premiership in 2010.

On 25 May we faced Leicester at the Millennium Stadium in Cardiff. We felt we were ready to win. We had lost one Heineken Cup final, and it was a big saying of Gaillimh's at the time that you have to lose one to win one. Anyway we all believed we'd served our apprenticeship and could take the final step. But we were up against a serious outfit. Leicester were the defending champions. They had a hard, streetwise forward pack that would basically do anything to win. They were captained by Martin Johnson, who would lead England to victory in the Rugby World Cup eighteen months later. Four of the Leicester pack in Cardiff played in that World Cup final, and a fifth, Martin Corry, was on the bench. You had your work cut out to grind down a pack of that calibre. They had a fierce survival instinct too. In the semi-final they beat Llanelli with a last-minute penalty from inside their own half. And in the final a year earlier they were on the ropes in the dying minutes against Stade Français, only to win it with a late try. Leicester were a great team at their peak when we met them; they had leaders everywhere and they knew what to do under pressure. I think in hindsight we lost to a team that knew how to win better than we did. It was another hard lesson, but we did learn from it. In later years we got a reputation too as survivors; a team that could hold its nerve and that knew how to win games even when we weren't playing well.

In 2002 we were not a naïve team, but I don't know if any of us would've had the pure balls to do what Neil Back did in the last minute. The game had loads of other incidents and controversies. The intensity and attrition was up there with any international.

But it will probably always be remembered for that incident at the end. I didn't see what happened. We were under their posts and had the put-in at the scrum. We were six points down and needed a try and conversion to win it. Next thing the scrum was breaking up and they were kicking the ball fifty yards downfield into touch. I can remember thinking, 'How the fuck did that ball end up there?' I knew that Frankie hadn't got the strike on it, so I figured it must've ricocheted off someone's leg or something. I only saw what actually happened later on television. Strings was presenting the ball for the put-in and Back, their openside flanker, was right beside him. And he just flicked the ball out of Stringer's hand and it bobbled back on the Leicester side. I'd say it was pure instinct by Back. A bit of inspired badness, you could call it. But it was done in the blink of an eye, a deadly quick bit of gamesmanship. The referee was on the other side of the scrum and Strings had his back to the touch judge, so he couldn't see it either. Next thing the game was over.

We were sore about it afterwards, of course we were, but we all knew too that if one of our lads had done it, we'd have been slapping him on the back. So it would've been hypocritical to make a big song and dance about it. And in the cold light of day we knew that we'd made lots of mistakes that had cost us long before that incident. Our lineout was demolished, and Leicester scored two tries on the day, whereas we scored none. It's only when you stand next to Neil Back that you realise how small he is. And this was at a time when it was all about having massive players in the back row. He didn't accept that he was too small to play international rugby. He wasn't an option in the lineout, but he was an option everywhere else around the field. He became something that England wanted and won a World Cup medal with them too. If he'd done what he did earlier in the game, I'd say we'd have pulverised him if we'd got half a chance. But he did it, and he got away with it, and there was nothing we could do about it.

There must've been 30,000 Munster supporters there that day. They made an incredible noise for us. The racket in the stadium was absolutely deafening down on the field. You couldn't hear yourself talk at times. Thousands of them were in Shannon Airport too when we came home that night, cheering us and clapping us and consoling us. It's actually a hard thing to go through, the emotion of it. You see what it means to so many people and how a result like that affects them. You couldn't but appreciate all the effort they made and how genuine they were. But, personally, I found it hard going because of the emotions involved. These occasions kind of felt like you were turning up at your own wake. It's a bit like being alive at your own funeral and looking at all these people mourning and thinking, 'Jeez, I must've been popular enough.' But you still don't want to be there.

The final was Claw's last game for Munster. Declan Kidney and Niall O'Donovan would now be moving on full time to the Ireland coaching team. For the rest of us, it was back to the drawing board. The learning curve would continue. We would start all over again the following season.

8

Ireland were playing Romania in a pre-season friendly at Thomond Park in September 2002. It was about five minutes in when we worked a lineout near the Romanian line. We won the ball, mauled it on, and the pack fell over the line in a heap. Grand job. First score of the game. I was on the edge of the maul, so I wasn't buried under a load of bodies. I got up and walked away. I was gone about five yards back by the time the last of the forwards had got up off the ground. But next thing, the fella on the PA announced that Ireland's try had been scored by John Hayes. I burst out laughing. I thought at first he was taking the mick, laying on a bit of crack for the home crowd. Because it was obvious I hadn't scored it. I wasn't even near the ball when the pack fell over the line. I was at the front and it had been slipped back to one of the back row forwards. It was Keith Gleeson who got up with the ball. He was the number seven, and when the pack crashed over, Keith touched it down. Sometimes in those situations there'd be a bit of confusion over who got the score; you could have two fellas wrestling on the ground and both trying to claim it. But there was no confusion over this one. Or if there was, it shouldn't have involved me anyway. I was sure that they'd check it and set the record straight. But they never did. I scored one try for Ireland.

On the IRFU website it says I scored two. But it gave us all a laugh on the day, Keith Gleeson included.

The other thing that had us in knots afterwards was Denis Hickie's anecdote about the abuse he kept getting from a few heads in the crowd. These lads were supposed to be supporting Ireland. Denis was actually a home player on the day, but some of them were holding onto their Munster loyalties. Denis was on the wing and every so often he'd hear one of them calling him 'a fuckin' fancy Dan'. He was used to getting it when he'd turn up in Limerick playing for Leinster or St Mary's. 'Go home ya fancy Dan ya!' But even the green jersey gave him no protection. He was laughing and shaking his head about it. Every time I meet him I still call him a fancy Dan and he still gets a laugh out of it.

There wasn't much else to laugh about that day because we were dire in the second half. Normally you wouldn't pass much remarks on a pre-season friendly against a weaker team, but it was also our only warm-up game before we faced into two World Cup qualifiers against Russia and Georgia later that month. We'd spent the month of June in New Zealand, where we lost both Test matches and came home with plenty of regrets. We had a chance to make history in the first of them. Ireland had never beaten New Zealand, and still haven't. But we let them off the hook that day in Dunedin. We were better than them in every facet of play except the all-important one of taking chances. They were clinical with the few chances they got, we weren't. We'd been positive and aggressive and pressured them into making an unbelievable amount of mistakes and turnovers. But we couldn't put them away. We came within fingertips of scoring a couple of tries; Geordan Murphy's try after half-time was disallowed on a hairline decision. They were booed off the field by their own supporters in the end, even though they'd done well to survive at all. Then they got hammered by their own press. Some of the reaction grated with us a bit. The insinuation behind a lot of it was that losing to Ireland should be unthinkable. How could the All Blacks come so close to being beaten by Ireland? It was a bit insulting to our performance on the day. Anyway, we had a fair idea that there'd be a backlash coming the following weekend, even though you wouldn't admit it to yourself. They beat us by thirty-two points in Auckland. I stayed on for a week's holidays and went back to Invercargill. I presented the Marist club with my Ireland jersey and met up with a lot of old friends and teammates. I wasn't long back in Ireland before I was packing the bags again, this time for Spala.

Twelve days after the Romania match they were packed again, this time for Siberia, of all places, where we were due to play Russia in our first play-off game. We were going to be crossing seven time zones, and management decided on a sort of hit-and-run strategy. The idea was to get us there as late as possible in the hope that the jet lag wouldn't have kicked in by the time the match was on. We were delayed in Moscow airport for three hours and it was like a scene out of a James Bond movie, with all these huge fellas in big overcoats sitting in Ladas on the tarmac and looking like they wanted to arrest us. The game was on Saturday. We landed at Krasnoyarsk airport at three in the morning on Friday. Someone had a map and reckoned we were about 200 miles north of Mongolia. It was a fairly grim part of the world. The stadium was a bit of a dungeon and the pitch was rougher than a cabbage patch. The Russian players were fairly rough too. They had a few fellas who played rugby in France and a couple of big South Africans in the pack who knew what they were doing. Thankfully, it was their summer, so at least we didn't have the Siberian cold to deal with too. We were all half-wrecked and not knowing what to expect; it was a matter of getting through it and getting back on the plane. It was a strange experience all told, but I looked on it as an adventure and took it all in. I doubt it if I'd have ever seen Siberia if I hadn't been a professional rugby player. I can't say I saw a lot of it either, but I probably saw enough to keep me going. A week later, and still up in a heap from all the travelling, we beat a poor Georgia team at Lansdowne Road.

Those games were all about qualifying for the World Cup in Australia twelve months down the line. Every international game from then on was played with one eye on that tournament. In November we had three Test matches on the bounce against Australia, Fiji and Argentina. It poured rain all day against Australia, and we knew they wouldn't fancy it. The conditions were right up our street. Ireland hadn't beaten the Aussies since 1979, but if ever there was a day to do it, this was it. We basically ploughed into them at every opportunity. Rog ran the show and kicked six penalties from six attempts, which was some going in those conditions. Australia couldn't cope with our intensity and passion on the day. We won 18–9: it was one of those performances that gives a team an awful lot of satisfaction.

From pre-season to late November we were almost completely taken up with Ireland duty, bar a couple of Heineken Cup games in October. The rest of the Munster lads had been plugging away in the Celtic League under our new coach, Alan Gaffney. It was coming up to Christmas, and the international players still hadn't started working with him properly at this stage. Personally, I learned something from every coach I worked with, but most of the time they left me alone and I left them alone. It wasn't that they were standoffish with me, or vice versa. It's just that there wasn't much need. If they told me to do something different, I'd try and do it. If they didn't, I kept doing what I was doing. Most of the time we didn't really get in each other's way.

Alan had been assistant coach to Matt Williams at Leinster for a couple of years before taking over from Declan Kidney at Munster. He was big into process: skills, technique, patterns, the mechanics of playing. Deccie obviously knew his technical and tactical stuff too, but his great strength was team psychology. He had a sort of intuition for getting us in the right frame of mind; he could say something that would touch a chord with the whole group and get an emotional response from us. Alan was much more about analysis and hard information. He'd do his homework on opposing teams, he'd dissect their performances and draw up game plans based on that analysis. Team meetings were a lot different to what we'd done before. The same was happening at international level. We were starting to get an awful lot more analysis and feedback. We were spending more and more time in front of television screens looking at edited footage from the previous game or at footage of our next opponents. We started doing one-on-one meetings with Mike Ford. He'd be in the team room with all the footage on his laptop and he'd be able to pull up sequences specifically involving each individual player. He'd show you things you did well, things you did wrong, missed tackles, incidents at rucks or whatever. The computerised technology made it easier for Mervyn Murphy to splice and edit whatever material he wanted from a game. Mervyn was and still is the Ireland video analyst and it's a wonder he hasn't gone blind from all the hours he has spent in front of laptops over the years. In the early days he worked off video tapes and it was literally a case of fast-forwarding and rewinding until you found the play you were looking for. Mervyn would tape the match and run off copies for the players. On the Tuesday or Wednesday after an international a courier would call to your house with the tape, and you'd watch it over a few times to see what you could pick up.

Alan was very much into this level of analysis too, and already had a fair bit of knowledge about us from his time with Leinster. While we were away on international duty some of the lads left behind felt they weren't getting the same level of coaching they needed to develop them as players. That it was a case of running them hard in training and not really working on tactics and game plans; more or less just holding the fort until the international players were back in the fold. There could've been up to ten of us away with the national squad at any one time, and I suppose there was a danger that the lads left behind felt a bit neglected or whatever. But I don't think there was ever any friction between us and the rest of the Munster squad. None of us ever felt we had a divine right to swan back into the Munster team as soon as we returned. There were plenty of examples from the past where a player away on international duty found he couldn't claim his place in the provincial team when he got back. And it happened again in our time. You could never take it for granted. But fellas who've been playing away in the Celtic League, and playing well, aren't going to be happy when the internationals arrive back and take their place. At the same time, any coach is going to want to put out his strongest fifteen when there's a big European match on the line. It's a difficult balancing act for a coach. Professional sport isn't easy, and players are going to get their feelings hurt. But if a player in position doesn't perform, no matter who he is, he won't be tolerated in the team for very long either.

In October 2002 we travelled to Gloucester for the first Heineken Cup game of the new campaign and got a proper trimming from the home team. A week later we were at home to Perpignan and the loss to Gloucester meant we were already on thin ice. I hadn't come across Renaud Peillard in the four years since we'd last clashed, and as soon as I saw his name in their team, that match took on an added significance for me. I wanted him to know I was a changed player from the raw recruit he'd mangled that day in the Stade Gilbert Brutus. As it turned out, I scored one of my rare tries on the day too in what was a fairly mixed performance by the team all round. I actually stepped inside a covering tackle on my way to the line, which of course led to a load of slagging in the dressing room afterwards. But Perpignan were a completely different animal when we met them the following January at their place. We couldn't cope with their intensity on the day. We were well beaten and fairly shellshocked for a few days afterwards. Gaffney said our second-half performance had been our worst forty minutes of the season. The result left us hanging by a thread in the group. The following week we'd have Gloucester at home. We'd have to score four tries and win by twenty-seven points to pip them for qualification. But our form was poor, we were struggling to score tries, and we had key players injured. Gloucester were a crack side; they were top of the Premiership table in England. We didn't spend the week talking about the mathematics of the situation, probably because it seemed too outlandish to achieve. There was no great science to our approach; we had to win and we had to keep going to the final whistle. We were in bad humour over our performance in France, and the intensity in training that week went way up. There was aggression and anger in the scrummaging sessions and various drills; the atmosphere was serious, the usual messing and joking had disappeared. It was because our backs were to the wall; we knew we were facing a do-or-die sort of situation. And it definitely intensified our focus and concentration. No one needed to say a whole lot; everyone could read between the lines.

On big match days in Thomond Park you can pick up the vibe from the crowd and nearly measure it. You can compare it to other days and register whether it's hotter or cooler. You can guarantee that there's always going to be a buzz, a hum in the air. But a lot depends on the occasion, the opponents, and what's at stake. Some days will be a bit more low-key than others. The Gloucester game was one of those days when all the ingredients came together and you could feel the electricity coming off the crowd. Now this was ninety minutes before the match kicked off. They had arrived early and they wanted something to happen. Maybe they half anticipated that something special could happen, that something special was possible. We had dropped our bags in the dressing room and gone for a walk around the pitch, as we normally do. The place was packed already, and we were all looking at each other because we were all picking up the same vibe from the crowd; we could sense their intent. This is why home and away makes such a difference. A week earlier the Perpignan players were on cloud nine in front of their own supporters. Now we were back at home and it was filling us with energy. But the atmosphere was above and beyond the norm this day, even by the standards of Thomond Park. There was only one other day in my career that I could compare it with, and that was the game against Sale three years later. Those two days stand out for the sheer intent that was in the crowd. Other days the supporters in some parts of the ground would still be coming in ten minutes before the match started. On both of these occasions the place was packed an hour before kick-off.

Alan had been trying to get us playing a more expansive game that season, and rightly so too, but this time it was going to be an old-fashioned blood-and-thunder Munster performance. We couldn't wait to get out of the dressing room. You could see it in everyone's eyes – every player was ready, we all knew what was coming. I can't remember how long the game was on when I cleaned someone out at a ruck, but it was early enough – and I was a bit late. We were attacking, they had a couple of fellas on the wrong side, and it was a blatant offence. But just as the referee was about to blow I horsed into this fella and flattened him. It wasn't dirty, but it was a bit late. Jim Williams was captain, but for some reason the referee, Joel Jutge, told Foley to tell me to calm down. It wasn't often I had to be told to calm down, but that was where we were at in our heads that day. Needless to say, Foley didn't bother telling me either.

We had two of the four tries we needed by half-time. They were probably hoping in their dressing room that the storm had blown itself out by then. We'd seen it ourselves with French teams, how they'd sag in the second half after a frenzy in the first. We had to keep going. Personally, I still didn't know the maths required. All I knew was that we needed four tries. And we left it late. As a team we were able to play with a clock in our heads; we were usually good for managing the time well. But Jesus we fairly flirted with it on this occasion. We didn't get the fourth try until the eightieth minute, and then Rog still had to land the conversion. But I don't think any of us knew that. The conversion made the final score

33–6. Four tries, a twenty-seven point margin, just what the doctor ordered. It was immediately christened the Miracle Match. I suppose it was just so improbable, the whole thing. Winning by twenty-seven points against a team of that calibre was a fairly tall order in the first place. And then to do it with the last kick of the game – the sheer drama of it all. They say it's a game that will go down in Munster folklore, and I suppose it will. But people forget that Gloucester had a simple chance to undo all our heroics with just seven or eight minutes to go. They were awarded a penalty more or less in front of the posts about thirty metres out. If they knocked it over we'd have had to score twice. The late try and conversion wouldn't have been enough. Instead they took a quick tap and it came to nothing. Maybe they hadn't done their maths either, or maybe their heads were scrambled by the atmosphere at that stage, I don't know. But it let us off the hook and set us up for that final twist in the tale.

It was nearly as hard getting off the pitch as it was in the collisions that day. The crowd had been our sixteenth man again. The noise at times was nearly hurting your ears. And they swarmed onto the field at the final whistle, batin' us into the dressing room with slaps on the back. I was shattered afterwards, between the emotion and the physicality of the game. We were a while in the dressing room when word came through that the crowd was still on the field. Normally they'd have been drifting away at this stage, but they wanted to savour the moment, I suppose. We went back out to acknowledge them, but the pitch was packed with people. We couldn't do a lap of honour, so we went up into the stand and applauded them from there. They returned the applause a thousand times more. I don't think you could've had a stronger bond between a team and its supporters than we had in those years.

The lads went out pubbing and clubbing that night, but I got into my car and headed home to Cappamore. A night out like that would've been insane with the crowds around you, and I wouldn't really have enjoyed it. This was around the time I started going home after games rather than making a night of it. I enjoyed plenty of good nights out over the years, but as I got older I found I preferred a bit of peace and quiet after a big game. I was never a big drinker, and eventually I gave it up altogether for the last six or seven years of my career. Some fellas wanted the high from a match like that to continue on, because it was genuinely hard to come down from it anyway; you couldn't just switch off the adrenaline that was running through your system; and one way of coping with it was going out on the tear. My way was to go home and get away from it all. That game is still a special memory, not just because of the result but because of the character and soul that the team showed that day.

We still hadn't won anything, though, and we had a chance two weeks later to get some silverware when we played Neath in the Celtic League final. We had lost the final a year before to Leinster, we had lost two Heineken Cup finals as well, and we were getting fed up being seen as the nearly men of rugby. You can get patronised very easily as a team of gallant losers if you start losing too many semi-finals and finals. There's a danger that it will start to become a habit too. And if you get a reputation for not being able to close the deal, other teams will fancy themselves against you when there's a trophy up for grabs. It can become a bit of a vicious circle. Winning a Celtic League mightn't be seen as a big deal in hindsight, but at the time it was important for us. We saw it as a stepping stone to greater things, we saw it as an opportunity to prove we could seal the deal when a trophy was on the line. We had to play Neath in the Millennium Stadium, which was effectively a home venue for them on the day, and we were well up for it. Rob Henderson's try on the hour mark ended the game as a contest. In fairness, we were in control for most of the match and were comfortable winners in the end. The biggest roar of the day came late on when Mick Galwey arrived in off the bench. This was going to be Gaillimh's last season as a player, and the supporters wanted to see him get his moment in the sun. We all did, and when the trophy was presented we made sure he was up there to receive it alongside Jim Williams. Gaillimh had been captain on a lot of other days, and it was great to see him receiving the silverware when it finally came.

The Heineken Cup quarter-final was fixed for the middle of April, ten weeks after the Celtic League final, against Leicester at Welford Road. Like Thomond Park, Welford Road was a fortress. They were going for a three-in-a-row of Heineken Cups. It was eleven months since the 2002 final and there was an awful lot of talk about Munster wanting revenge for Neil Back and all that. But it wasn't a motivational tool for us the week of the game. There was no point; what happened the year before was done and dusted. Revenge would be a sort of negative motivation anyway. We wanted to win the competition and this was just another step along the way. There was definite intent that we could win on the road; we had proven it in France and England in the years before that. As usual they had a seriously powerful forward pack but we met them head on. The mantra all week had been to meet fire with fire. You couldn't take a backward step against an outfit like that or they'd bully you off the park. It made for a fairly raw encounter; it was rough and rugged stuff. But we finished up dictating terms to them. Late in the game we even marched them backwards in a maul for about 40 metres.

But it took us a long time to turn the edge we had into scores on the board. We were only 6–0 up when they took the lead on the hour. Seven or eight minutes later came the turning point. And it involved their out-half on the day, Austin Healey. I can't say many of us knew the fella personally but he always came across as a cocky so-and-so. Anyway, they had the put-in at a scrum. Rob Henderson lined him up and poleaxed him with a ferocious tackle. Healey was hurt and disorientated. He was limping on one leg. They were going to take him off; they had a stretcher ready for him and all. But he decided to play on. We had the scrum this time and we knew exactly what we were going to do: we were going straight for Healey. We went charging down his channel and piled into him. He was in no condition to make a tackle. And from that move we manufactured the try that swung the game our way. Healey was taken off then, but it was too late. He should've gone off after Hendo's hit. He'd been down getting treatment for about five minutes. He knew we'd be going for him; it's what you do. If you see an opponent getting treatment for a damaged shoulder, say, you're going to target that shoulder as soon as you can, see if it can take a tackle. So if you stay on the field, you'd better be able to do your job. There's no excuse. Otherwise you're letting your team down. Healey made a bad decision and got punished for it. Now, there might've been a bit of extra incentive for us to go after him, because it was him in particular, but it would've been the same if it was any other player either. A fella said to me afterwards we were like a pack of lions going after the wounded calf in a herd of zebra or something. I don't know about that, it's a dramatic way of putting it, but there is a bit of the law of the jungle about rugby all the same. And that Leicester team was as ruthless as any team I came across. They'd have done the same to us, and so would any team worth its salt.

The reward for winning at Welford Road was Toulouse in Toulouse two weeks later. Out of the frying pan and into the fire. We put in a massive effort on the day. The work rate of everyone was huge. We were actually the stronger side in the first half and dictated a lot of the play, but they found another gear in the second half and started coming at us in wave after wave. We went into hold-out mode; hold out at all costs; we tackled and ran ourselves to a standstill. We made it very hard for them to break us down. We were still leading by six points with an hour gone, but eventually we cracked. They got the only try of the game with about five minutes to go. I'd say it was fatigue as much as anything that put us under. We just couldn't hold out any longer. Their financial clout told as well: they had a lot of talent on the bench and they used it. Toulouse brought on six subs, we brought on one. I think the effort from our lads was immense, and we came very close to pulling it off against serious odds. That's what killed us about that game, coming so close and only coming up short by the narrowest of margins.

In a game like that you're only talking about inches between winning and losing, and I was responsible for a Toulouse penalty that turned out to be vital, right on the stroke of half-time. Maybe I was thinking about the dressing room, I don't know, but they were awarded a scrum and I was penalised for collapsing it. It was a lapse in concentration. I wasn't fully ready for the hit, the pressure came on, I hit the deck, and the referee singled me out for collapsing it.

There was huge disappointment after that game, and a lot of people were starting to wonder if Munster would ever go the distance in the European Cup. We had now lost a final and two semi-finals by a solitary point. People were saying that we were good, but not good enough. That we were big on heart and guts but lacking in the necessary class. We definitely did have issues in terms of being able to create tries against the best teams. We didn't really look like scoring a try against Toulouse that day. And we needed more depth in the squad against teams who could roll out big guns off the bench when they were needed.

But we never stopped believing that we could do it. It wasn't blind faith on our part, or false optimism. We were a realistic bunch of lads and fairly self-critical too. We were obviously shattered after the Toulouse game, but in time we took the positives out of it too. And we were entitled to: they went on to win the Heineken Cup, yet we had come within a point of them on their own ground in the south of France. We had beaten Leicester, the two-time champions, at Welford Road. We knew we were close. We just had to keep working and keep believing.

9

You couldn't take it all in. There was so much drama happening at such speed it was impossible to take it all in. The chaos on the pitch, the noise around the stadium, you were in danger of having a meltdown. And that was just the last ten minutes.

It was the Six Nations game against Wales at the Millennium Stadium in March 2003. We had already beaten Scotland, Italy and France. A win against Wales would set up a Grand Slam decider against England the following weekend. There was nothing in it for Wales. They were heading for the wooden spoon. They'd caused a sensation by losing to Italy in the opening round. Then they lost to England and Scotland. We were hot favourites, they were written off, which of course suited them an awful lot more than it suited us. With nothing to lose, they came at us with all guns blazing. With everything to lose, we underperformed.

It's an issue in Irish sport, I suppose, not just rugby, being able to deal with expectations. It was an issue that cropped up plenty of times during my time in the Irish team. The lesson I learned from playing with Munster was that the more times you put yourself in that position, the more comfortable you become with expectations. If you don't win games, you'll never become favourites for anything. The best way of dealing with the favourites' tag is the best way of dealing with anything in sport: practise it, get used to it, and eventually it becomes less of a burden. It shouldn't be a burden at all because it's a recognition of your ability and achievements. The downside is that you're always going to be open to an ambush on a one-off day against underdogs, especially in a competition like the Six Nations. But Irish sides in all sports traditionally like the underdog role, and it's a hard habit to break.

I'd imagine that Wales, despite their poor form, were quietly fancying a crack at us all week leading up to this match. They hit the ground running and kept coming at us. But we did what favourites under pressure often do – we took our chances against the run of play. Keith Gleeson got in for a try before half-time, and just after half-time he got in for another. We were leading 19–7 and seemed to have knocked the wind out of their sails. We were still leading 22–14 when Gareth Thomas took the roof off with his try eleven minutes from time. Stephen Jones converted; there was just a point between us. And that was when the mayhem started. It was just a frenzy for the last ten minutes. Wales were driving at us for all they were worth, and with about five minutes to go won a penalty. Jones missed the kick and it looked like we were off the hook. But what happened next was heart attack stuff. And this was all in injury time. Jones struck a drop goal to give them the lead. Rog had just come on ten minutes earlier and his re-start was brilliantly won by Malcolm O'Kelly. That led to the drop goal chance which Rog landed from about 40 metres. That was surely it now, I thought. But the referee, Steve Lander, didn't blow his whistle. Wales came barrelling through us again and Justin Bishop, out of desperation, knocked on a Welsh pass. It should've been a penalty, more or less in front of our posts. But Lander didn't call it; he played advantage instead and then awarded them a scrum. From the scrum they engineered another drop goal. Jones got the shot off, but out of nowhere Denis Hickie threw himself at the ball and managed to block it down. The whistle went and fellas on both sides were left in a state of shock.

Like I say, you couldn't take all that in. You were too busy just trying to hang in there, struggling to keep up with the play. It was incredible that so much action and drama could be condensed into such a short space of time. People have a lot of memories there to choose from, but the thing I remember most is none of those moments. What I remember clearest is Donncha O'Callaghan's big mop of hair. He had come on for Leo Cullen with ten minutes to go. It was his senior Ireland debut. Donners was wired, a young buck mad for action. He was exploding out of his pants to get onto the field, and when he got there he made a huge impact. The rest of us were struggling for air, but he was charging around the place. He must've made about five tackles in two minutes. At one stage he made a tackle and I was running onto the next play, and he came sprinting past me with this big bush of hair on his head to make another tackle. He had been on the ground and had got up and was tearing past me. And I just remember thinking, 'I can't let that happen again, I need to get my arse in gear here now.' I was conscious that he'd made a tackle and was beating me now to the next tackle. That fired me up. It re-ignited me again. And that's the difference a good sub can make to a team that's running out of steam. The energy and attitude can spark you into life again.

We sat in the dressing room in the Millennium Stadium, knowing we were going back to Dublin for a shot at the Grand Slam. The win over Wales had cleared the decks. We hadn't spoken about a Grand Slam the week before Cardiff; it was a taboo subject. But it was out in the open now; everyone was talking about it as soon as the final whistle was blown. And when we got back to Ireland there was no getting away from it. Ireland hadn't won one since 1948. England had lost Grand Slam deciders against Wales in '99, Scotland in 2000 and Ireland in 2001. And I think psychologically this was what gave them the edge. The pain of losing those games, the insult at being called chokers – they weren't going to let that happen again. A coach can plan for every eventuality in a game, but if a team is hurting more than yours is, it gives them an emotional cause that you can't manufacture for your side. England weren't going to be denied. As much as we wanted it, they wanted it more. They turned on the power that day. We felt it as early as the eighth minute when they whip-wheeled us at a scrum in front of our own posts. I can remember it. Their front row was Graham Rowntree, Steve Thompson and Jason Leonard; they had Martin Johnson and Ben Kay in the second row. It was our put-in and we got a good hit; there was nothing wrong with it. But they didn't actually drive us straight, they wheeled it round on my side, Rowntree walked me round. But you could still deal with that; you could lose your angle on your own ball and still hold onto it. But we lost control of the ball; it shot out and Matt Dawson pounced on it and sent Lawrence Dallaglio over for a try that was far too easy. It was a sucker punch against us, but we rallied and played well for the rest of the half. We had our spells of possession but couldn't break them down. They had a very strong and well-organised defence, and I suppose we ran out of ideas and ran out of juice in the end. They broke us open in the last twenty minutes and ran in four tries. The final scoreline was the real sickener, 42–6; it's very hard to take a losing margin like that. But they weren't going to spare us once they got the run at us, and rightly so too.

England were in a ruthless humour that day and it was summed up by Johnson before the game had even started. Everyone remembers the shenanigans on the red carpet that day. It's not actually carpet, it's a red plastic sort of walkway. Anyway, England took their place for the anthems on the wrong side of the line; that was supposed to be our side. We did our huddle on the field and then walked down to take our place in the line only to see the English lads there. Some of our lads talked about what we should do; we definitely didn't want to lose face by giving into them, so Brian O'Driscoll said we should still go down our side and stand to the left of the England team. We stood there while some fella in charge of the match protocol spoke to Johnson and asked him to move. Johnson stood his ground. He told yer man he wasn't moving and that was it. There was a delay for a couple of minutes but it couldn't go on; you couldn't have a stand-off like that with an international match about to be played. We'd look fierce stupid for starters, both teams. So we remained in our place, further down the same line from England, which meant that President Mary McAleese would have to step off the walkway and onto the grass to shake hands with us. It didn't become an issue for us because there wasn't time for it to become an issue. The president came out, the anthems were played and bang, the game was on. I don't think Johnson deliberately set out to insult people or cause a diplomatic row. He says he lined up on the side they'd be playing in the first half, and once he was told it was the wrong side it was too late to do anything about it. He felt he'd also be losing face if he gave in. I can understand that too. You'd nearly have to admire him for being so brazen and stubborn about it. He did the right thing for his team by refusing to back down, and it summed up the mood they were in that day.

Two weeks after that Johnson was captain of the Leicester team that Munster beat in the Heineken Cup quarter-final at Welford Road. The word was that our supporters were taunting him afterwards about the incident at Lansdowne Road. Fellas were shouting at him that they had a red carpet for sale – 'only half used!' The following November he led that England team to victory in the World Cup in Australia. They backed down from no one there either.

Ireland's countdown to the same World Cup began with a summer tour of Australia, Tonga and Samoa. But while the lads were sauntering around the Pacific Islands I was back tipping around the farm in Cappamore. I had a wear-and-tear injury on the pubic bone. I could play with it, but it was getting sorer after every game, and the prognosis was rest. I'd have to rehab it over the summer and make sure it was ready for the new season. It's a tricky injury, it needed a lot of work. I spent the summer working on my core, strengthening all the lower abdominal and groin muscles just to take the pressure off and get everything pulling in the right direction. I was still rehabbing it when we went to Spala again for pre-season, and wasn't deemed fit enough for the first game of the season, a friendly against Wales in the middle of August. The next match would be against Italy in Thomond Park two weeks later, and I was pencilled in to play in that one. Four or five days before it we were doing a scrummaging session at the University of Limerick when I popped my calf in the scrum. I could feel it straightaway. I'm unbelievably lucky in that it was the one and only time I ever pulled a muscle in my whole career. When I think of the grief and anguish that other fellas went through with injuries, I was absolutely blessed. But of course I didn't feel that way at the time.

A scan showed there was a massive bleed right in the middle of the calf. I was looking at six to eight weeks to get back into the action. I'd miss the Italy game, the Scotland game a week after that, and a week of warm-weather training in Bilbao scheduled for after the match in Murrayfield. The squad was due to depart for Australia on September 29. I was in serious danger of missing that too. In November I would be thirty years of age. I hadn't made the 1999 World Cup and I was desperate not to miss this one. There was no guarantee that I'd be around for the next one four years later.

While the lads were off sunning themselves in Spain, I was sent to Dublin for a couple of weeks to work with a rehab-specialist, Mark McCabe. It was bloody torture, on the treatment table and off it. I was staying in the Grand Hotel in Malahide, not far from Mark's clinic. I spent my days getting beaten up on the treatment table. It'd be a two-hour session in the morning and another two-hour session in the afternoon, him digging into the calf until I was fit to roar. For fitness, he had me cycling up and down the hills around north Dublin. Mark would go with me. He was a triathlete, and there was black smoke blowing out of me trying to keep up with him. Fellas with long-term injuries will tell you it's a lonely road. They're on their own for months on end, and it can be soul-destroying. I only had two weeks of it and I found it hard going, not knowing anyone and not talking to anyone apart from Mark and the hotel staff. I'd have my dinner in the dining room every evening, and then it was up to the bedroom to watch television for the night with an ice pack on the leg. But Mark's treatment programme did the business. I was back doing light jogging two days ahead of schedule and eventually made the flight to Australia.

I got twenty minutes off the bench against Romania in our first game of the tournament and started against Namibia and Argentina. It was four years earlier, but the famous loss to Argentina in Lens at the previous World Cup had left people still a bit spooked about them. There was a lot of anxiety coming into that match in Adelaide, and a lot of anxiety during it too. It was a nervy performance. We just about scraped home, by a point in the end, and poor old Quinny paid a big price for it. He scored the only try of the game and busted his shoulder doing it. That was the end of his World Cup. Quinny reckons we all owe him our jobs for his heroics that day: he saved Irish rugby and ended up a martyr to the cause. The win meant we'd qualified out of the group with a game to spare. That was against Australia in the Telstra Dome in Melbourne, another one of those big games that we left behind with more than a few regrets. We had the beating of them; we played with a lot more freedom than we did against Argentina and frightened the bejaysus out of them. I was right behind David Humphreys when he launched his drop goal attempt late in the game. I was sure it was on target, but it just faded wide at the death. Being the host nation, it wasn't in the script for Australia to come out of their group as the second-placed qualifiers. A couple of crunch decisions went against us, and I got the impression it was nearly a case that Australia couldn't be allowed to lose this match. Anyway, it was another one of those could've-should've defeats that leave you frustrated and pissed-off for days. My thirtieth birthday was the next day and all my relations in Melbourne turned up for a big party barbecue organised by my Uncle Dan and his wife Marcella at their home. It was a great day and a welcome bit of enjoyment after the disappointment of the day before.

The result meant that Australia would have Scotland in their quarter-final while we'd be facing France, also in the Telstra Dome. The game was over by half-time. They just blew us away. It was one of those nights when the French were in the mood for serious rugby. The whole thing got a bit embarrassing at one stage. It was a massive anti-climax on our part. We scored a few late tries, but I reckon the French were already thinking about their coffee and cigarettes at that point. It was a shame that this was how Keith Wood's Ireland career ended. You could see the respect everyone in world rugby had for him at that tournament. He had taken an awful lot of punishment over the years, and his body was basically breaking down by then. He'd put in a huge effort to get himself physically ready for the World Cup. It ended with Fabien Galthié, the French captain, giving him a big hug after the final whistle. I think he was acknowledging Woody's great contribution to the game, his stature amongst his peers.

Woody was way ahead of his time when he started out. The things he did as a hooker, the speed and skills he had, set him apart from probably everyone else in the world who was playing that position. And then there was his personality as well; he didn't care what people said or thought, he was going to do things his way. Woody could talk for Ireland, but as captain he led by his actions, and as a player he was up there among the best I ever played with or against.

*

Ireland had beaten France in the 2000, 2001 and 2003 Six Nations campaigns. It's starting to look like a mini-golden era because they've more or less dominated us in the decade since. Three months after their win in Melbourne they had the upper hand again at the Stade de France in the first round of the 2004 Six Nations. The going was tough in the front row that day. The going was always tough against France in the front row, but we were really under the cosh here, especially in the early exchanges. I was up against my old friend Marconnet. There was a series of collapses and resets, and every time there's a reset it drains another bit of power and energy out of you. They won a strike against the head and we went under in a few other scrums. Mentally, I was able to deal with it though. I had solid belief in myself, and I'd keep positive. I'd try and fix it on the hoof during matches if it was a matter of technique or concentration. The more experience I got the more I understood that a few bad scrums early on didn't mean the end of your day. You'd get other chances; you'd figure out what your opposite number was doing; you'd keep going and stick with it. And usually something positive would happen; usually you could turn it around. The important thing was to keep faith in yourself and not let it undermine your self-belief if you got rocked a few times.

Niall O'Donovan and I would talk about this a lot. Niallo was a great mentor to me over the years. I trusted his judgement; he knew what kind of fella I was; he knew what things to say. We did a lot of work together on scrummaging. The scrums that went wrong in a game were reviewed and analysed. If I got seven right out of ten, he'd be looking at the three that went wrong. He used to say to aim for eight or nine right the next game. Ideally, it should be ten out of ten in every game but there's a fella across from you on the other team who's looking to get ten out of ten too. A lot of the time with Niallo it was just reinforcing what you already knew about the importance of concentration and technique. There was no great science to it, but I respected his opinion, and a bit of remedial work on the training ground generally got your confidence up and had you looking forward to the next game.

There seemed to be a consensus about me, whenever I had problems in the scrum, that it all harked back to the fact that I'd taken up rugby late in life compared to most international players. I think it was a valid explanation in my early years, but I never wanted to use it as an excuse, especially as I got older. I probably was playing catch-up, especially when I started out at international level, but when I got to thirty or forty caps I didn't want to hear about it. I felt I was given enough opportunities to catch up. Personally, I never once used it as an excuse. Looking back now, maybe there was something to it. Maybe the lack of a foundation showed up from time to time. But I couldn't afford to dwell on that while I was playing. The whole thing for me was to improve and keep improving. Not just from game to game, but even within a game itself. That was why, if I had a poor start to a game, I'd take a lot of positives from it if I'd finished well. I never used a personal sports psychologist. I didn't have anything against the idea but I was fairly self-reliant when it came to my own confidence and inner thoughts. I found I was able naturally to get the balance right between self-criticism and self-belief. There were plenty of times when I hit rock bottom over bad performances. I'd be beating myself up after games when it didn't go well for me. You couldn't deny a bad personal performance or delude yourself that you'd played better than you did. You were only codding yourself going down that road. But I never went completely negative on myself either. In that situation you were coming close to secretly hoping that you'd get dropped for the next game; that it'd be a blessing in disguise if you didn't have to face the music again next week. If that happened, you were in a dangerous place. Generally I'd suck it up if I played badly; I'd watch the video, see the scrums and accept the evidence. Then I'd take the positives out of it too – a few good scrums or tackles or carries or whatever – and I'd hold onto them as well. After a few days then it was a matter of looking forward; getting back out the next day, playing better and putting things right.

You had to have that balance, and you had to have that bit of optimism, otherwise you wouldn't survive. If you go too far down, or too far up, you're not in a realistic place. When you win you're not the best player in the world, and when you lose you're not the worst either. It doesn't matter what anyone else says, it's what you believe yourself. I stayed in the middle because that's where reality is. And that's where you have to stay, through good times and bad. I don't know how other fellas coped, all I can say is that it worked for me. I'd like to think that I was resilient, that I did come round and didn't hide when the going got tough. I learned a lot about myself through playing the game at that level. How to deal with adversity and disappointment and low moods – and how to rally out of them and come back for more. It was a character-forming experience and it made the good days taste all the sweeter when they came round. And that's what I'd like to say to any young fella who is going through the mill in professional rugby, especially in a position like the front row. You will get your share of bad days, but if you stick with it and keep going, you'll come out the other side a better player and a stronger character.

A week after the France game we met Wales in Lansdowne Road. The Welsh coach, Steven Hansen, made no secret that he was intending to target me in the scrum. He dropped the prop forward who had played against Scotland the week before and replaced him with Iestyn Thomas, the Llanelli loose-head. It was a surprise decision but Hansen explained that it was a 'horses-for-courses' selection. In other words, he felt that Thomas would have my number in the scrums. I was properly pissed-off about what was being implied here. I played against Iestyn Thomas loads of times and got to know him a bit over the years – I found him a very nice fella. But I honestly believed there was no basis to

Hansen's reasoning. And it was too obvious to be ignored; I knew exactly what he was implying by that selection. Needless to say, I was fired up for that encounter. It turned out that our forward pack dominated; we mauled them off the park and we were rock solid in the scrums too. No one likes being taken for granted or underestimated, especially in public.

I think England seriously underestimated us a fortnight later in Twickenham. This was to be their homecoming party after winning the World Cup the previous November. It was supposed to be a celebration; they would be parading the William Webb Ellis trophy; and they were supposed to be invincible in Twickenham. We came into the game completely under the radar. We weren't one bit happy about being dismissed before a ball had even been kicked. It was completely set up for us; we felt England would be distracted by the carnival atmosphere; they were sitting ducks as far as we were concerned. What's more, Jonny Wilkinson was injured and Martin Johnson had retired. Johnson's leadership would be missed by them, but so would his presence in the lineout. We dismantled their lineout that day. I even caught a few of their throws myself, at the back of the lineout. Paul O'Connell and Malcolm O'Kelly had their homework done on England's lineouts. It was no accident; it never is an accident when the opposition lineout is consistently disrupted and stolen.

Over the years O'Connell has put in a huge amount of hours working on the lineout. It's an awful lot more sophisticated an operation than it was when I started out. The amount of time spent on video analysis by every team nowadays means that your lineout has to keep evolving all the time. You have to have all sorts of variations in the movement to keep it unpredictable and keep your opponents guessing. So there's a fair amount of choreography to it, between the lineout caller, the hooker who's throwing in the ball and the rest of the forwards. Everyone has to know his job and the timing has to be spot-on between the thrower, the jumpers and the lifters. There's a lot of moving parts in a lineout manoeuvre, and if the timing isn't precise from everyone then you can easily lose the ball. And that's just on your own throw. A lot of time would be spent analysing the opposition in the run-up to a big game. You'd be looking for patterns in how they defend against the opponents' throw, and the patterns in their own throw. If you see the same pattern in a number of previous games, you will make a note of it and plan to target it if you recognise it happening in real time during a match. The research has to be fairly up-to-date because teams are all the time changing and improvising.

All this analysis and planning meant we spent hours on the practice ground, rehearsing our own moves over and over until the timing was smooth and everyone knew their jobs. Then rehearsing moves to disrupt their throw. It was sheer practice, doing it repeatedly until everyone was satisfied. Before a big Munster or Ireland game O'Connell would have done a lot of research on his laptop. He'd print the information on handouts and give them out to us to learn. It was one facet of the game I found came easy to me. You had to be able to pick up a new variation fairly quick and get on with it in practice. I spent a lot of time over the years lifting the likes of Mal and Paulie into the air. The more you worked with a fella the more you understood his moves and what he wanted. The co-ordination would come easier. Occasionally in a game you wouldn't hear the lineout call for whatever reason, but with someone like O'Connell I knew by his movements what he was going to do anyway and was able to get him up in the air.

Some fellas had a better spring than others. Foley and Gaillimh, they weren't exactly salmons when it came to leaping into the air. Gaillimh needed to take a bit of a skip first, to get his jumping action going; he needed that bit of momentum to get him off the ground at all. So you had to give him the boost at exactly the right moment, when he'd taken that first small jump. Otherwise you were lifting him deadweight, and I can tell you there was some lifting in that. I remember a few times in training myself and Clohessy taking the mick with Gaillimh. If the call was on Gaillimh, Claw and me would be in front and behind him, ready to give him the boost. Next thing Claw would turn around and give me the wink. The ball would be thrown in, Gaillimh would go to make his jump, and neither of us would move a hand to lift him. Gaillimh would get about two inches into the air and everyone would be falling about the place laughing. He'd be effing and blinding us for showing up how bad the jump was. Mind you, if you got him into the air, he was generally going to win the ball no matter what way it came. Gaillimh had come up in a time when there was no law and order in the lineouts, so if any fella tried interfering with the ball in midair, he was liable to get a box or a belt of an elbow for his troubles.

Lifting fellas in wet weather can be difficult because basically it's harder to get a grip on them. That's when the ledges you'll see someone like O'Connell wearing come in handy. The ledges are strapped into the wrapping around their thighs, and that's what they're there for – to give you grip when you're throwing them up in the air. And the heights they reach when they're at full stretch are fairly impressive. I often came off a pitch with stud marks on my chest from the boot of whatever player I was lifting. When they're up at that height it's your responsibility to get them back down to ground safely. If a fella gets spun in the air or knocked sideways he won't have much control coming back down, so you have to be mindful of that. Sometimes an opponent will blow the legs from under them when they're up there and players can get injured then in the fall. It's the lifter's job to make sure that he comes back down in one piece, instead of falling from a height and getting banged up.

All our lineout preparations for the game in Twickenham worked a treat on the day. It's not often that something you've specifically worked on in training comes off in a match situation to the degree it did on that occasion. Girvan Dempsey's match-winning try was a training ground move that worked like clockwork as well. There's huge satisfaction for everyone in something like that: the coaches and players know how many hours were spent practising it, and when it comes off it's like all your work has been rewarded. The England game in 2004 was one of those days when pretty much everything came together. It was the day too that Gordon D'Arcy announced himself on the international stage with a brilliant individual performance. In fairness, I don't think England could've picked a worse team to spoil the party. We were roaring and shouting and singing like lunatics afterwards. The Irish supporters in the crowd were in great form after it too. It was one of those great occasions and one of the best results of my international career.

And it was proof too of how the sport can pull you from one emotional extreme to another within the space of a game or two. Down in the dumps for a few days after the France match and now high as a kite after the England match. It's exactly why the middle ground is the safest place to be when you're trying to cope with these kinds of swings.

Then, as if to prove the point, along came Italy to Lansdowne Road fully intending to take us down a peg or two. Certainly intending to take our front row down a peg or two. It was unbelievable what they tried to do that day. They had the kick-off to start the game and their out-half, Roland de Marigny, dribbled it along the ground just a couple of metres in front of him. It was done deliberately to engineer a scrum. We copped straightaway what the plan was. They were throwing down the gauntlet to us. They obviously reckoned they could drill us in the scrum, so they didn't want to wait around for one; they wanted to get stuck into us straight from the bell. Now, if that doesn't piss you off or fire you up as a forward, nothing will. If you've an ounce of character at all in you, you're going to react to something like that. Their front row was Lo Cicero, Ongaro and Castrogiovanni. Reggie

Corrigan and Shane Byrne were alongside me. We knew the Italians always prided themselves on their scrum, but this was ridiculous. I was thinking, they must've fuck all else to their game if this is what they're up to. They weren't as good as they thought they were, and to be honest we weren't long about showing it either. There were no words between Reggie and Munch and me. They were pissed off too, and we hammered into the first scrum. The Italians didn't budge us an inch. It backfired completely on them. They had put all their eggs in this basket and it came to nothing.

The game was ruined by the wind. At one stage I saw the corner flags bent over, horizontal to the ground. We all knew it was going to make for a scrappy match against a limited team. The Italians had a rugged, powerful scrummaging unit in those days, I wouldn't take that from them. But that move they made from the kick-off was the worst thing they ever did, because it didn't just annoy the front row, it pissed off the whole team. We pulverised them in the mauls and drilled them every chance we got. I wouldn't mind, but they were the finest fellas you could meet after a match.

They managed to score just a penalty in the whole game and the win left us with a match against Scotland a week later for the Triple Crown. Ireland hadn't won it since 1985; there was history in the making and we all knew it. I didn't train all week and came very close to missing out. I barely even walked all week. A nerve in my back was damaged; there was this shooting pain going down my hip and into my leg. I slept on the floor in my hotel room for five solid nights. Gary O'Driscoll was the team doctor, and in fairness to him he gave me every chance to make the cut. But on the Friday he was told he'd have to make a decision. The match was just twenty-four hours away. We were staying in the Radisson Hotel in Stillorgan and Gary took me out walking. All that week I couldn't walk for more than five minutes with the pain of it. But I had to keep walking this day. It was getting worse with every stride, but I just kept going and going until eventually it didn't get any worse. I told him I'd be all right if I got a good dose of anti-inflammatory tablets into me. He passed me fit and I took my place the next day. Scotland rattled us for the guts of an hour, but we finally cut loose and ran in three tries to win it pretty comfortably in the end. I remember thinking when I saw Reggie being replaced with about twenty minutes left that I wanted to stay on the field. I wanted to be there when the whistle blew and history was made. And in fact I was going fine at the time too. The painkillers were still working and I was getting around the field no problem. It was agony again that night when the adrenaline wore off, so while the lads were out celebrating I was tucked up in bed. I know it has gone down in general value and prestige since, but winning a Triple Crown that time was huge for us as a team. It meant a lot to the public too. Ireland had only ever won six of them, and this was the first for nineteen years, so it wasn't like we could afford to get too sniffy about Triple Crowns at this stage. It was a big deal and a personal milestone for all the players on that team.

We were gone off the boil by the time we turned up in Bloemfontein to play South Africa in June. And Bloemfontein isn't the place to be if you're not a team at the peak of your form. It's a fairly rough spot and South African teams well know that they're supposed to win every time they play there. On the other hand, visiting teams are left under no illusions that they're never supposed to win there. Getting off the bus that day for the game there was absolute hatred coming from the local supporters. They were well tanked up, giving us the fingers and roaring abuse at us. We got more stick getting back on the bus afterwards, and Brian O'Driscoll was singled out for a fair amount of it. In between we had to cope with a massive South African forward pack. You could feel the size and strength of them in the scrums, just the sheer weight of them coming against you. I was up against the legendary

Os du Randt. It was his first game for the Springboks in five years. He was hugely popular with the fans and you could see why. He is a massive man. I mean, I'd be considered fairly big, but Os was wider and heavier again. A pack like that can scrummage using pure weight and power; they don't have to bother with much technique at all if they don't want to. South Africa pulled away from us in the second half.

The season ended with the second Test in Cape Town. We'd been on the go for the guts of eleven months at that stage, World Cup included, and there wasn't much left in the tank by then. We managed actually to come within a score of them in the last quarter, so we finished a lot more competitively than we had in Bloemfontein.

There was the usual malarkey on that tour with fines and court sessions and fellas acting as judges handing down penalties. If a player was late for something or wore the wrong gear or said the wrong thing, he was fined by the appointed judges in our own kangaroo court. I was the hired muscle, so to speak, delegated to collect the money which would all go into the kitty for the end-of-tour party. You could be fined for pretty much anything, but sometimes the penalty wasn't just financial. If two fellas had a row in training, the court would tell them to kiss and make up. Literally kiss and make up, and on the lips too not just the cheek. Fellas can get very bored and very silly on tour. Now, some people who've never played the game apparently reckon that it's a bit gay anyway, especially in the scrums. I think they have this idea that the second row forwards stick their heads between the legs of the lads in the front row. For the record, they don't. They stick their heads between the hips of the hooker and the props. Mind you, they do stick their hands between your legs and grip the waistband on your togs so that they don't disengage from the front row. But you don't even notice it or think of it. Obviously there have been gay rugby players over the years and very few of them have come out. Gareth Thomas, the Welsh player, is probably the most famous to come out and I think he got a lot of respect among rugby players everywhere for having the guts to do it. But I can honestly say that a rugby scrum is not the place to go if you're a bloke looking for a date. There's fellas trying to kill you in there rather than chat you up. And it'd be fairly hard to get any romantic notions, even if you wanted to, with fuckin' Os du Randt and the likes of him looking across at you, trying to break you in half.

The end-of-tour party in Cape Town coincided with my stag party. Needless to say, they were pouring the drink into me back at the team hotel. And who should land in among the middle of us but Colin Farrell, the film star. He was making a film in South Africa at the time and was in town for the night. He was wearing his Irish jersey too and wasn't long about getting stuck in to the party. Farrell was good crack and well able to hold his liquor. Everyone was taking the piss, congratulating me on getting Colin Farrell to come to my stag and wondering how I did it. The next morning I was wondering how I even made it to my room. It was a great night at the end of a long, hard season.

I'd met Fiona Steed during the foot and mouth crisis in the spring of 2001. I know it's not the most romantic way of expressing it, but I suppose I wouldn't be great on the romance side of things anyway. I wouldn't be an expert on flowers and chocolates, put it that way.

It helped from the start that Fiona was also a rugby player, and a very good one at that. She was playing for Shannon, Munster and Ireland at the time. One of her teammates was Rosie Foley, sister of Anthony. I knew Rosie through Axel, and apparently she thought that Fiona and I might be well suited, if ever we met up. Anyway Rosie mentioned it to Axel and of course Axel mentioned it to everyone – Gaillimh, Stringer and Quinny included. But I was none the wiser.

The Ireland management team arranged a squad camp in Limerick during the foot and mouth. One night a few of us decided to go to the cinema, myself and the three amigos mentioned above. And it so happened that Fiona and her friend Siobhán Cusack also had the same idea the same night. So we bumped into each other. I didn't know her, but Gaillimh did. He wasted no time making the introductions; Quinny and Strings were having a bit of a chuckle behind my back. Naturally I played it cool, passed no remarks. A week or two later we met again in Shannon rugby club after an AIL game. So we arranged an ould dinner date for the night after and that, as the man says, was more or less that.

Fiona is from the parish of Ballinaclough, outside of Nenagh. After school she went to university in Middlesbrough to study physiotherapy. She worked in England for a number of years after college. She'd come home the year before we met. During her time in England she went out of her way to keep her international career going with Ireland. She travelled at her own expense several times a year to train and play. She was dedicated to it and I admired that. I think it showed a lot of mental strength in the first place to leave home so young and go to university in a different country where she knew nobody. She played in the back row for Ireland, number seven, and showed the same attitude on the field. When we started going out I went along to some of her games. Unfortunately they lost more games than they won in those years, so she had to spend a lot of time tackling and defending. I'm not just saying this, you could see she was exceptional. She played for Ireland sixty-three times, which was a record at the time. At one time I think we jointly held the record for most-capped Irish players in the men's and women's game.

I never had to explain to her about the commitment demanded in top level rugby. She knew more about it than me. This was someone who was paying for her own flights to train and play for her country – and trying to hold down a job at the same time. So she understood why I was away so often. She understood that the relationship would have to work around rugby, not vice versa. And she understood winning and losing.

We were married in Ballinaclough Church, where Fiona had also made her communion and confirmation, on 1 July 2004. It was a summer wedding; it had to be a summer wedding because it was during the off-season. Virtually every fella I played with got married in the last week of June or the first week of July. Most of us have our wedding anniversaries within a week or two of each other. My speech at the wedding may well be another record, for the shortest bridegroom's speech in history. I had nothing written down. I had a few things in my head to say, and I reckoned once I got them said I'd think of other things to say. It would flow from there. Jesus, was I wrong. I said my few bits and then the well ran dry. Someone switched off the tap. I stood there cringing. So I thanked everybody for coming and sat down. I'd say the whole thing lasted thirty seconds. We got over it. I don't think they were expecting miracles anyway. The speech was an ordeal, but inside I was a very happy man.

10

It was the 2004 Heineken Cup semi-final against London Wasps at Lansdowne Road. It was our fifth semi-final in a row; it was their first. We weren't in Thomond Park, but we were still at home. The 48,000 crowd was a record attendance for a semi-final, and the vast majority of them were cheering on Munster.

It was all set up for us. By any measure of experience and cup rugby know-how, we were in pole position. What's more, midway through the second half we scored two tries and led by ten points with twenty minutes to play. Our tails were up, we had momentum, we were looking good to seal the deal.

Wasps had thrown the kitchen sink at us all afternoon, but with those two tries it looked like we'd weathered the storm. But we hadn't. Wasps were the English champions and they were a hell of a good team. They had broken Leicester's stranglehold in England; they were blowing teams out of the water that season. Lawrence Dallaglio was their captain, and they turned up in Dublin not one bit intimidated by the crowd or their opponents. We helped them too by shooting ourselves in the foot in the last quarter. Two of our lads ended up in the sin bin during that period, we missed tackles and made mistakes. We were still leading by seven with just five minutes left in the game, but they broke us apart with two tries in two minutes. It was a famous victory for them and they went on to beat Toulouse in the final as well. So hats off to that Wasps team.

Pretty much everyone reckoned it was a classic match; some people were saying it was one of the greatest games of rugby ever played. You had two teams going at it hell for leather for the full eighty minutes, the momentum swinging one way then the other, and loads of dramatic moments. That was all fine and dandy, except that we were the ones on the losing side. But you couldn't argue with the result: they had scored five tries to our two.

But what really disappointed us when we sat down for the end-of-season review was that Wasps had been fitter than us. They were fitter, stronger, more dynamic. That really troubled us at the time because we thought we were a very professional outfit by then. And we were; our whole approach had been transformed over the previous three or four years. What happened was that Wasps had come along and raised the bar. They had pushed physical preparation to the next level. We were hearing rumours that the English teams were using full-time dieticians and bulking up not just in the gym but with the use of supplements too. Whatever the factors, Wasps were fitter than us, and that was something we'd have to address. Personally, I never went in for supplements or protein drinks or specialist diets and the like. I didn't need to bulk up, I didn't need to be any heavier than I was. In the last few years of my career I began taking recovery drinks after training sessions, but that was about it. I did my weights programmes in the gym too, but it was always about trying to develop more explosive power, not about wanting to bulk up any further.

We were behind in the lack of a specialist defence coach too. Wasps had one in Shaun Edwards. Apart from the five conceded against them, we'd also conceded four against Stade Français in the quarter-final. That was nine tries in two games, a sequence we didn't want becoming a habit the following season. We'd also scored four tries against Stade Français. The lesson from the previous season was that we needed to be a bit more expansive with ball in hand. We hadn't been prolific enough in terms of creating chances and finishing them. With that in mind, Munster in the summer of '03 had signed one of the greatest try scorers in world rugby at the time, Christian Cullen. I was actually in New Zealand when Cullen broke onto the national stage in or around 1995. Even by their standards he was a sensational talent. He was only twenty when he made his debut for the All-Blacks. By the time he joined us he'd scored forty-six tries in fifty-eight Tests for New Zealand. He was still only twenty-seven when he landed in Munster. It was a huge feather in our cap to get a world star of the game in our dressing room.

When I think about it now, it must've been a bit of a culture shock for the likes of Cully. I don't mean the rugby side of things; I mean the slagging side of things. He was an exceptionally shy, quiet fella. And he walked into a dressing room where there were bullets flying in every direction. If you put your head up at all, you were liable to get it shot down by some other smartarse. Anyone who walked into the Munster set-up, he had to leave his feelings at the door.

One of the great things about a professional rugby career is that you get to play with a lot of different fellas from different parts of the world. The mixture of personalities and backgrounds is good for any squad; it shakes things up a bit. The foreign lads bring their own life experience and way of thinking into the mix, and it all helps to broaden your horizons a bit, on the pitch and off it. But whether they were from Australia, New Zealand, South Africa or wherever, most of them would be taken aback initially by the abuse and insults and one-liners that'd be thrown around. I remember Wian du Preez saying once that if a fella back in South Africa came out with some of the stuff we were saying, he'd get his lights knocked out fairly lively. Over here everyone just laughed no matter what was said. He couldn't believe some of the stuff we were coming out with. But anything was fair game as far as we were concerned, nothing was sacred. And fellas would keep pushing the boat out. If someone said something cutting, someone else would have to come back with something worse. There was always someone raising the bar when it came to saying something outrageous. Or lowering the bar, I suppose is what it really was.

For example, if a fella got dropped from the team and was feeling sorry for himself, someone else would be in fairly quick to rub salt into the wound. It'd be said in a roundabout sort of a way, putting a bit of spin on it: 'Sure, don't worry about it, you'll have the weekend off and you'll be grand.' And then some other fella would add to it: 'Yah, sure you'll be able to go shopping with the missus now.' It might sound a bit heartless, but actually it was meant to break the ice if someone was in a bad mood, turn it into a joke. He'd tell you to fuck off and start laughing, knowing well that you were winding him up. It was better than tiptoeing round an awkward subject, walking on eggshells and trying not to hurt someone's feelings. No subject was ever tiptoed around; it was straight out and slag them and get it over with. There were so many remarks made over the years I can hardly remember any of them, but I do remember Will Chambers's reaction the first morning he turned up in the gym for training. Will had come over from Australia on a short-term contract in October 2011. He came into the gym and there was myself, Marcus and O'Connell giving Jerry Flannery a bit of treatment about being out injured for so long. Poor old Fla had been going through the horrors with injuries for a couple of years at that stage. It eventually forced him into premature retirement early in 2012. And there we were jibing away, reminding him how much the game had changed since the last time he'd played. 'You know there's lifting in the lineouts nowadays, Fla?' 'Yah, you can lift a fella nowadays.' 'And there has to be a gap now in the lineout, a metre between the teams.' 'Yah, it's changed a lot over the years, in fairness.' Fla was smiling away, sucking it up, but Will couldn't believe it. He was going, 'How could you say that to an injured player? He's going through hell to try and get back and you're taking the piss with him?!'

But Fla knew the score, and we knew he wouldn't take offence. I played with lots of good hookers; they all had different strengths, but I'd have to say Fla was the best when it came to connecting with a lineout. He was a brilliant thrower of the ball. It was just down to hours and hours of practice. With so much movement and strategy and counter-movement in the modern lineout, the hooker has to be absolutely spot-on with his throws. Fla used to fire them in with such pace and precision they were very hard for any opposition to do anything about.

And he was a good man himself when it came to dishing out the verbals. He'd bury you with a comment. O'Connell, Marcus, Quinny were usually among the ring leaders too. They'd be the ones shouting stuff around the gym when we were lifting weights. The fitness staff would say that the forwards were worse than the backs when it came to dishing out the abuse. And Donncha O'Callaghan reckoned there was even a divide between the Cork and Limerick lads – that the Limerick lads were a lot worse! He reckoned the mindset was a bit more supportive in Cork. If any of the lads was trying to do a big lift in the gym in Cork, the rest of them would be encouraging him, whereas in Limerick we'd be undermining him. If a fella did a big lift, we'd say he was cheating, or he was fresh and able to do it because he'd been dropped the previous weekend. Everyone was chopped down; no one was getting any kind of a confidence booster at all.

Most of the foreign lads copped on fairly quick that it was a kind of a sink-or-swim scenario. You had to be able to fight your corner when the slagging started. Even someone as quiet as Cully started coming back with a few quick remarks and it always sounded funnier coming from someone like him. Wian as well, he got the hang of it fairly quick, and again you'd enjoy it more coming from him. Cully was a lovely fella, absolutely no airs and graces about him even though he was one of the most brilliant rugby players in the world. Unfortunately, we never got to see the best of him in Munster. The fella was just cursed with injuries. He arrived over with a shoulder injury, and then he had a back problem and it ruined most of that first season. The pattern continued from there over the next three seasons. I don't know whether it was because he'd played too much rugby too young, but by the age of twenty-seven, twenty-eight he was almost constantly suffering from injury problems. Shaun Payne's arrival at the same time was overshadowed by Christian's, but he had the complete opposite experience. Shaun never got injured, played five full seasons and is still with Munster as part of the staff to this day.

Graham Steadman, a former rugby league international with Great Britain, was brought on board as a defence coach in the summer of '04. Jim Williams stepped down as captain and Anthony Foley took over. Denis Leamy had been with us for a couple of seasons and was breaking through now, while Fla, who had joined us from Connacht the year before, was also knocking on the door. Paul Burke had been signed as cover for Rog at out-half. As usual by now, the internationals were absent for a good part of the early season, but were back in harness for the first round of the Heineken Cup, against Harlequins at Thomond Park in October.

The day after the game myself and Foley headed into University of Limerick for a recovery session in the swimming pool. We were walking from the car park when a man with his young son stopped us and asked for autographs. We were standing there signing our names when another fella walked past. Next thing yer man remarked: 'If ye keep playing like yesterday, there won't be anyone looking for your autograph.' And he kept going. It was like something that'd be said in our own dressing room. Maybe that's why the slagging among the Limerick players was close to the bone at times – it's in the air down here! But a comment like that from a passing stranger, it'd sting a bit. You'd remember it. In Limerick they keep the pressure on their rugby players. They'll let you know about it if you haven't played well. That was an example of the kind of expectation that's always there. And it's good for you; it keeps you on your toes; you know you won't get away with too many shoddy performances. And we'd been middling at best against Harlequins. The match was played in woeful conditions, desperate wind and rain. Harlequins made a dogfight of it and gave us a proper scare. Leamy and Anthony Horgan scored a try each in the first half and it was a case of battening down the hatches against the wind in the second half. We didn't score at all in the second half, but held out for a 15–9 win.

The next time we faced Harlequins it was in the final round of pool games in January 2005 at Twickenham. Our form had been up and down in the meantime, getting a great win away to the Neath-Swansea Ospreys and then losing away to Castres in December. The upshot was that we needed a bonus point win at Twickenham to get a home venue in the quarter-final. We won, but it was another nervy performance. We were struggling again to score tries this season and only managed two on the day. The final shake-up of results meant that we were left facing Biarritz in the quarter-final in the south of France. In fact, it turned out to be over the border in Spain. Biarritz moved the match to Real Sociedad's soccer stadium in San Sebastian. Taking on an assignment like that, you needed everything to be going well, but our form had been mixed and we had picked up injuries along the way too. O'Gara was out, Leamy was out, Cullen was out. Alan Gaffney had signed the Samoan Brian Lima as a stop-gap option at short notice, and he wasn't in Munster a week until he was ruled out with an injury too. Biarritz were stuffed with top-quality talent from Harinordoquy to Betsen, Thion, Traille, Brusque and Yachvili. They had too much for us on the day.

This one wasn't a hard-luck story. It was our own fault. We'd made it too hard for ourselves by having to play a French side away from home in a quarter-final. It was a bit of a damp squib of a season, really, even if we signed off by winning the Celtic Cup

final in May, against Llanelli at Lansdowne Road. It was Alan
Gaffney's last match in charge. He was heading home to Australia.
The Celtic Cup was nice to win, but it wasn't the Heineken Cup.

Declan Kidney took over from Alan at the start of the '05/06
season. We were happy to see him back. We knew him and he
knew us pretty well. Mind you, there'd been a fair turnover in
players during the three years he'd been away; but there was a good
core of us still there from his previous stint in charge. Deccie had
done two years as assistant coach to Eddie O'Sullivan with the
national team and one year as head coach with Leinster. No more
than ourselves, he had developed and learned a lot from the old
amateur days. The squad was freshened up too in a big way; all of
a sudden you had several new faces about the place. Trevor
Halstead was signed from South Africa; Federico Pucciariello was
brought in as front row cover from Bourgoin; the English rugby
league legend Gary Connolly arrived, and Mick O'Driscoll was re-
signed after his two-year stint with Perpignan. Then you had a
clatter of young home-grown lads starting to push hard for a place
in the team, fellas like Barry Murphy, Ian Dowling and Tomás
O'Leary.

There was plenty of optimism and energy about the place as the
new season got underway. At least there was until Sale Sharks
battered into us in the first round of the Heineken in October.
The match was played on a filthy evening at Edgeley Park and
Sale's forward pack was revved up for a big confrontation. It was
a seriously powerful unit with the likes of Andrew Sheridan,
Sebastien Chabal, Jason White and Ignacio Fernandez Lobbe.
Charlie Hodgson was their out-half and they had a cutting edge to
their backline in Jason Robinson and Mark Cueto. Robinson's try
with twelve minutes to go put the match beyond us. When you
lose a first round match you're in a tight corner for the rest of the
group campaign, but that Sale game was costly in more ways than
one. Quinny did the cruciate in his knee and would be gone for

more or less the rest of the season; a neck injury to Frankie ruled him out for the season too. Flannery replaced Frankie that night and it was a turning point in his career. Fla took his chance, and by the following spring he was playing for Ireland. We had cover for Quinny in the back row with Leamy, Foley and Wallace, but it was an awful blow to him at the time.

Eight days later we put forty-two points on Castres at Thomond Park. The pressure was on; there was always going to be a reaction. In December we were away and at home to Newport Gwent Dragons in the space of seven days. In the build-up to the first game their prop forward Rhys Thomas said we were an ageing side. He added that we were probably one of the weakest Munster teams of recent years. We were in Wales the day before the game and one of the local newspapers had decided to have a bit of fun with his comments. They did a mock-up with a couple of our heads superimposed on the characters out of *Dad's Army*. I got the ould fella with the glasses and the hat. We had a good laugh at it, but we were wondering why Thomas said it at all because Munster wasn't an old team by any stretch of the imagination. It was a stupid comment to make because it only got us more revved up. It wasn't a vintage performance, we didn't get a bonus point, but they were sticky opponents and we were happy to come away from Rodney Parade with the victory. The problem was that we didn't get a bonus point in Thomond Park a week later either. In fact, they were leading by a point with ten minutes to go. O'Gara knocked over two penalties and Flannery scored a try in the eight-ieth minute to make the game safe. But as a team we weren't firing on all cylinders; we were still scratching around for our best form.

We got the reality check we deserved a fortnight later, on New Year's Eve, in a Celtic League game against Leinster in the RDS. They outclassed us on the day. We looked one-dimensional and mediocre. It was a sickener of a performance because of all the things going on around it: the huge public interest, the rivalry between both sets of supporters and the fact that we knew so many of the Leinster lads from the international squad too. It's never a game you want to lose. Their out-half Felipe Contepomi finished the match with two tries and twenty-five points. He picked up a yellow card too and that was no surprise because there was a bit of an edge between him and some of our lads. On his day he was a brilliant player, and this was one of his days. But he could be got at too psychologically, and if he missed a kick or whatever, a few of our fellas wouldn't be long reminding him about it. There was usually an extra bit of spice to a match if Contepomi was playing.

I wouldn't say the Leinster result led to a crisis in the camp, but it was a hard one to swallow and there was a lot of soul-searching done after it. We'd been doing just enough to get by in the Heineken Cup games, but we weren't scoring enough tries and we weren't picking up bonus points. Leinster had scored four tries to our one. We knew something would have to change. We were coming up short. We had to find another gear and an extra couple of per cent to get us further down the road. Then all of a sudden we found it, two weeks later against Castres in France. It helped that they were out of the running for qualification, so they hadn't a huge incentive to make a battle of it. But if you gave them a sniff, they could get their tails up in no time. We weren't taking any chances anyway – we had to get our act together no matter who we were playing. Deccie had done a lot of thinking since the Leinster game too and decided to give Barry Murphy and Ian Dowling their first starts in Europe. It was his way of shaking things up, and it did bring an injection of youthful energy into the side. O'Connell was also back for his first game in Europe, having been out injured for three months. We scored seven tries against Castres. We went to town on them. A lot of pent-up hurt and frustration was poured into that performance. I think we turned a corner in that game. It released a lot of the worry and anxiety and pumped us up with a lot of confidence. The timing was just about perfect: a week later we'd have Sale at home in the final round. A win would take us into the quarter-finals, a loss and we were out. A win with a bonus point would put us in the frame for a home quarter-final. But you couldn't be thinking about bonus points against a team of that calibre – Sale were top of the English Premier League at the time.

You'd often wonder why we made it so hard on ourselves at times, putting ourselves into a scenario like that. Maybe it was a subconscious thing, knowing that we'd find the extra shot of emotional energy you need when your back is to the wall. We were at our best when we played with full-on intensity and maybe we needed that sort of emotion to find that level of intensity. You can't summon it up for every game. It'd take too much out of you. You can only really find that kind of maximum intensity a couple of times in a season. This was a game where everything was on the line, and it suited us that way. It suited the crowd too. An hour before the match Thomond Park felt exactly like it did against Gloucester three years earlier. The place was electric, and we were soaking it up like sponges. It was wiring us. By the time we left the dressing room we were near enough psycho. Sale felt it too in the opening exchanges. They lost their cool early on, some punches were thrown, and Lobbe ended up in the sin bin. Then twelve minutes in we descended on Chabal. He was their figurehead, I suppose, an absolute powerhouse of a man who loved to make the big tackle and the big carry. Hodgson had landed a penalty and Rog hung the restart up high. Chabal was under it and by the time he caught it O'Connell had arrived. I'd say Chabal knew what was coming. He had to keep his eye on the ball; he was a sitting duck. O'Connell wrapped him up, and the pack piled in behind him and drove him back a good 20 metres. The crowd went berserk. They reckoned it was a symbolic moment; it probably was, but you still had to keep a clear head and go about your work with brains as well as brawn. We had three tries scored by half-time and had to wait the whole of the second half until the fourth one came. They had a scrum inside their twenty-two. We got a good angle on them and turned them round. Chabal tried to pick and go, but their scrum was retreating and our back row was flooding onto him in a flash. He was penalised for not releasing and we had the put-in now. Stringer moved the ball wide from that scrum and David Wallace went over from a ruck. It was the eighty-second minute, a bit too close for comfort, but we had our bonus point and topped the group. The end result after all the other permutations were sorted was that we would have a home quarter-final against Perpignan on 1 April. It would be played at Lansdowne Road.

In the meantime we'd have the usual issue of breaking up for the Six Nations to deal with. By the time we got back we badly needed a warm-up match, and the Celtic League game against Llanelli in late March was earmarked for that purpose. We travelled to Wales, got ready for the match at Stradey Park only to have it called off less than an hour before kick-off. The pitch was flooded; the referee felt it was too much of a risk. It meant we'd be going in rusty against Perpignan and it worried us. But everyone had to put aside those worries for a couple of days because we were coming home from Wales to the funeral of a young rugby player whom we'd all known and liked. Conrad O'Sullivan had played with Cork Con and he'd been in the Munster squad for a couple of years. He was a cousin of Mick O'Driscoll and a great friend of Denis Leamy. The Cork lads in particular knew him well. The news of his death had cast a pall over everything in the lead-up to the Llanelli game. The funeral was on a Sunday, and on Monday we had to try and get back to work. On the Tuesday a short practice match in training erupted into a full-on, full-contact situation. I think a lot of fellas were a bit tense and cranky. We needed a blow-out and we were trying to simulate the intensity of a knock-out cup game. It was on the back pitch at Thomond Park and it was a case of stand back and let them at it.

Fellas were piling into rucks and clean-outs and tackles. It was as much as we could do to try and get some bit of match sharpness into our game. We needed every ounce of it too, because Perpignan, unlike other French sides over the years, turned up to play. They had a beast of a pack and they turned it into a grinding battle for most of the eighty minutes. O'Connell scored our only try of the game. Perpignan had their chances too, but we did enough to keep the lid on them and see it out safely.

Lansdowne was packed to capacity that afternoon, an absolute sea of red. Munster's popularity in those years was breaking new ground. The popularity of the game in general seemed to be breaking new ground. The television viewing figures for the big rugby games were apparently breaking new records. You wouldn't have thought the hype and excitement around the Heineken Cup could have got any bigger, but it went into another stratosphere altogether after the other result on the same day. Leinster had gone down to Toulouse and beaten them in a thriller of a match. It meant both sides would be back in Lansdowne three weeks later to meet in a Heineken Cup semi-final that had all the trappings of a GAA All-Ireland final. It caught the public imagination in a way probably that no rugby match played in the country ever had. Everyone was talking about it, everywhere you went. It was an awkward one for the players on both sides because we knew each other so well. So many of them were teammates of ours from the international squad. It gave a personal edge to the match that you don't often get in professional rugby. The fella you were facing was a friend of yours, but that makes it worse in a way. It adds more pressure, because the last person you want to lose to is a friend.

Maybe what separated us on the day was that we were on the road longer as a team. We'd been knocking on the door for years and we couldn't contemplate coming up short again. We also had the beating they gave us at Christmas in our minds too. On the day we were absolutely manic in our intensity. Every man knew what he had to do. It was one of those games where every single player played well. And some of our lads played out of their skins. It was close enough to a complete performance. It probably helped that Leinster were favourites. They'd been brilliant against Toulouse; their backs had cut them to shreds. That was the big danger for us. We ended up putting David Wallace in midfield on their lineouts to clog up the space for their runners. It meant I'd have to get a jumper into the air on my own. I didn't mind; we'd been doing it for years at that stage. You'd have to get your timing exactly right with the jumper, because if you were a fraction out there wouldn't be a second prop there to gather him up. But with enough practice and familiarity it works nearly as well as a two-man lift. It's something that can confuse your opponents. If they see just you there, they'll be inclined to think that you're not going to be lifting anyone, and it can catch them out. On the day against Leinster we were just trying to throw a spanner in the works; we had to try and come up with something different against a team that knew us so well. With a backline of their calibre they'd have wanted to call full lineouts to drag in all our forwards and leave more space for their backs. They'd have copped on fairly quickly that we were leaving Wally out in midfield, so the surprise wouldn't have lasted long; but little tactics like that give you extra confidence going into a game.

Vin Nally, my old friend from Invercargill, was at the game that day. He and his wife Jan were over in Ireland for my sister Rosemary's wedding. Vin had been at hundreds of big games in New Zealand over the years. He said he'd never experienced an atmosphere like it before. He was in the East Stand. The noise, the colour, the emotion, he said actually he'd never been at a sporting occasion like it. Vin was on a high afterwards. He wasn't alone, obviously. The Munster fans were fairly happy too. They'd managed to take over the stadium on the day. It was meant to be more or less 50/50 red and blue, but when we walked out we could see far more red than blue. It was a great omen for us and got our adrenaline going even more.

We were on top for most of the afternoon, but it was only when Rog scored his try with three or four minutes to go that you could finally relax a little bit. The Munster supporters were in full voice at that stage, and it was a weird sort of feeling, jogging around nice and relaxed with three or four minutes still to go when you'd been pent-up about it for the guts of three weeks. The pressure was finally lifted. Then Halstead ran in his intercept try to put the tin hat on it altogether. Trevor made a huge impact that season. He was all power and no frills attached, but very consistent in defence and attack. He was one of those fellas with the ability to give you go-forward ball every time he got it. He was massively strong, you were always getting impetus when he got the ball in his hands, and he had the skills to offload out of the tackle. He just did it time and again. And he led the defence as well with big tackles. He brought a physical presence and maturity in the centre position that was vital for us that season.

At the final whistle I left the pitch early and headed for the dressing rooms. Reggie Corrigan had been carried off injured with about ten minutes to go, and I didn't know what had happened to him. I had a lot of time for Reggie, I'd known him a good few years at that stage. He was my opposite number in the scrum that day; we both went flat out, but once it's over it's over. I knocked on the Leinster dressing room door and a few of their lads were already back. They let me in and I went over and had a chat with Reggie. Some people would like to think that there'd be bad blood between the players on both sides, but that's nonsense. There was a lot of respect and friendship. I stayed there for a couple of minutes before their dressing room started to fill up and then headed back down to ours. The place was like paradise with all the happiness and contentment floating around it. It was only a semi-final, and in theory you're not supposed to get too emotional over a semi-final, but you couldn't pretend that this game was just another hurdle to get over. It was the most talked-about game of rugby that was probably ever played in Ireland. It was the derby to end all derbies. You couldn't pretend it wasn't something special; you had to take it all in and enjoy it before moving on. There was none of us going to lose the run of ourselves anyway. We'd been around too long for that and had got bitten too often in the past. In four weeks' time we'd be playing our third Heineken Cup final. It'd be against Biarritz in the Millennium Stadium. We had lots of time to come down from the high of Lansdowne Road and get ready for another tilt at the big one.

There was a lot of talk in the build-up that Munster's time had come, that we had served our apprenticeship and done our time. There was none of that in our camp. People were saying that we had earned the right to win a European Cup; that we deserved one after all the heartbreak and all that. Well, Biarritz weren't saying it. They weren't thinking that we deserved one. You deserve what you get, no more and no less, and we knew that only too well. But what you did have now was a serious group of players with a lot of experience in the bank. We had knowledge and mental toughness, and in hindsight I think you can say that we were coming to the peak of our powers around that time. But we still had to win it. We still had to do it.

Quinny made it back in the nick of time, seven months after doing his cruciate. He came off the bench for the last two Celtic League games before the final and was selected for the match-day twenty-two. Frankie didn't make it back and Barry Murphy was out too. Barry had scored a brilliant individual try in the Sale game in January, but then broke his leg a month before the Leinster match and was gone for the season. It's a lonely enough station for fellas like that, especially when everyone else is celebrating a major victory like the one in Lansdowne Road. And it's worse, I'd imagine, when everyone else around them is preparing for a massive match. They'd only be too happy to go through the nerves and sickness you feel in the days and hours before kick-off. It's a killer, the way time slows down on you and every minute feels like ten. Generally I was able to get a good night's sleep the night before a big game. I'd be able to get in a good breakfast the next morning too, which probably isn't a big surprise to anyone, but the last few hours would play hell with the nerves. Many a time I threw up in the dressing room just before going out on the field. You'd be hydrating all morning, pouring the water into you, and next thing it'd come up in a flood. Retching pure liquid. Sometimes the old chicken and pasta came up too. And it would've been hard enough to get down in the first place. But you had to go through with it, you had to embrace the nerves and look on them as a good sign that your system was ready to go when the whistle blew. As soon as the game was on I found I was grand. I'd be supping away at the water every chance I got.

Seventeen minutes into the final, Halstead scored our first try. They reckon there were about 60,000 Munster fans in the stadium that day. The roof was closed. The noise they made when Trevor went over was frightening. I can say without a doubt that it was the loudest roar I have ever experienced on a rugby pitch. And I heard a fair few loud ones over the years. But this was one in a different league altogether. I remember it clear as day: turning round and walking back and this wave of sound rolling around the stands like thunder. You could nearly have done with ear muffs it was so loud. You literally couldn't have heard someone a metre away from you. You would have to use eye contact and hand signals if you wanted to get a message to someone. I think it came out of relief as much as joy or euphoria. Biarritz had scored a try after three minutes and there was this desperate sort of quiet tension among the Munster fans. So when we scored there was just this explosion. I played in another Heineken Cup final at the same venue two years later; the Grand Slam game in 2009 also at the Millennium; the England game in Croke Park. In my personal experience, Halstead's try broke the sound barrier. I'll never forget it.

We hadn't panicked after their try. There was another seventy-seven minutes still to play. There was no fear. We were clear-headed and calm. That was the benefit of experience kicking in. We knew what we had to do, and knew we could do it. That's not hindsight talking. Everyone was calm and clear. We went about our work, found our rhythm and turned up the pressure. We got penalties that were kickable and turned them down to go to the corner instead. We'd made up our minds in the days before that we weren't going to lose it through caution or the fear of taking risks. We'd need tries to win, and we'd go after them rather than playing the percentage game. We didn't score the tries from those situations, but we were making a statement, to ourselves as well as them. But you can only plan for so much. Things happen, fellas do things in the heat of the moment, a game takes on a life of its own.

No one saw Peter Stringer's try coming. I mean no one. I didn't even see it until I watched it on television after the game. That's what happens when you're in the front row of a scrum. The ball is gone and play has resumed while you're still extricating yourself from the pile-up. Or there could be a knock-on or something, and you're getting up from one scrum and going straight into another without knowing why. There are things you miss, and you only find out what happened on television afterwards. The first I saw of Stringer's try was him getting up off the ground with the ball and our lads running over to congratulate him and the crowd going wild. I didn't know how it happened or if he'd gone left or right. Biarritz were absolutely stunned to have coughed up a try as soft as this in a game as big as this. A try like that is not supposed to happen at that level. I'd imagine they switched off because of their pre-match analysis, or maybe over-analysis. They'd have seen Strings over the years and decided there was no chance he'd break and snipe like that. They'd have looked at Munster over their previous ten or twenty matches and reckoned that in this situation there was no need to leave a winger there to defend the blind side. And the way Strings stood over the ball at the back of the scrum, it looked for all the world like he was going to throw it out left to O'Gara or someone. You could see on TV their winger, Bobo, drifting in from his corner and leaving a gap. But they still had Serge Betsen on the blindside of their scrum patrolling that space. He had his head up, looking at Stringer, and I think he bought the dummy too. Betsen put his head down for a split second, and next thing Strings was scurrying by him like a mouse getting away from a cat. The like of that would be very embarrassing for a flanker, to be caught out like that. But it took serious balls for Strings to do what he did. He was doing it on his own, he'd have been totally isolated, and if Betsen had caught him he'd have thrown him into the stand. Betsen looked totally shocked after it happened. He looked like a fella that was thinking, 'What the fuck happened there?' He wasn't alone; I was thinking the same thing myself.

Three minutes into the second half Rog landed a penalty to leave us 20–10 in front. Then we had our worst period of the game. We didn't score for half an hour. Dimitri Yachvili kicked three penalties to leave them just a point behind with ten minutes to play. Yachvili is a brilliant, dangerous player and I could never understand why French teams kept dropping him and subbing him.

I'd say we tightened up in that second half. It's not something you want to do; ideally, you just want to keep playing your own game irrespective of the occasion. But it's human nature. You see it all the time. The nearer a team gets to the prize they've been chasing for so long, the more they're going to be feeling the pressure. And the first time is always the hardest. You want it so badly you can't help but tighten up in yourself. I can remember the thoughts going through my own head in the week before the game. I was thinking to myself that if we were to lose this game, there was no way I was going to go up on the rostrum for another losers' medal. They could keep it as far as I was concerned. I know I shouldn't have been thinking those negative thoughts, but I was. I had my mind made up that if we lost I was walking straight off the pitch. It is disgusting to have to go up and receive a losers' medal. I have no idea where my two are, and I couldn't care less if I never saw them again. A third time would have been unbearable.

That was the pressure we were under that day, some of us anyway. But we were just about battle-hardened enough to cope with it. With an hour gone, we were struggling. Then there was a break in play and suddenly the giant screen in the stadium was flashing up images from O'Connell Street in Limerick. The street was a sea of red. The crowd in Limerick erupted and the crowd in the stadium erupted at the same time. I saw it and it was impressive. I didn't stand there admiring it, but it gave us a shot of energy and inspiration when we needed it. But Biarritz still had all the momentum, and we were still under the cosh. Seven minutes from time we finally got a reprieve. They were penalised for coming in from the side and O'Gara was handed the penalty. We badly needed the points for breathing space. The anxiety was desperate. Rog struck it perfectly and over it sailed. Our paths crossed as we were running back for the restart; I gave him the outstretched hand just to acknowledge what he'd done. I didn't normally go in for gestures like that but it was out of pure admiration.

The amount of times Rog has stood over crucial kicks for us, you couldn't but admire the man. You could take the piss plenty with him too, but deep down I had nothing but respect for his strength of character and all-round class. He missed kicks, he wouldn't deny that himself, but he never collapsed. You wouldn't be worrying if he missed one, because you knew he'd be able to fix what went wrong when he stepped up the next one. And in general you'd be relaxed as he went through his routine, because there was always a better chance than not that it was going to go over. A lot of the time you wouldn't be looking at him at all when he was lining up a conversion. You'd be in a huddle getting ready for the next play, trying to make sure we didn't concede a try just after we'd scored one, which often happens to teams. You can't invest much emotion in a kick at goal anyway. It's out of your control.

You can't let it damage your morale if it doesn't go over; you just can't let that happen. The only thing that matters is what's going to happen next.

But I'd be lying if I said there wasn't some bit of fear in me when Rog was addressing that particular kick. It was just so badly needed. Watching it going over gave us a great sense of relief. It must be such an isolated place to be, standing there on your own in front of 80,000 people and millions more watching on TV, then putting down the ball, stepping back and looking at the posts. Years and years of practice have gone into a moment like that. But it still has to be executed, in those circumstances, under that amount of pressure. I don't think you could do that job unless you really wanted to do it. There's lots of fellas who could take a ball in training and drive it between the posts from the half-way line. But doing it when it matters, and wanting to do it – you have to be a certain kind of character. They say that in team sports no team should be dependent on any one player. That's all right in theory, but nearly every great team has a special player that in reality they can't do without. Not in a major final anyway. Kilkenny have Henry Shefflin, Barcelona have Messi, Man United have Rooney. If there wasn't such a thing as a special player, it would level the playing field for an awful lot of other teams. O'Gara in his temperament and leadership and game-management was special.

Biarritz threw everything at us in the last seven minutes. It was a matter of keeping our concentration and making tackle after tackle until time ran out. There were fellas crying and hugging on the pitch after the final whistle. And the Munster crowd was going bananas. It was a lovely thing to see all that happiness, walking round the field and waving to people you knew in the crowd. I'd say for the younger lads like Flannery and Dowling it was just pure joy. They hadn't been around for six or seven years trying to win this bloody thing. That's why there was as much relief for me as elation. The feeling of relief was huge. I wouldn't have to be walking up for another losers' medal. We were finally there. The Biarritz lads would have to make that horrible walk this time. I can remember watching them, waiting around to go up and get their medals. Yachvili came up to me and offered his hand. I could see the devastation in his face. I don't know if he understood me, he has some English because I've spoken to him a few times over the years, but I told him that I knew how he felt. It wasn't just hollow words I was speaking. I did know how he felt, and I had sympathy for him. I well remembered the sick, empty feeling I had after 2000 and 2002. The contrast with how I was feeling now was night and day. The sheer extremes between one feeling and the other. But that's what sport gives and takes away, I suppose.

We left the Millennium Stadium and eventually got back to the airport in Cardiff for the flight home that night. The supporters were going nuts everywhere we met them, and most of the players weren't that far behind them. Everyone was on a complete high. The lads partied on for days, but I had other things on my mind. Fiona was a few days away from going into labour. I told Deccie that I'd be peeling away from the celebrations as soon as we got home. I drove straight from Shannon to Nenagh, where we were living at the time. Fiona had watched the match at home on television. Five days later our first daughter, Sally, was born. I suppose if you're going to ask for one great week in your life, it doesn't get much better than that one.

Winning the Heineken Cup for the first time, the satisfaction you got from it went deep. The sense of fulfilment it gave you was a brilliant thing to experience. It was a huge part of my life. I woke up for days afterwards with a smile on my face. But for me the birth of a child is more special. I don't think about that final, or the 2008 final, every day of the week, but I think of Sally and her sister Róisín every day. One is sport, I suppose, and the other is life. But I know where my winners' medals are, and I never want to lose them either.

11

The shoe was on the other foot when South Africa turned up in Dublin five months after they'd done the double on us in Bloemfontein and Cape Town. It was November 2004, Ireland's first game of the new international season.

I can't deny there were tears in my eyes during the national anthem, because there are photographs and TV pictures to prove it. I don't really know what came over me but I used to get goosebumps any time I stood for *Amhrán na bhFiann* anyway. I think there were tears in Drico's eyes too! It might have had something to do with comments the South African coach Jake White had made. During our summer tour he'd said that of the Irish players only Drico would make the South African team, and that Paul O'Connell and Malcolm O'Kelly might make their squad. And he stood over those remarks the week of the match in November. White was basically dismissing an entire team, bar a couple of players. The previous March we had beaten England, the world champions, in Twickenham. We'd won the Triple Crown that season; we felt we were a good team that was going places.

Apart from being disrespectful, it was a stupid thing to say. Because any team hearing it is going to be galvanised into action; it's going to hurt and it's going to motivate you. I can never understand why players or coaches come out with stuff the week before a game that's going to antagonise their opponents. I couldn't understand what Jake White thought he was trying to achieve. I mean, even if they had beaten us, would he have achieved anything more than if he hadn't said anything? It was a brainless thing to say. Eddie O'Sullivan didn't have to use White's comments as motivation, because there was no need. They had bullied us in those games in South Africa, and that was another reason we were wound up. We won 17–12 and it was a sweet victory.

I got to know Os du Randt a little bit at the dinner that night. They put me sitting beside him. And, like a lot of opponents I met over the years, he was a sound fella. Rack of lamb was on the menu that night. There were extra portions going round, and needless to say Os and myself helped ourselves to more. Some of the other lads at the table got a bit giddy and decided to gather all the bones left over from the other plates. They piled them onto one massive plate and presented it in front of the two of us. There must've been about forty bones on the plate. It looked like me and Os had eaten a whole lamb between us, or maybe two. Fiona has a photo of us hiding behind this mountain of bones. In fairness, I don't think there were many vegetarians ever played rugby, and probably fewer who played in the front row. I swapped jerseys with du Randt on the pitch after the game and it was one opponent's jersey I was happy to get. I had huge respect for him, a world-class player and a legend of South African rugby. He'd won a World Cup with them in 1995 and would win another in 2007 after a gap of twelve years. That was some achievement.

I swapped a fair few jerseys over the years; I never refused, but generally I didn't do the asking. That was because of what happened in November 2001 when we played New Zealand at Lansdowne Road. I was still a rookie international at that stage. After the game I went into their dressing room to swap with my direct opponent that day, Greg Feek, who happens to be the current Leinster scrum coach. I asked him and he said no, and I felt a bit embarrassed. Not everyone swaps jerseys, it wasn't unheard of, but it left me feeling a bit awkward and naïve. I walked out of that dressing room and vowed there and then that I'd never go into an opposition dressing room again looking to swap jerseys. I didn't know at that time whether I'd get any more caps, but it turned out that I got a lot more; but still, I never did it again.

The first game of the 2005 Six Nations was away to Italy. Two days before the match Niall O'Donovan took me out for a walk around the streets of Rome. It wasn't to see the sights. It was to give me a pep talk. Niallo reminded me that this was a Lions year and there was a big opportunity for me if I had a good Six Nations campaign. We all knew that the British & Irish Lions would be touring New Zealand that summer, but O'Donovan was planting it in my head as a target. I hadn't set it as a goal, the same way I hadn't really set any goals along the way. For me it was always about playing and performing and letting whoever the selectors were make their judgements after that. But Niallo said there was more in me than maybe I was showing; if I had a good Six Nations, I'd be in with a shout of making the Lions squad. It got me thinking, it got me motivated. We beat Italy; I upped my performance and got around the field to make myself a bit more prominent in the loose. That's the thing about nearly anything you go to do, I suppose: there's always a bit more in you than maybe you realise. You think you're giving 100 per cent but there's probably a few per cent more that you can give if you have the right motivation. Sometimes it just needs someone to say the right thing at the right time. A week later I scored the only try of my international career, against Scotland at Murrayfield. And that's including the one I 'scored' against Romania in 2002. It was near the end of the game; we were well ahead at the time. I was on the blindside of a ruck close to their line. Malcolm took the pass from

Strings, he gave it to me, and I more or less fell over the line. Can't say it was a thing of beauty. I got to my feet only to find the lads laughing their heads off. They were easily amused.

They weren't the only ones who saw the funny side of it. We were in camp for the England game a fortnight later, staying in the Citywest Hotel in Dublin. Word went around that Christy Moore would be coming in to play for us one night, and we were all looking forward to it because Christy had done a gig for us years earlier when Warren Gatland was in charge. That time we were staying in the Glenview Hotel in Wicklow, and we were out in a bar/restaurant for dinner in Greystones one night when Christy walked in. Rala, our baggage manager, had organised it as a surprise. His proper name is Paddy O'Reilly, but everyone knows him as Rala. A great character and a friend to all the players, if ever you were stuck for anything, you'd go to Rala. Anyway it turned into a great night. Christy sang seven or eight songs and some of the lads joined in. Trevor Brennan sang with him and then several lads persuaded Woody to have a go. He didn't want to, but he gave in. Woody was about to launch into his song when next thing Claw pipes up. It was something like, 'This is the only chance we'll ever get to hear Christy Moore singing for us, and you're going to fuckin' ruin it. Shut the fuck up and let Christy sing!' Typical Claw; everyone was in knots. In the Citywest Christy landed in with his brother, the singer-songwriter Luka Bloom. We had a function room in the hotel to ourselves. Christy did some of his old favourites, Reggie sang a song, and so did Donners. Then Luka took over. And he said he had written a song specially for the occasion. It was called *Weapon of Mass Destruction* and it was about one of the players on the team. Grand. Everyone assumed it'd be about Drico or O'Connell or someone like that. But he was only a few lines into it when everyone realised the song was about me. Oh, Jesus, no. The whole place just erupted. They were cheering and roaring, but I was red in the face with embarrassment. I hated being the centre of attention. I just sank down into my chair. And the further he went on the worse it got. He had lines in it about the Scotland game and the try I scored. And the chorus was that Hayes should be playing on the wing because he was the weapon of mass destruction. The lads cheered him on to the last note and then erupted all over again. I'll never forget the embarrassment of it. Luka had written the words on a sheet of paper and I made damn sure to get it off him before the night was out. I didn't want it leaking out anywhere else! Luka was happy to hand it over and I was happier to get hold of it. I got him to sign it, and Christy to sign it. I brought it home and got it framed, and I have it to this day. It's a nice memento to have, and I've fond memories of the night now. But I wasn't the better of it for a couple of days.

We wanted to put two wins back-to-back against England, and we did. That was the big theme that week: beating them for the second year in a row to prove that the win in Twickenham wasn't just a flash in the pan. The next game up was France, also at home, and the talk had already started about going one better than the Triple Crown the year before: the Grand Slam, in other words. Then France swanned into Dublin and turned us over. And that tore the arse out of our grand plans for another season. The Slam was won that year all right, but it was by Wales, not us. We had to go to Cardiff on the last day of the campaign, and there was going to be no stopping them at home. A season that had started out well ended in a big anti-climax.

The Lions management had sent out letters and forms during the Six Nations to every player from the four home unions that was in with a chance of being selected. I filled mine in and sent it back and heard no more of it until the touring squad was announced live on Sky TV on 11 April. I watched the live broadcast at home in Nenagh. I didn't have high hopes after the Six Nations. It had started out well, but we'd tapered off in the last two games, and the feeling was that the momentum had swung away from us. The players were announced in alphabetical order and I was a relieved, happy man when my name was read out. Eleven Irish players were named in the squad of forty-four, which was the largest Lions squad ever assembled. The tour would cover eleven games in six weeks. A warm-up match against Argentina at the Millennium Stadium was arranged for 23 May. It was supposed to be a handy-enough loosener, but their players hadn't read the script. Argentina were well up for it on the night and got stuck into us. We were a thrown-together outfit, a lot of players were unavailable for one reason or another, and we struggled to perform as a team. It took a penalty from Jonny Wilkinson with the last kick of the game to draw the match. It wasn't a great start for the squad, and for me personally it was even worse. The scrum was under pressure and I was substituted after fifty-one minutes. It was one of the worst games of my life. I couldn't get into it at all. It passed me by. I was demoralised that night and for the next few nights. I'd personally been building up to the Lions tour since the day they announced the squad. I was determined to give it everything. I'd done a lot of extra fitness sessions to be in the best possible shape. I wanted a massive performance on my first start, and then the opposite happened. I'd say in hindsight my mentality was wrong. Instead of treating it as another game I got too wound up about it. I was in a whole new environment with different players and different coaches, and I think it all threw me a bit. I wasn't calm and relaxed enough going into the game. That performance in Cardiff damaged my chances of making the Test team twenty-two in New Zealand.

The first game was against Bay of Plenty in Rotorua. If Argentina was an omen, then losing a leader like Lawrence Dallaglio was another. He was gone from the tour, injured after twenty minutes against Bay of Plenty. The next one up was a match for the midweek squad against Taranaki. We had our own midweek coaching staff in Ian McGeechan, Gareth Jenkins and Mike Ford. Clive Woodward was the brains behind the whole operation. He had led England to the World Cup in 2003 and had planned everything with military precision. It was a serious exercise in logistics, travel arrangements and personnel. Apart from bringing a squad of this size, he also had something like thirty backup staff on board too. It was a major expedition. No expense was spared, no detail was overlooked; we were treated like kings.

I couldn't wait to get onto the field against Taranaki. It was my chance to put things right after the Argentina game. But if anything it went worse. Any provincial side worth its salt will always be wired taking on a touring Lions side. It's a massive match for them. Taranaki were no different. They threw everything at us in the first half, but were a spent force for much of the second. By that time I was gone; I'd got the shepherd's hook again after fifty minutes. The scrum had struggled again, and I'd made no impact around the field. I was in a state of depression that night. We were all rooming on our own, and I spent most of it awake, tossing and turning. I never lost confidence in myself during my career, thank God, but I came close to it at the time. I'd always bounced back from a poor or middling performance in the very next game; that was my way of fixing things. But it didn't work this time. And when something that has worked for you before stops working, it's hard to know what to do or where to turn. The thing that I was fearing most of all was the perception among my peers. I was playing with English fellas, Welsh fellas, Scottish fellas, and I felt I was letting myself down in front of them. I wanted to do myself justice and earn their respect. That's all I ever wanted really. It was the most important thing for me. I'd heard stories over the years about players on Lions tours who'd gone into their shells after a bad performance and become passengers for the rest of the tour. They just more or less cut themselves adrift and ended up not getting selected for even the midweek team. You'd have Test match players doubling up for the midweek games as well. And I can remember thinking, 'Fuck it, I can't let that happen to me. I have to do something about this, I have to try and get my form back.' We beat Taranaki, but it was one of the lowest nights of my career.

Part of Woodward's strategy for the tour was to make a conscious effort to win over the locals wherever we went. And we ended up covering a fair amount of New Zealand, from Rotorua to New Plymouth, Hamilton, Wellington, Dunedin, Palmerston North, Invercargill, Auckland and Christchurch. But there was a fair contrast between a Lions tour and an Irish tour. With Ireland you got a great reception wherever you turned up. Everywhere we went now we were called 'fucking Poms'. I remember saying to myself, 'I'm not a fucking Pom,' but it didn't matter; we were all tarred with the one brush. It probably had something to do with England winning the World Cup and then dominating the Lions squad, which you'd have expected given their success. You'd hear some fella calling a radio phone-in show and referring to us as Poms, and the radio host would be saying they're not just Poms, there's Welsh and Scots and Irish there too. But for the ordinary punter we were Poms, and they didn't like us. Every town we played in there were school visits and community events and public training sessions organised. It was a PR kind of initiative, to win over hearts and minds, as they say. You'd have six players lined up for one event and another six lined up for another one, and so on. And because I wasn't getting as many games, I was rounded up for a fair few of them. I felt like a fella who had committed some petty crime or other and was sentenced to a hundred hours community service for my sins. I wouldn't mind, but everywhere we went they were only looking for one fella anyway – Jonny Wilkinson. You'd be signing autographs in a school or some place and all you'd hear is, 'Where's Jonny?' 'Is Jonny not here today?'

At the same time, then, while all this PR was going on, there was a bit of paranoia behind the scenes. We were based in

Auckland for the first two weeks or so, and management had ordered this big 7 or 8 ft temporary fence to be erected around the training ground. We had three or four security men with us too, ex-British military, I think, and real hardcore types. There were so many players and staff that it took two buses to transport us to training every day, and the security lads would be there first, running around, checking things out, looking this way and that, like they were casing the place for spies. It was all a bit over the top. The biggest problem on that tour, I felt, wasn't the different nationalities and trying to get the right chemistry for the Test team; it was the size of the squad and the staff. It was too big. Clive had picked two squads, basically, so that they could alternate between games; each one would get a week to prepare for whatever game they were selected to play. But it just split the whole thing. You had so many players you couldn't have them all on the pitch, or in the gym, at the same time. So you ended up with two separate teams almost, training at different times and coming and going from the hotel at different times. The Test squad would stay behind while the midweek squad headed off for one of their matches. We'd stay behind and train while the Test squad headed off, and we might only arrive at the venue an hour or so before their game. The thing was too fragmented. It was hard to build up the proper unity you need in a Lions squad in circumstances like that.

Personally, the tour turned around for me in Invercargill, my old stomping ground. I was probably the only player who was looking forward to going to Invercargill. I loved the place, I had a lot of friends there and for me it was like going home. We were playing Southland; I was familiar with the stadium, and my family was arriving from Ireland for the game too. I had happy memories of my time there and the thought of going back relaxed me and got me in the right frame of mind. I had dinner with the Nallys the night before the game at their house, like I had many times before. Some of my old workmates called into the team hotel the morning of the game. I was buzzing again; I couldn't wait for the match to start. It would be my first game since Taranaki and I was determined not to give the selectors any reason to discard me for the rest of the tour. It wasn't a great team performance but we won and I had a good night. I wouldn't even say that I played brilliantly; I just played like I could. I gave an honest account of myself. Aaron Dempsey was still playing; he lined out for Southland that night. Nine years earlier Aaron was my direct opponent the first time I ever packed down in a front row. He was still a tight-head, but so was I; we didn't have to butt heads this time round. I had a big smile on my face when it was over. That was where my Lions tour really began. Aaron came into our dressing room afterwards. It was great to meet him again. We swapped jerseys and sat down and had a good old chat. It's those sorts of friendships and connections that make rugby the game it is.

At the official dinner that night O'Gara was up to his usual mischief. Bill Beaumont was the Lions tour manager, and Bill was old school, a great character who enjoyed the crack. Rog was telling Bill over dinner that I wanted to make a speech because I was back in Invercargill, knowing full well it was the last thing I wanted to do. Andy Leslie was high up in the New Zealand Rugby Union at the time, and Bill was in on the joke too; he passed the message onto Andy. So when Leslie finished his speech he announced to the whole room that John Hayes wanted to say a few words. Most people thought it was serious; they started clapping and cheering. All eyes were on me, but I looked over, and there was O'Gara laughing his head off. I went up anyway and thanked everyone for the welcome they gave me and the team. Fiona said I spoke longer than I did at our wedding, which wouldn't have been hard to do anyway. But I was so delighted with the way the game went I'd have sung a song if they'd asked me.

*

Because the squad was so big, and because Woodward was mainly involved with the Test team, I didn't get to talk to him much on tour. He had a lot on his plate, and I didn't mind too badly one way or another. But to get to know fellas a bit better he set aside one night each week to go to dinner with a bunch of different players. O'Callagan and myself went to the cinema one day in Auckland, and by the time we got back to the hotel he was late for his dinner appointment with Clive. So we ran back down the street and bumped into Clive and the other chosen lads in the foyer of the hotel. Donners went over and joined them. I tried to keep my head down and head for the lift. Donners the bollocks knew well I hadn't much interest in joining them, so of course the first thing he said to Clive was that I would love to join them for dinner. So Clive looked over and told me I'd be more than welcome to join them. I muttered something about having to meet someone else and flew up the stairs before he could ask me a second time. Woodward was famous in England at the time because of the 2003 World Cup. At one stage of the tour Prince William turned up to meet him at training one day. William is a big rugby fan and he came into our dressing room after one of the games and went round shaking our hands. I was sitting next to O'Connell. William told him he'd heard of Limerick rugby and the legendary Thomond Park. So Paulie said to him he should come over for a game some time. William said he'd love to but it wouldn't be easy; a visit like that to Ireland would take a bit of organising. And quick as a flash O'Connell fired back, 'Some of your ancestors hadn't much problem coming over to Ireland.' He kinda half said it under his breath so I wasn't sure if Prince William had heard it or not. But I had, and I nearly fell off my seat laughing. It was a deadly line.

One of the interesting things that came out of that tour was that the Irish set-up was way ahead of the Lions in terms of video analysis and defensive planning. In all the years I worked with Mervyn Murphy, he was always one step ahead of you. If you wanted some video footage of upcoming opponents, he always had something stored on his laptop. If you wanted to review your performance the morning after a match, Mervyn would have the relevant footage edited and ready. With the Lions you'd have to wait. And I remember looking for some material on the opposition for one game and they had very little. We also discovered that the defensive presentations we were getting from Mike Ford were streets ahead of what they were getting anywhere else in the home nations.

By the time we got to the Southland game the midweek squad had developed a bond of its own. There was great fun and banter among the players, and a lot of good photos were taken at various stages along the way. Fellas like Graham Rowntree, Michael Owen, Martyn Williams, Ben Kay, Simon Shaw, were easy to get on with and good company. Josh Lewsey had family friends in Kilkee and used to go there on holidays when he was a young lad. We talked about having a jar in Kilkee some time. Most fellas were dying to get home at that stage, but I was loving it, I could've toured on for another three weeks. I'd hit rock bottom, but had turned a corner and was really enjoying it now. We played our last game against Auckland at Eden Park, between the second and third Test match, and won a tight encounter against a quality side. I didn't get to play the Test games against the All Blacks, but I'd made my peace with that a long time earlier. The 2005 Lions tour started out in misery for me but ended up being one of the best experiences of my career.

12

You have to hang in. I'm only repeating it because it's true. No matter how bad things are in a match, you have to hang in and keep going. In rugby you can get humiliated very quickly if you let the head drop. But you can't let it drop because you have to hold onto your self-respect as a team at all costs.

France in Paris in 2006 is as good an example as you'll find. Ireland were trailing 43–3 ten minutes into the second half. We were making mistake after mistake and the French were capitalising every time. They scored six tries. It was embarrassing, a desperate state of affairs. Our credibility as a team was on the line. We could've been a laughing stock. But we kept going. We started putting some attacks together. Some would say that France took their foot off the gas with such a big lead. But maybe they had punched themselves out at that stage, which French teams so often do. One thing's for sure: they thought we were gone. They thought they could coast to the final whistle. They were in for a surprise. O'Gara got in for a try, then D'Arcy, O'Callaghan and Andrew Trimble. Four tries in the space of twelve minutes. It was mad stuff. We had further chances too in the last ten minutes, but weren't able to convert them. The French were out on their feet by the end. Their tongues were hanging out. They were ragged in the scrums. It ended 43–31, one of the craziest games I was ever involved in. We didn't win it, but that last half-hour was vital to us as a team. We salvaged our pride. If we had collapsed completely in that match, the bottom could've fallen out of our whole season. It could've had serious implications for Eddie O'Sullivan and the management team. Even when a game looks dead and buried, there can be a lot riding on how you respond as a team.

We took a lot of momentum out of that turnaround in Paris and rolled it on into wins over Wales, Scotland and England for our second Triple Crown in three seasons. The win at Twickenham will probably be remembered for Shane Horgan's last-gasp try. Shaggy had the telescopic extension attached to his right arm that day. He just stretched every inch of his frame to get the ball down one-handed in the corner. It was the day after St Patrick's Day and a grand way to celebrate it. Ten weeks later those of us who'd toured with the Lions the year before were back in New Zealand, this time with the national team. We brought a lot of self-belief with us from the Six Nations campaign, and it showed in our performances. The previous November, in the autumn international, the All Blacks had put forty-five points on us in Lansdowne Road. And unlike France, they didn't let us back into it. That's the difference: New Zealand keep the foot on your neck, no matter how much of a lead they have.

Seven months later we were facing them again, but we were in a much better frame of mind this time. We played well, we were resilient, we went toe to toe with them in Hamilton in the first Test. Drico scored a lovely try, Rog was kicking his penalties, we led 16–8 at the break. They scored a try early in the second half, but Trimble replied with a great try and we were still leading with nine minutes remaining. They went in front with a penalty and then killed us off with a late try to win 34–23. It wasn't just a blood-and-guts Irish performance, although there was plenty of that too. We played some good rugby; the tries were well created and executed. But we came up short, just like every Ireland team before us. Losing this one was a sickener. We had a chance to make history. We didn't want to be another hard-luck story. We wanted to change the traditional pattern of Irish teams in the past, playing well for an hour and then going under to a late blitz from the All Blacks.

But there's no team harder to keep down. If you leave the door open, they'll come through it. We were nine minutes away but couldn't hold them out. They have serious power. They always seem to be able to get over the gain line. Their backs are as big as their back row players, the same height and weight more or less, but usually with pace to burn. There's no magic formula to how they operate. They do things at a very fast tempo, they do everything at pace, and they generally make the right decisions on the ball. That's a key ingredient, their decision-making in possession. They can look spectacular at times, but generally they're just very efficient, they do the basics well. They'll run hard lines, take it hard into contact, clear it out and away they go again. They'll repeat that until they've opened up a bit of space, and then they go for the jugular. They did it to us again in the second Test a week later in Auckland. It was pissing rain that night, awful weather conditions. They hit us with two tries in the first half and were leading 17–0, but again we hung tough. O'Connell barged over for a try before half-time and Flannery got our second from a line-out drive. We were within three points, but then Luke McAlister crashed over for them with less than ten minutes left. That was it. Both of those performances were admirable in their own way, but we couldn't keep them at bay for the full eighty minutes. We couldn't take the final step and actually beat them. We were a very frustrated squad leaving New Zealand. And still the season wasn't over, because we had to travel from there to Perth on Australia's west coast for the final Test match of the season. It took us the most of a day's travelling to get there. This was the last week in June at this stage. It was our third hard game in three weeks.

O'Gara and Neil Best scored great tries after half-time to give us a four-point lead. But we had nothing left in the tank; we had run out of juice. Australia ran in four tries in the last twenty minutes. We played some brilliant rugby on that tour, we poured our guts into those games against the All Blacks, but we came back from the southern hemisphere nought from three.

An Ireland team will beat New Zealand some day. I'd prefer if it were sooner rather than later, but it will happen. I don't think we have an inferiority complex about them. It's more a lack of familiarity with their style of play. You have to get used to coping with their power and pace. Australia and South Africa can beat them because they're used to playing them, not just at national level but provincial level. Australian and South African players come up against them all the time playing for various sides in the Super 14. And they don't always perform like world-beaters in the Super 14. But when they put on the black jersey it puts them under pressure to perform better. I saw that from my own time living in New Zealand. There's an expectation that they will raise their game. They have to win, they have to play better, when they're representing the All Blacks. Ireland and the home nations in general will always be at a disadvantage because they don't get to play them often enough. We gave it a good shot in my time, but I hope an Irish team will come along that goes the distance and finally breaks that particular hoodoo.

The results on the '06 summer tour were hard to take, but once the disappointment faded there was a lot of positive feedback to be taken from the performances. A good squad had been built over the previous few seasons, we were playing quality rugby, and our confidence was growing. The following November we had dominant wins over South Africa, Australia and the Pacific Islands in the autumn internationals. South Africa fielded a weakened team, but any day you beat the Springboks is a good day. Australia were the team we wanted. Twelve months earlier we'd bombed against them in Dublin; we were disgusted with ourselves over that performance. This time round we wanted to make amends and delivered a top class overall display. There was a great buzz around the squad and among Irish rugby supporters at this stage. The 2007 World Cup was twelve months away, and we all had a sense that we were building nicely to that tournament.

Rugby was in the news for more reasons than that at the time. The old Lansdowne Road stadium was about to be demolished, and the national team was going to need a temporary home while the new stadium was being built. In 2005 the GAA had taken the historic decision to open Croke Park to rugby and soccer internationals. The Six Nations fixture with France in February 2007 would be the first rugby game ever to take place at Croke Park. We had a match against Wales in the Millennium Stadium to worry about first. We got off to a great start, Drico blocking down a clearance in the opening minute and Rory Best picking up the loose ball for a handy try. Wales put us under heavy pressure at times, but we took our chances well and pounced for two more tries while we kept our own try line intact. It was a good win, and it set us up perfectly for the French a week later.

Coming from a GAA background, I was thrilled at the prospect of playing in Croke Park. There had been a lot of debate about it in the years before the GAA made their landmark decision. Even if I never played rugby, I would definitely have been in favour of it. Twenty years earlier, maybe even ten years earlier, I don't think it would have happened. But times had changed, mindsets had changed. Most ordinary GAA people I knew were in favour of it. Of course, the slagging started once the decision was made. Comments were flying around about a Limerick player finally getting to play in Croke Park. The Tipp lads, Quinny and Leamy, were rubbing it in big time. A few weeks before the France game we had our first training session in the stadium. I took a round ball onto the field and went on a solo run. I must've thought I was Jack O'Shea or someone. But I wanted to be able to say I scored a point in Croke Park. I made sure I got good and close to the posts before I let fly. I scored my point; I was delighted with myself. It's a massive stadium, and when you're standing in the middle of the field on your own it looks even bigger. We couldn't wait to get out there when it was packed with over 80,000 people.

There was a theory floated at the time that we lost because we got a bit distracted by the occasion. There was so much talk about us playing in Croke Park that we forgot about playing France. I don't buy that. We had control of that game when it mattered. We were four points up with two minutes to play and we made the capital mistake of losing concentration. O'Gara's penalty in the seventy-seventh minute gave us that four-point cushion and all we had to do was see it out. But you don't fall in love with yourself when you get a score on the board. The golden rule is to get your head back on and get ready for what happens next. But we didn't do that. Rog's penalty meant a drop goal or a penalty wasn't going to be any good to them, and the thought crept into our heads that we were safe. We didn't win the restart and next thing they were coming at us with all guns blazing. They punched a hole deep into our twenty-two, set up a couple of rucks towards the right-hand corner and then came left. They threw a long skip pass to Vincent Clerc. He had men over, but I'd say his eyes lit up when he saw me in front of him. I'd ended up more or less in the outside centre position. It happens in phase play; you get scattered around the field after three or four phases and that's where I happened to end up at that moment. Clerc went for the gap between myself and Neil Best. I thought I had him; I got a hand on him, but he just skimmed me on the outside. I hit the ground trying to make the tackle, and as I rolled over I looked up in time just to see him going over the line. I was shellshocked. It was a desperate kick in the guts. There's nothing more sickening than losing a big game in the last minute. It'd drive you demented. That was one of those games that cut you to the bone.

The only positive that came out of it was an absolute commitment to making sure it didn't happen in the next game. It was bad enough losing our very first match in Croke Park. It was unthinkable that we'd lose a second on the trot. Especially when it was against England. No, that couldn't happen. This was the game that really caught the public imagination. It was just the whole history and politics of it: the Bloody Sunday massacre in the stadium in 1920, the flying of the English flag over Croke Park and the playing of *God Save the Queen*. It was the talk of the country for months. And in the weeks leading up to it you couldn't turn on a radio or television without hearing it being discussed. You couldn't go anywhere without people wanting to talk about it. In theory it was only a game, but this went way beyond sport. It was a national occasion; the whole country would be tuning in to watch it.

I suppose the whole thing got to me a bit. I got a bit emotional during the playing of the anthems, and I saw afterwards that the bloody television cameras focused in on me several times while we were standing in the lineup. I lost count of the number of people who mentioned it to me in the weeks and months after. Some of them said that when they saw me with tears in my eyes, it got them going too. I was a bit self-conscious about it, showing my emotions like that. I'm not sorry it happened, but I'd hope it's not the only thing I'm remembered for. It was the whole Croke Park mystique, I suppose. The history and reputation of the place. Growing up playing Gaelic games and watching All-Ireland finals on the telly. And there was me standing for the national anthem on the pitch, waiting to play England there. It was just a bit overwhelming. I felt the weight of the responsibility too: we were trusted to look after the place and not let the country down. And the missed tackle on Clerc had been haunting me as well. I took personal responsibility for that, and I'd carried it with me for the following two weeks. I badly wanted to make amends. So the whole day took on an extra bit of meaning for me. I can only say that when the waterworks came, I was as surprised as anyone. It just happened.

I know that all the players felt a sense of responsibility too, to the stadium, to GAA people and the country in general. That was why there was huge intensity in everything we did on the field. It was one of those rare days where every single player played well. It was like all this pressure had been dammed up for two weeks and now we were releasing it. We led 23–3 at the break. We were on fire in that first half. But at half-time the message was hammered home not to stop. We didn't want to let them back into it, we didn't want to limp our way to a victory. We'd put on a show in that first half and we wanted to continue it. The margin in the end was thirty points, a new Irish record in games against England. It was one of those days when just about everything went well. The crowd, the atmosphere and the performance all came together. It was as close as you'll get to a perfect day in sport. I suppose it's a part of history now, a day that will always be remembered, and I feel very privileged to have been on the field while it was happening.

Most of the lads went on the town that night, but I would've been just as happy to get into the car and drive home. You couldn't do that because there was the official dinner to attend and speeches to be made and all that carry-on. Everyone was on cloud nine, but I was brought back to earth with a bang. Sally was about nine months old at the time. She was with me and Fiona in our hotel room and she woke with an ear infection. She was crying with the pain, and I'd have given anything to make it go away. It shows the difference between sport and what's real in life. I wasn't long forgetting about the happy scenes in Croke Park that day. I just wanted her to be better. We got Gary O'Driscoll to have a look at her. We eventually calmed her down and took her home the next day.

Two weeks after England we had Scotland in Murrayfield, and we were vulnerable. After the high of a performance like that, there's always going to be a slump. You can't replicate that level of intensity two games running. It's not humanly possible. You have to produce a strong professional performance, that's the bottom line, but you won't often be able to tap into the sort of emotions we did in Croke Park. On top of that, we were away from home, and Scotland would be lining up an ambush for us. That's always the way in the Six Nations. A team comes up with a massive performance in one match, and their next opponents, no matter how bad their own form is, raise their game. We've done it many a time ourselves. Against Scotland we were sitting ducks. In the circumstances we did well to get out of Murrayfield with a one-point win. It gave us our third Triple Crown in four years but at this stage the novelty was wearing thin. We wanted the big one, but France had put paid to that. Rog got a bit of a fright late in the game. He got caught at the bottom of a ruck. I'd been in on the other side of the ruck and landed on the ground near him. I knew he was in trouble because I could hear him gasping for breath. I could hear these grunts, and then they stopped. I went to get him out and roll him over on his side. I think he was unconscious. I put him in the recovery position and checked to see if he'd swallowed his tongue. He started breathing again more or less straightaway. It was all over in a couple of seconds. The doctor and physio were on the scene in a flash too and they took over. He was grand; he came around very quickly, and shortly after that the final whistle went.

We had an outside chance of winning the championship on the last day. There were complicated mathematical equations involved; they were complicated for me anyway. We had to beat Italy by a big margin, in Rome, and hope that Scotland did us a favour against France. As it turned out, it was all a bit of a cliffhanger in the end. We scored eight tries and put fifty-one points on the Italians. We let them in for a try in injury time, and, as it happened, that was the try that swung it on points difference for France. The Scots scored a late try, but France scored an even later one and pipped us at the post. It would've been nice to win the championship, it would've been progress from winning Triple Crowns, but it wasn't the be-all and end-all either. We'd blown it against France that day in Croke Park, and in our eyes that was what had cost us.

A two-match visit to Argentina was scheduled for June, but most of the front line players were kept at home. The World Cup was in September. The plan was to wrap up the season with our provinces in early May and then rest up for a month. We'd come back refreshed and ready to go for the new season in mid-June. At that point, the countdown to the World Cup would begin.

The first week of pre-season for those of us who hadn't travelled to Argentina was in the middle of June, and it was spent in Spala. We then did another week in Spala the second week in July as part of an extended forty-six-man squad. The cryotherapy chamber was still torture, but it was worth it; it was all part of the programme to have us at our fittest come September. We were being pushed hard in the weights and fitness sessions and we wanted to be pushed hard. The results were showing up in our tests: fitness, speed and power levels were all high throughout the squad. We spent a few weeks back with our provinces before going into camp in Limerick for a week at the end of July. The operation was then moved to Dublin in preparation for our first warm-up game of the season, against Scotland at Murrayfield. There was a buzz in the camp, morale was good, everyone was optimistic and excited about our prospects. There was even talk of us having a proper crack at winning the World Cup.

The team selected to play Scotland had a fairly mixed, experimental look about it, and Scotland took full advantage, scoring five tries and winning by ten points. But there was no panic. You couldn't read too much into it because this was early days; it was our first blow-out of the season and we were all a bit ring rusty. After Murrayfield we shipped out to the south of France for a week of warm-weather training in Capbreton. It was a beautiful spot with lovely sunshine and all was well. A match against the Bayonne club was arranged and Eddie went with a full-strength selection on the night. For us it would be a useful workout, but it turned out to be a lot more important to them. It's hard to know what their motivation was, but they were clearly intent on making it a dogfight from the start – and a fairly nasty one at that. They started clattering us with cheap shots and all sorts of sly digs. It was insane what was going on. The crowd was baying for blood too. And we couldn't retaliate because we couldn't afford to get sent off. So we just had to take it. I got a few clatters and at one stage I was coming out of a maul when one of their players took a swipe at me. It didn't even hurt, but it was just the intent behind it and the lack of any good reason. I was startled. I just looked at him. I'd have loved to have taken his head off with a box, but I couldn't touch him. It was a no-win situation. Drico was done in an off-the-ball incident and carted off to hospital in an ambulance. He'd been punched in the face, and the panic was that he'd got a fractured cheekbone. Instead it was a fractured sinus, but it was bad enough this close to the tournament. We hammered them on the night, but we just wanted to get the hell out of there by the time it was over.

After that it was back to Ireland for our final warm-up game before the tournament began, against Italy at Ravenhill. We hadn't clicked yet, but we were convinced it was only a matter of time. We were fairly confident it would happen against Italy, but instead we stalled. We were very lucky to beat them in the end. They scored a try in injury-time to give them the lead. O'Gara replied with a try, and a dodgy one at that, even deeper into injury time to save our blushes. Maybe in hindsight we might've been as well off losing to Italy. It might've forced us to face the fact that we weren't right, that there was something missing. You could say in hindsight that the writing was on the wall that night in Ravenhill, but we didn't sense it at the time. The alarm bells weren't ringing. We still had two weeks to go. We had relatively easy games up first in our World Cup pool, against Namibia and Georgia, before the big one against France on 21 September. We figured, I suppose, that those two games would clear the system of whatever rust was there.

But the omens were starting to stack up, and the hotel we were booked into for the first phase of the tournament wasn't a great sign either. It certainly didn't lighten the mood. It wasn't a dump, it was a decent enough place, basically a motorway hotel for sales reps and the like to put their head down for the night before moving on again. It wasn't a place to be stuck in for three weeks, with nowhere to go and not a lot to do. If the location was bad, the food was shocking. Most of the lads ended up living off sandwiches and salads. Lunch and dinner were atrocious as far as I was concerned. I just bypassed the hot buffet every evening and went straight to the salad and cold meats counter. I couldn't eat the hot dinners they were serving up; the meat was horrible, the sauces and veg were terrible. Eddie and the backup staff tried to improve it. Ruth Wood-Martin, the IRFU's nutritionist, came down and tried to sort things out with the chefs, but nothing changed. I know that French food is supposed to be world-renowned, but I never liked it. In all my time going there with Munster and Ireland, I always found the food unpleasant. I'm not saying the food in this hotel was a typical example of French cuisine. I'm sure it's a lot better than that, and in fairness it'd need to be. I used to wonder about the chefs. They'd be standing there every night watching us looking at the dinner they'd prepared and ignoring it. Like, if I gave the cattle back at home silage, and it was still there the next day, I'd know straightaway there was something wrong with it. Here you had thirty lads walking by their food every night and the penny never dropped with them. People might say it's a minor enough issue, but it's not. You obviously need to be eating good food to get the proper nutrition if you're going to be training hard every day and playing top-level games of rugby. And you need it for the morale of a team too. If the grub isn't good night after night, it doesn't help the mood at all.

Maybe we'd have been better off if we'd had to face France in our first match. It might've changed our mindset that summer, knowing that we'd have to be right at the top of our form for that one. We would've had to hit the ground running straightaway. But at the time we thought the draw was ideally graded for us, starting off with a handy-enough opener against Namibia, then building it up for a stiffer test against Georgia, and taking the momentum from big wins against them into the clash with France. We'd be flying by the time we got to the France game. That was the thinking and it was logical at the time. Namibia had just six full-time professional players in their ranks. They were basically an amateur side. Ireland had beaten them by fifty-seven points in the previous World Cup. It should've been a rout. Instead we were flat and patchy and made far too many mistakes. They scored two tries in the second half and the French crowd in the stadium got totally behind them. They never looked like beating us, but we looked fairly ordinary on the day. We won 32–17. In a World Cup tournament you want a good start to give you momentum going into the next game because it's such an intense, compacted period of time. You don't get two weeks between games to rest and recuperate. You have to bounce from one game straight into another, and the more impetus you have the better. We had none after Namibia, or not a lot anyway. But still there wasn't any panic. There might have been a warning light flashing, but there was no warning bell ringing. We hadn't played well, but there was every chance it'd all come together in the next game.

Instead it nearly all fell apart against Georgia. They dominated the last quarter. We were leading 14–10 and somehow that's how it stayed until the final whistle. We didn't score for the last twenty-five minutes. Georgia just battered us up front in that last quarter. They weren't the most technical of players, but they were huge, strong men. Some of them were absolutely massive, and they could sense they had a famous victory there for the taking. Every ruck and maul was a full-on wrestling match. We were under siege. They had two drop goal attempts which both went wide. Then two minutes from time they got over the line only for the TMO to rule that Leamy had held them up; they hadn't grounded the ball. If they'd scored that try, it would probably have caused one of the biggest shocks in World Cup history. The warning bells were ringing now. They were nearly deafening. We'd kept hoping that the performance would come. We knew it was there. It'd been there in the Six Nations. But where the hell was it? That's what we were wondering. We thought we had ticked every box. Our summer preparation, our fitness levels, were the best they'd ever been. There was no one shirking any blame. No one was pointing any fingers. The forwards were saying they had more to do, the backs were saying the same, individuals were saying the same. Everyone was accepting responsibility, but nobody was coming up with any answers. Eddie wasn't rearing up. He wasn't going ballistic. He was having meetings with his staff and trying to get to the bottom of it, just like us.

Six days later we limped into the showdown with France in Paris. This was our third game in twelve days. Our confidence was shot. And to make matters worse France needed to win. They had lost to Argentina in the first game, and that result had put the cat among the pigeons. Argentina had hit form like they'd never hit form before in their lives. They took the momentum from that win over France and rolled it all the way to the semi-finals. We were the opposite. We had hit form too like we'd never hit form before, but only in the opposite direction. We actually played better and put it up to France for long periods, but were well beaten in the end, 25–3. We could only manage a solitary drop goal in the eighty minutes. I actually played well that night, and there was a reason why. I hadn't trained all that week, and I was fresher than I had been for a long time. I'd got a kick on the calf muscle, and so I sat out training. And I can remember feeling better for the rest. I felt fresh in myself that day in the dressing room. We'd been doing massive, long training sessions. We were trying to put it right on the training ground. Basically we were trying to solve the problem by throwing more sweat at it. And I wouldn't blame Eddie or his coaching staff for that either. If I was coaching a team at a World Cup and we'd played poorly in one game, would I have said to the lads, 'Take Monday and Tuesday off and we'll see you Wednesday'? I doubt it. If things had been going well, we'd have been ticking over in training, getting our rest and generally relaxing. But when you're in a crisis situation no one feels like relaxing; you're stressing out, trying to figure out how to fix it.

At this stage we were hearing about all sorts of rumours that were flying around back in Ireland. Word got back to us that there was widespread speculation about disharmony in the camp. I heard one rumour that I was supposed to have had a fight with David Wallace. Me and Wally! It was so stupid it was a joke. You couldn't have found two fellas less likely to have a row with anyone, never mind each other. Then stories broke in the press about Rog's private life. That was wrong, totally wrong; he shouldn't have had to put up with that. You can criticise a player's performance on the field, but that should be as far as it goes. A line was crossed when that sort of personal stuff was being put into the papers and discussed on the airwaves. A few newspapers were desperate for angles. We were doing a recovery session in the swimming pool beside the hotel after training one day. A photograph was taken and an article appeared beside it the next day saying that we were lying about the place, sunning ourselves, when we should've been hard at work. It was a completely false picture of what actually was happening. As an Irish team we had never experienced this sort of reaction before. The rumours, the stories, the speculation, it was more like what you'd find around the England soccer team. It was crazy stuff. Between what was happening on the field and off it, it's no wonder a siege mentality crept into the camp. The whole thing was turning into a miserable experience.

*

We had Argentina in our final game. We were hanging on by a thread. If we were to qualify out of the group we'd have to score four tries to get the bonus point, and prevent Argentina from getting a bonus point. But we weren't playing fluidly enough to score tries. Moves were breaking down all the time, we were struggling to put phases together and our confidence had ebbed away. Argentina won the collisions and eventually ended up taking control of the game. They were always awkward to play against, they loved the trench warfare, and they were mad for battle this day. It was just non-stop tackling and grappling up front. As a forward you'll always have your highest tackle count against Argentina because they'll pick and go from rucks all day if they can. They'll maul and ruck and scrummage and continually challenge you up front. Most teams will move the ball wide when they get a chance and attack the space. Argentina will keep it tight and attack the opposing players instead. But, in fairness, that was a fine team at the peak of its powers at the time. The harsh reality was that we in the forward pack had been beaten up by Georgia, France and Argentina. The team in general was stale and out of sorts. It was a pattern of continuous deterioration from Scotland to Italy to Namibia to Georgia, France and Argentina.

The closest thing to a plausible explanation is that we overtrained, fitness-wise, and were undercooked in terms of rugby sharpness. That we did too much fitness work through fitness work and not enough through rugby. I didn't travel to the 2011 World Cup, but I was involved in the pre-tournament training schedule. Most of our fitness work was done through rugby because at the end of the day you are a rugby player, not a long distance runner. We did our cardio work with the ball in hand, playing games in training most of the time. Ireland played four international games and another against Connacht before they headed to New Zealand. The lesson had been learned from four years earlier. There was a post mortem done after the debacle in France, and the general consensus was that we'd got the balance wrong. We'd had a long lead-in to the tournament, starting back in mid-June, and had gone overboard with physical fitness as opposed to pure rugby training. We had over-trained and weren't able to raise a gallop when it counted.

The 2007 World Cup was a lost opportunity. A lot of players were at the peak of their careers. World Cups only come around once every four years, so when the chance is gone, it's gone for good. You can lose a big Heineken Cup or Six Nations game and you can put it in the bank as a useful lesson. You'll have a chance to put it right the next year. But it was hard to take anything good away from France in '07. There was no upside to going home with your tail between your legs like that.

Four months later we were back in France again, this time for the second round of the 2008 Six Nations campaign. We had stumbled over Italy in the first round. In Paris it was business as usual, you could say, with the French running amok for a lot of the first half, Ireland making loads of mistakes and generally being off the pace. Vincent Clerc scored a hat-trick of tries in the first half; France led 26–6 ten minutes into the second. Then we rallied. It might seem a predictable pattern to some people, France going into a big lead and us making a gallant comeback only to leave it too late. But it still takes a lot of guts and heart to do it. I don't think it should be underestimated. You won't make any sort of a comeback against a team like France, away from home, if you're not a genuine team. There were lots of things missing with us at the World Cup, but honesty wasn't one of them.

The last half hour at the Stade de France belonged to us. We forced a penalty try after three scrums in succession that had the French buckling under the pressure. That was a nice victory for the front row. Wally got over for a try four minutes later, and suddenly there were only eight points between us. Rog hit a late penalty to narrow the gap to five, but we couldn't convert all that pressure into a winning score. A fortnight later we comfortably beat Scotland in Dublin and were at home to Wales in the following game too. The turning point came in the twenty-third minute when Shane Horgan looked certain to score. But Mike Phillips just managed to hold him up short, and I think the momentum swung after that. I suppose our confidence was still fairly fragile, and we needed that try to drive us on. Not getting it rattled us a bit, while it had the opposite effect on Wales. They took control of the game, and we didn't really threaten their line afterwards. Shane Williams's try was the difference in the end. A week later we crashed out against England at Twickenham. We actually led 0–10 seven minutes into the game, but it was all downhill after that. We didn't score for the rest of the match. England turned the screw and eventually cut loose in the last quarter. We were beaten by twenty-three points.

Wales had had a poor World Cup too; they'd also failed to qualify out of their group. But they turned it around by winning the Grand Slam. That was the sort of reaction we'd been looking for too, but it never materialised. The result against England left us fourth in the table, the first time we'd finished outside the top three since it became the Six Nations in 2000. The pressure had been building on Eddie since the World Cup; the result against Wales in Dublin only added to it, and our performance against England turned out to be the end. He stepped down a few days later.

I think the World Cup took its toll on him. He was always a very confident kind of fella, but I'd imagine it went hard on him. He deserved another Six Nations to try and put it right. We had won three Triple Crowns in four years under Eddie. We had beaten England four years in a row. We had put in some great performances during his six years plus in charge. For a lot of that time the squad was happy and in a good place. But the time had probably come for a parting of the ways after how the 2008 Six Nations panned out.

Eddie didn't do chit-chat or small talk. If you passed him in the corridor, you'd keep going. I'd have had a few chats with him over the years, but mostly he kept his distance and I kept mine. He didn't try to be your friend, he wasn't one for hanging out with the lads, and I think most of us preferred it that way. But he wasn't a robot either, he wasn't a brick wall. He was approachable and he was capable of a personal touch if it was needed. A few days after Sally was born in 2006 the squad was due to meet up for a week or so before flying out to New Zealand for the summer tour. We were supposed to meet up on the Saturday, as far as I can remember, but Eddie rang me earlier that week and told me to stay at home until the following Tuesday. I hadn't asked him for a few days' extra leave, and he had a lot of other things on his plate to be worrying about. But he still thought to make the phone call and give me a bit of leeway. It was a nice gesture, and I appreciated it at the time.

The general impression of his management style was that he was a bit of a control freak. I wouldn't go that far. He had a strong personality, which I think you need to have in a job like that. The coach of a national team is almost like the CEO of a small company nowadays. He has thirty or forty players under his care and a sizeable backroom staff as well. He has to select the team and keep a lot of players onside who won't be happy when they're not getting picked. Then he has to take the rap when results go wrong and face the music when all the criticism is coming his way. Eddie was well able for all of that. And fellas could have their say. There would be a leadership group among the players, and if we were complaining about anything they could go to him and put the case to him. He would listen, and he would definitely argue the point if he disagreed. But if he saw they had a good case, he'd take it on board. As a coach and a man manager I liked Eddie; I thought he was sound.

The bottom line, anyway, for professional players is that you have a contract to fulfil no matter who is in charge. The World Cup was over and the Six Nations had ended on a sour note. We would have to pick up the pieces and, as Eddie himself used to say, get back on the horse.

13

At Munster we had a spring in our step going into 2006/07 pre-season. We were champions of Europe. It was new territory for us, and it was a nice place to be. We were more used to starting out still hurting badly from a semi-final or final at the end of the previous season. And then you'd have to start all over again from the bottom of the mountain.

This time we were starting at the top of the mountain, and it was nice to be able to enjoy the view. We'd been years trying to get there in the first place. Of course we were well aware it's a dangerous place to be. Everyone wants to knock you off it. And there's always the risk that you'll end up enjoying the view too much, instead of getting back to the grind. So we said all the right things as we looked forward to the new season. We wouldn't get complacent, we'd train even harder, we'd put two titles back to back to prove we weren't just one-hit wonders.

We couldn't have had a much harder start to the defence of the title than an away game at Leicester in October. Welford Road was packed, the rain was teeming down, it was a long day in the trenches. But we toughed it out, and O'Gara showed all his bottle and class to land a match-winning penalty from the halfway line in the eightieth minute. We'd played six Magners League games at this stage and lost four of them. But the European Cup was what mattered, and this was a major win on the road; our season was up and running. A week later we beat Bourgoin at Thomond Park, and in December we beat Cardiff home and away on successive weekends. Bourgoin were bottom of the table by the time we met them in the return game in January. They had nothing to play for in terms of qualifying out of the group, and we were half expecting them to go through the motions. But you can never know what way a French side is thinking, and this was the day they decided to play as if everything was on the line. The match was played in Geneva, and it was riddled with loads of mistakes and turnovers and incidents. The lead switched hands several times, and we were lucky to get some key decisions from the referee.

Lifeimi Mafi had been signed from New Zealand in the pre-season. He wasn't a big-name signing, but Mafs turned out to be a shrewd bit of business by Munster. There's not a lot of him there when you see him in his street clothes, but he had a ferocious tackle and quick feet in a tight corner. Mafi scored a crucial try fifteen minutes from time to give us a seven-point cushion. The game looked safe when Rog kicked a penalty with six minutes left. But they came back again with another converted try. We held out for a 27–30 win but it was far too close for comfort. The result guaranteed us a place in the quarter-finals. We had Leicester at home a week later and either side would top the group with a win. It would be Munster's last game at Thomond Park before the old stadium was demolished to make way for a new one. The place was our fortress; we had never been beaten there in European rugby and we didn't expect it to happen now, especially on its last day. But that's what happened. Leicester turned up and did a demolition job on us. They battered us up front, and that's the long and the short of it. The conditions were desperate, driving wind and rain, but they had the hard-nosed forwards to get through it. We didn't bring our usual intensity to the party. Maybe the fact that we'd already qualified had softened us a bit. Or maybe it was all the talk about this being the last day out for the old stadium. One way or another we took our eye off the ball. We didn't want it enough. We didn't want it as badly as they did anyway. Leicester had to win to guarantee their place in the knock-out stages; we didn't. It gave them an edge that we couldn't match. Leicester fronted up at the breakdown, in the scrum, everywhere. We were a point down in the second half when we were awarded a penalty. The lads turned it down and opted for the scrum. But we were shoved off the ball and they forced a turnover. A moment like that can be a big turning point in a game. It was a horrible feeling, knowing we were second best up front, with no sign of it changing either. We drove like demons at them late in the game to try and rescue the situation, but it was too late. The crowd left the old Thomond Park quiet that night, and so did we.

The upshot was that we'd have to do it the hard way; we'd have to go to Stradey Park for the quarter-final. Llanelli were flying that season. They'd won six out of six, including home and away wins over Toulouse. But we had time to regroup. The quarter-final was nine weeks away. There was a Six Nations campaign to get through first for the international players. There shouldn't have been any hangover from the Leicester game. I don't know if there was, but Llanelli beat us comfortably on the night. Maybe the hangover was that Llanelli sensed we were vulnerable now. They'd seen what Leicester had done to us and maybe fancied their chances a bit more. They played like a team whose confidence was sky-high, while we played like a team that had lost its way a bit. Stradey Park was a bear pit on the night too, a bit like Thomond Park on the great nights there, and the Welsh tore into us. They led by seventeen points at the break and kept us at bay for most of the second half. We didn't play anywhere near our best; we didn't go down fighting. We were back at the bottom of the mountain, along with the rest of the also-rans. It was a fairly tame way to surrender our crown.

We finished the Magners League that season halfway up the table, or halfway down the table, depending how you looked at it. Halfway down the table is how we looked at it. But it was a pretty accurate reflection of what had been a mediocre season. Maybe being champions had taken our edge away; the same hunger and bitterness wasn't there; we didn't have a cause, so we didn't go deep enough into ourselves. It's hard to quantify these things, but you do know when that manic sort of desire is missing. It was missing a couple of times in the games that mattered that season.

For those of us involved with the international squad, Munster was put on hold through the summer and autumn until after the 2007 World Cup. London Wasps took over from Munster as Heineken Cup champions in May '07, and they were our first opponents of the new campaign, which began later than usual in November. I'm told it was a great match. I played in it, but can't remember much about it because I got knocked out five minutes before half-time. I was carted off concussed, replaced by Tony Buckley, who had started to come through the previous season. Wasps edged us by a point at the Ricoh Arena in Coventry. We were in a brutal group that season, alongside Clermont Auvergne, Llanelli and the defending champions. Losing your first game always put you in a tight spot, but this result practically put us in a straitjacket from there on. Next up was Clermont at home a week later. Once again the French had their own logic coming into a fixture like this: they made fourteen changes to the team that had beaten Llanelli the previous weekend. We beat them well, scored five tries and picked up the all-important bonus point. Next up were Llanelli away and at home in the space of eight days in December. Not surprisingly, we had huge motivation going back to Stradey Park after our non-performance there the previous March. We ground out a 16–29 win in some of the worst conditions we ever had to face. There was ice-cold wind and rain; the game was actually stopped for a while in the second half when this shower of hailstones came hammering down. Llanelli had lost three from three at this stage and were already eliminated in terms of qualifying out of the group. But they turned up to play the following week and gave us a serious fright. It got very hairy when Stephen Jones reduced our lead to four points inside the final quarter and Marcus Horan then got sinbinned. Brian Carney scored the insurance try for us seven minutes from time, but there was no bonus point on the day. We were relieved enough to have won it in the end.

Two days after Christmas John Kelly played his last game for Munster. Rags was retiring after ten years with the team. He was a fella I had huge respect for, on and off the field. Everyone had massive respect for him. When he spoke people listened. He was a very thoughtful fella, in what he did on the field and what he'd say in the dressing room.

There were always players coming and going and this season was no different. Carney had arrived in the summer along with Paul Warwick and Rua Tipoki. In January '08 Dougie Howlett arrived, the All Blacks' record try scorer in Tests and a class player in everything he did. Tipoki made a big difference that season. He wasn't as big and powerful as Trevor Halstead, but he had a real presence in midfield too. He was an intelligent player, an organiser in attack and defence who gave us real impetus in that position.

Clermont took us apart in the return match at their place in January. They took us apart for most of the first half anyway. Nothing new there, away in France, but there were times here when we were hanging by a thread. We needed to come away with a losing bonus point, at least, if we were going to get out of the group. Clermont were rampant, doing everything at a hundred miles an hour, trying to inflict as much damage as they could while they were in this sort of frenzy. At one stage they led by seventeen points. We were getting buckled in the scrum. That was part of the deal too in a place like this, in a game like this. For French teams at home, the scrum is a barometer of their intensity.

They will target the visiting scrum. Any scrum anywhere on the field is going to be full-on. They don't take any of them easy. Sometimes against other teams you'll get fellas taking a breather. There'll be a certain kind of scrum where there isn't much danger to either side, maybe in midfield or out near a touchline, and the packs won't give it the full 100 per cent intensity. But, on a day like this against Clermont, they were going to target us all day. It was their way of laying down a statement. They had a fairly formidable front row in Laurent Emmanuelli, Mario Ledesma and Martin Scelzo. Emmanuelli was trying to walk around me all day on our ball. He was trying to slip out of the bind instead of driving straight under me. If I didn't keep him pinned down, he'd step outside and then Ledesma, the hooker, would be attacking me on the inside shoulder. So you were dealing with a two-on-one situation. In some ways it's physically easier to deal with, because the loose-head isn't exerting heavy pressure on you. Someone like Olivier Milloud, who played for France and Bourgoin, would drive straight through you. He would back his power and technique and drive straight into your chest. What Emmanuelli was at was a different way of scrummaging. You weren't being bent under the pressure. He was trying to take away my angle instead. He was trying to walk around the outside of me, and when that happens their back row gets in on top of our back row, and your number eight and scrum half are under pressure to get the ball away. You end up with a shitty ball, and there's not a lot you can do with it except kick it away. I never went in for those kinds of tactics myself. Generally I played it straight. I was probably too honest in some ways, but it never really occurred to me to do it any other way.

Clermont was a hard day at the office, but I can guarantee the scrum levelled out eventually. It always does, because they always run out of puff at some stage and we get a second wind. That's what happened in the second half in general. We turned the tide and got the upper hand. Mafi scored a try off a brilliant counterattack, and Rog kicked a couple of penalties to reduce the deficit to seven points. That was what we needed for the losing bonus point. They came hell for leather late in the game to get the score that would leave us empty-handed. Brock James struck for a drop goal deep in injury time, but it drifted wide of the posts. We left with the bonus point. We were beaten, but we'd survived.

Thomond Park was literally a building site when Wasps turned up for the final game in the group. Only one team would make it out of the group. Again there were mathematical permutations to do with tries and bonus points, but a win by a decent margin would see us through. It was another match played in pouring rain. Twelve months on from the shock defeat against Leicester, we had a half-built new stadium and a team that was in a far healthier state of mind. Unlike then, we needed to win now. Wasps didn't go down without a fight. It took us until the seventy-fourth minute to finally breach their line, and that was after a siege that went through some twenty-two phases. We won 19–3; we had clawed our way to the top of the group. It was the tenth year in a row that Munster had reached the Heineken Cup quarter-finals.

If we were to make it to the final, we'd have to do it the hard way again, on the road, in hostile venues. We faced Gloucester, who were top of the English Premiership, in Kingsholm. These games always look handier in hindsight than they felt when you were in the middle of them at the time. We won 3–16; they didn't score for an hour, but Chris Paterson had an off day with the boot and missed three kickable penalties in the first half. Ian Dowling finished off a great move three minutes before half-time, and Declan Kidney reared up on him afterwards for celebrating to the crowd before he'd touched down. Gestures like that wouldn't be Deccie's style. Ian was told in no uncertain terms to make sure he'd scored first before waving to the fans.

It wasn't Deccie's style to hurt anyone's feelings either. That was one of his strengths as a man manager; he was sensitive about how he spoke to fellas and how he generally dealt with them. But he wasn't afraid to make big decisions either, and he showed it in his team selection for the Gloucester game. Shaun Payne and Peter Stringer were dropped, for Denis Hurley and Tomás O'Leary respectively. He gambled with two inexperienced players for a Heineken Cup quarter-final away from home. Anthony Foley got a few minutes at the end of the match. Axel was thirty-four by then; we pretty much knew this was going to be his last season. But he'd started in those crunch pool games against Clermont and Wasps in January; he was still capable of doing a vital job for us. He was one of Munster's all-time greats, but there was no senti-ment where he was concerned either. Donncha Ryan had established himself in the squad, Axel didn't even make the match-day twenty-two for either the semi-final or final. The changes in personnel for the Gloucester game meant that we had a new-look backline all of a sudden, with Hurley, Howlett, Tipoki and O'Leary now in the mix. Mafi and Dowling hadn't been around for years either.

We got away by the skin of our teeth against Saracens in the semi-final at the Ricoh Arena. It was unbelievably nervy as the second half wore on and our game deteriorated. We led 15–7 at the break, but could manage only a single penalty in the second half. They kicked three second-half penalties and we were hanging onto a two-point lead with ten minutes left. Sarries could easily have been awarded a penalty in injury time for Munster infringing at a ruck close to our line. Instead they were penalised for not releasing. We got away with it. Sarries were coached by Alan Gaffney, and he had them revved up big time for it.

A Magners League match against Glasgow in Musgrave Park turned out to be Foley's last game for Munster. We had an idea it would be, but the Heineken Cup final had still to be played, and there was a chance he'd still be involved. All it'd take was one injury to somebody else. You'd have loved to have turned on the style and send him out on a high, but a lot of fellas had one eye on the final and one eye on Glasgow. They ended up beating us, and it wasn't a great way for him to sign off. But I don't think it bothered him badly – Axel's mind was on the final too.

He wasn't the only one who was going to be retiring or moving on at the end of the season. Kidney had been appointed the new Ireland coach a few weeks before the final. Jim Williams was moving back to Australia. Shaun Payne was stepping down as a player to take over as Munster manager. And John Kelly had retired at Christmas. They all got the send-off they wanted on 24 May.

I have a few standout memories from the final. One is the scrum that led to Leamy's try seven minutes before half-time. There was talk in the weeks leading up to it that Toulouse would be targeting our scrum. In fairness, I think the Munster front row really stood up on the day. We knew it was going to be a key battle. We'd concentrated really hard on getting it right in training, and we were full of intent to take on the Toulouse front row. Marcus Horan was up against the Italian prop Salvatore Perugini. I was facing this big South African, Daan Human. Marcus was totally pumped up, and he fairly drilled it into Perugini that day. He was giving it to him in a big way, and I could feel it on the other side of the scrum. They had the put-in on a 5-metre scrum on their line, and those are the situations where both forward packs give it hammer and tongs. We upped the ante on the hit and drove them back. It allowed O'Leary in on top of Sowerby, their number eight, as soon as he picked up the ball at the base. Quinny wasn't far behind him. Sowerby was penalised, and we had the put-in. From there we rumbled a few times, and Leamy was driven over. It was a huge moment for us, as a team, as a front row. Obviously the try and conversion were badly needed because Toulouse had dominated for the first twenty-five minutes or so. But it was a big confidence boost for the rest of the game, knowing that the scrum was going well.

We had done a lot of analysis on their scrum and lineout. O'Connell, and Jim Williams as forwards coach, didn't leave any stone unturned in terms of reviewing Toulouse's games that season. They had spotted that Toulouse had a very effective maul off a specific lineout move. They used this move to get their maul going. It was a pattern. They'd have had a name for it. They'd line up in the same way and throw it to the same player if they were going to use the maul. So we rehearsed a move to disrupt it. A few minutes into the second half they got a lineout in or around our twenty-two. This was exactly the situation they were waiting for. I can remember walking into that lineout knowing that they were going to try it here. We all knew it, we all recognised it. They were going to set up their maul off it and engineer a try or a penalty off it. Our plan was to get Quinny up in the air and contest the throw. The only problem was that it was a gamble on our part. If they didn't do what we expected, we were going to be exposed. But they went for it. Quinny got into the air and tapped it back. We tidied it up and cleared it. In the battle between the two forward packs, that incident broke them. I believe it was a turning point. You could see they were rattled by it. This was something that had always worked for them, and suddenly it didn't work. They knew that we had read their play book. It's very demoralising for a team when you know that your opponents have sussed you out. That moment is one of the best examples I can think of where home-work paid off at the highest level of the game. That lineout was won weeks before the final.

The next big moment couldn't be analysed ahead of schedule, or predicted in any way, unless there was footage somewhere of Fabien Pelous kicking an opponent up the arse. But that's what he did to Quinny in the fifty-first minute. We were standing there more or less in midfield, waiting for a scrum to be reset. The two packs were gathered either side of the gap, but Quinny had wandered into the

What's seldom is wonderful: scoring my one and only international try, against Scotland in the 2005 Six Nations.

Taking the Triple Crown after beating England in 2006. As you can see, the novelty hadn't quite worn off just yet.

The Munster fans took over the stadium at the Heineken Cup semi-final against Leinster in 2006.

We managed to pay them back by winning the final against Biarritz a month later.

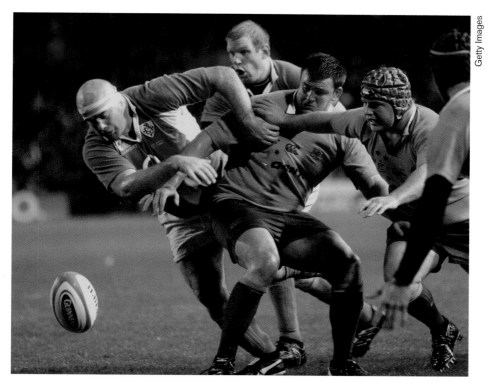

Grappling with Australia at Lansdowne Road in 2006.

Day of history: Croke Park, Ireland v England, 24 February 2007.

With a slightly
worried-looking
Jerry Flannery
at the 2007
World Cup caps
presentation.

As the final whistle
is blown at the
Heineken Cup final
against Toulouse,
I don't think the
realisation has
dawned on me yet.

Arriving back in
Shannon Airport
with the Heineken
Cup, we were
mobbed by fans.
The lads partied
for days, but I
snuck home to
Fiona.

Playing Italy during our 2009
Grand Slam campaign,
Ireland's first clean sweep in
61 years.

On tour with the Lions in South Africa. I was delighted to finish off that part of my career on a high note.

Sent out onto the field all alone for my 100th international cap, against England at Twickenham.

My 105th and final cap, in my last Six Nations match, against Scotland at Murrayfield.

Goodbye to all that. The Munster fans give me an emotional send-off in my final game of rugby, at Thomond Park. Fiona and our kids are my life now.

middle of theirs. He was yakking at Byron Kelleher, their scrum half. He'd been trying to get into Kelleher's head all day, because Kelleher was a fiery customer and Quinny thought he could get some change out of him. But Pelous was usually above all that. He was an icon of French rugby, a class player and generally very disciplined. Anyway, Quinny was making his way back to our side when he and Pelous threw an arm at each other. Quinny turned around, and Pelous followed up by aiming a kick at him and catching him in the backside. It was actually very funny. I was standing there in the front row and I saw it. I can remember thinking, 'What has he done to make Pelous kick him up the hole?!' Quinny was a pain in the hole to lots of opposing players over the years; he was always annoying fellas. But this time he was literally on the receiving end. Mind you, Pelous didn't reef him; it wasn't a full-blooded drive. But it was enough to grab the linesman's attention. Quinny grabbed the back of his leg and limped around the place before going down. He copped himself on and got back up pretty quickly, but the linesman notified the referee, Nigel Owens, and Owens showed Pelous the yellow card. It was their put-in on the scrum, but suddenly we had a penalty, which Rog converted to give us a 13–6 lead.

You could argue it was rough justice on Toulouse, but a kick at someone is still a kick. They probably felt that justice was done when they scored a try with Pelous off the field. The conversion levelled the match. O'Gara's penalty ten minutes later edged us in front again, 16–13. There were fifteen minutes still to go. I don't know what got into us after that. Nerves took over, I suppose, the tension of the occasion, with everything at stake and such a slender lead. We were afraid to move the ball wide for fear of an intercept or a turnover or something. We more or less put the ball up our jumper for the last eight or so minutes. It was a long time, too long; we'd have been better off if we'd kept playing. But the more the minutes ticked down the more nervous we were of throwing the ball around. The forwards just went through phase

after phase, recycling it over and over. It was pick and jam, pick
and jam, pick and jam. We weren't really going anywhere, just a
few metres forward, a few metres back, all the time eating up the
minutes and seconds. It was conservative stuff; some people said it
was downright negative. But it was bloody high-risk too. We
could've knocked it on, we could've popped it out in a tackle, we
could've been penalised for sealing off the ball. If they had scored,
we'd have had to come out of that defensive mindset and go back
on the attack again, and that would've been hard to do. It worked
for us, but I wouldn't be recommending it. I think it changed the
way the authorities implemented the rules afterwards. If a team
was trying to close out a match in that way, referees became very
quick at penalising them for preventing contact and sealing off the
ball. I think we were the better team on the day anyway. We
played harder, we wanted it more, we went deeper into ourselves
than they did. We were full value for that three-point margin in
the finish.

Owens finally blew his whistle with O'Connell at the bottom of
a ruck. He and O'Gara had had a big conference over what to do
with a penalty in the last half minute. Eventually Rog tapped and
threw it to O'Connell who took it into contact. I arrived into the
ruck when the whistle went. I got up and walked away. Marcus
was beside me, and he had the ball in his hands when Owens blew.
He threw the ball into the air in celebration. It bounced straight in
front of me as I was walking away. I grabbed it and said to myself,
'I'll have that.' And I have it still. The ball from the 2008
Heineken Cup final. I should've got the twenty-two on the day to
sign it, but if you handed it around the dressing room like that
you might never have got it back. I gave it to the baggage man, Ian
Fleming, to hold onto, and he kept it for me.

In my mind I find it hard to separate the two European Cups. The
first one was pure joy and relief, the second one brought a lot
of satisfaction. I think it confirmed the stature of that team. It

cemented our place in the history of the competition and left a stronger legacy. We'd poured our hearts into it for the guts of ten years. We felt we deserved a second title, but you still had to go out and earn it. We did it the hard way that season; I don't think anyone can doubt that we earned it.

Just like two years earlier, Cardiff was again bananas that night. It was hugs and handshakes and back-slapping everywhere you went. Fellas singing and drinking and cheering everywhere you turned. We could hardly get through the crowds at Cardiff Airport for the flight home. It was the same in the arrivals hall at Shannon. We got the bus to the team hotel in Limerick, and people came out waving and beeping their car horns along the route. There was another massive crowd waiting for us at the hotel. I had the car parked up at the hotel. I got my bag, slipped out of the bus and drove home to Cappamore.

14

It wasn't easy keeping up with Jamie Heaslip that day in Croke Park. He was going fast, for starters, and stepping this way and that, but believe it or not I managed to hang onto his shoulder. You could nearly say I was going fast too.

It was against France in the first game of the 2009 Six Nations. Jamie had taken the ball from O'Connell in midfield, about thirty metres out from the posts. Next thing he took off and didn't stop until he was falling over the line. I happened to be the nearest man to him when he got the ball. Maybe that's why he decided to go it alone. But I was there in the van, ready for my moment of glory. I was sure he was going to be brought down. All he'd have to do is pop it back, and I'd finish it off. I would've loved that, scoring a try against France in Croke Park. It didn't happen, but prop forwards are entitled to the odd notion too, every now and again. Jamie did brilliant to finish it all on his own. And I went back to the mullocking.

We won a great match that day. France played some fantastic rugby, but we hit top form too. Drico slashed through the cover for one of his trademark finishes after half-time, but France came back with a try and a drop goal. The match was on a knife edge until Gordon D'Arcy swivelled his way over with fourteen minutes left. Beating France was a big monkey off our backs; we'd lost seven games in a row since defeating them in 2003. It gave us a great injection of confidence. It'd been almost two years since we felt this sort of buzz in the camp. The '07 World Cup and '08 Six Nations had left us at a fairly low ebb. When Kidney took over in the summer of '08 we were badly in need of a lift. It's often said that a new voice in the dressing room can freshen things up a lot. Deccie wasn't exactly a new voice to the Munster lads in the Ireland squad, but it was a different environment, and that in itself changes things. He also recruited a new coaching staff with Alan Gaffney, Les Kiss and Gert Smal. So all of a sudden we were getting a range of new voices and new ideas.

Gert carried a lot of authority with him from the start; he had been the forwards coach with the South Africa team that had won the 2007 World Cup. Ireland had played South Africa on tour and in autumn internationals while he was with them, and he had done a lot of analysis on us for those games. So now we were getting a look at ourselves from the outside. We were finding out what the Springboks thought of us and how they felt they could beat us, and that was a valuable insight to get. Any time we turned up for camp, Gert would be straight down to business. It'd be in the door, drop your bags in your room and come down for a meeting. He'd have the schedule planned, his printouts ready and a rundown of our work for the week: lineouts, scrums, breakdown, all the drills that were needed. He was meticulous about the details. He brought the South African mentality to the collisions. He'd go through all the technical aspects of forward play, but it always came back to the collisions. That was the fundamental. It was all about aggression and physicality and trying to dominate your opponents. We all knew how important that sort of physical intensity was anyway, but it was good to have it reinforced over and over. He used to say to me that I was too quiet and needed to make my voice heard more. I was a senior player by then, and if I felt fellas weren't doing things right, I should be revving them out of it. He probably had a point. I used to always look at myself first if things weren't going well, and I wouldn't go round giving out to other fellas. But at the same time if I felt it wasn't just me to blame, then I would say something.

Les Kiss brought a lot of expertise as a defence specialist from his time in both rugby league and rugby union in Australia. Alan Gaffney was working with the backs and Paul McNaughton was the new team manager. Then you had a new wave of young players coming through since the World Cup, the likes of Heaslip, Rob Kearney, Luke Fitzgerald, Tomás O'Leary and Stephen Ferris. This was the season they really made their mark. They brought a bit of energy and fearlessness to the dressing room which lifted the longer-serving players too.

At international level the players are supposed to have a fairly high baseline when it comes to ability anyway. Winning at this level is a matter of getting them performing close to the best of that ability. If every individual is finding a couple of per cent more and feeding it into the overall collective, you've a team with a good chance of winning things. The trick is getting it out of them. The senior players have to show leadership and set the right example too, but it's up to the coach and staff to create a good environment where players are happy and feel confident in themselves. One of Deccie's great strengths was getting the best out of players. He was good at pressing the right buttons, saying the right things, finding out how fellas ticked. There's an element of personal chemistry, I suppose, in it all.

The upshot, anyway, of all the changes and new faces was that the mood improved, the energy was positive and there was a bit of optimism in the air going into the '09 Six Nations. The previous November Ireland had been well beaten by the All Blacks in Croke Park. Three days later in Thomond Park Munster came within four minutes of pulling off an amazing victory over the All Blacks. It was more or less New Zealand's second string team, but

Munster had fielded a load of squad players too. And they were outstanding on the night; they played with unbelievable courage and heart against a team that on paper was far superior. It took a late try from Joe Rokocoko to finally break them. A few weeks later the Ireland squad had a training camp in Enfield, Co Meath. I don't know whether it was the contrast in displays against New Zealand, but Rob Kearney raised a fairly sensitive subject at a team forum. It was one of these talking shops where the squad is broken into groups of five or six and players are encouraged to bring up whatever is bothering them. Someone in each group is nominated as the leader – I was the leader in our group – and you made a note of whatever points were raised. If enough fellas raised the same issue, then you shared it with the rest of the room when each group came back with its findings. O'Gara was leader of his group and he said that one fella had questioned whether Munster players brought the same passion to the Ireland jersey as they did to the Munster cause. Then Rob put up his hand and owned up to asking the question. In fairness, no one jumped down his neck for raising it. But personally I didn't believe it. I was 100 per cent sure in myself that I brought the same attitude to Ireland as to Munster games. I never made that distinction, consciously or unconsciously. All the other Munster players in the room were of the same belief and said it. I was completely unaware that there might even have been this perception out there. So it was good that it was brought out into the open and discussed. If there's some sort of undercurrent like that in a dressing room, it's the best way to deal with it: bring it up, thrash it out and get rid of it. That's what happened in the hotel that night in Enfield. It was put to bed and never became an issue again.

Other stuff came up too, like the sense that there was a lack of clarity over the team game plan. It wasn't 100 per cent clear, our patterns and structures; there was uncertainty among some players. This was discussed and thrashed out too. Rob was only a young fella at the time, and he earned a lot of respect for having the bottle to bring up such a delicate subject. But I think its significance was overstated in retrospect. Mind you, the meeting was a very healthy exercise overall. It cleared the air and had the effect of bonding the players that bit closer together.

There's nothing like a big win, though, to bring a team together, and that's what the France result did for us. We took that confidence with us to Rome a week later and beat Italy by twenty-nine points. It was the usual scrappy, niggly dogfight upfront with the Italians. One of their former props, Massimo Cuttitta, was quoted earlier in the week as saying that Martin Castrogiovanni, their tight-head, was going to give Marcus Horan a hard time in the scrums. Needless to say, Marcus was ready for battle that day. And Donncha O'Callaghan, who was pushing behind Marcus, wasn't going to take a backward step either. Then the first scrum collapsed, and Castrogiovanni decided to have a few words with Horan. I heard him saying it, something like, 'It's going to be a long day for you.' He was trying to look all menacing as well. Castrogiovanni is a good player but a bit of a bullshitter. I told him to shut the fuck up, and I wasn't the only one. There was fellas queuing up to have their say. The funny thing was that he had to go off injured himself about twenty minutes later. He got a right volley of abuse in his ear going off. ''Twas a fairly fuckin' short day for you!' And stuff like that. Then Salvatore Perugini got injured in the second half, and Castrogiovanni had to come back on again. He got another flurry of fucks fired into him when he arrived back on again.

Brian O'Driscoll scored a late try that day. It wouldn't have affected the final result. He scored a try against England in Dublin a fortnight later that was crucial to the final result. He just managed to burrow over from close range on the England line. He had the power and speed to do it. A few minutes earlier he'd taken a high, late wallop that would've finished a lesser man. Drico can take a terrible amount of punishment and carry on. I don't think

I've played with a better player. He had world-class levels of pace and flair and skill, but he wanted to be the complete player. He knew he could beat anyone on the outside with his speed. He could carve up any defence with his sidesteps and ability to find space. But then he turned himself into an extra back row forward too. I think he didn't want anyone to say that he had a single weakness in his game. That he was a great attacking player, for example, but couldn't defend as well. So he worked on that aspect of his game too and became a ferocious defender. That's what made him unique. Other players with his sort of natural talent, it wouldn't have even occurred to them to do that sort of donkey work too.

That's how Drico reinvented the centre position. He had the physical strength and mental attitude to play like an extra flanker. When he locked onto a ball at the breakdown it was impossible to knock him off it. He was low to the ground and freakishly strong. I remember one incident in the 2006 Heineken Cup semi-final at Lansdowne Road. One of the Munster players carried the ball into contact. Drico locked onto him and was trying to poach the ball. I went in to clean him out, but I didn't go low enough. It'd be hard to go as low as him anyway. The thing is, even if you don't go low enough you can still dislodge a fella off the ball with sheer force and weight, if he's not strong enough. But Drico absorbed the hit and held on. I actually skidded off his back and went over the other side. The ref penalised Munster for not releasing. Time and again he has won turnovers with that kind of play.

For a bonus, he keeps his speeches brief too at the official dinners the night of a match. They're an awful dose, the dinners and the speeches. I mean the grub is grand, but sitting there in a monkey suit, waiting for the two captains and the two union presidents to get through all their rigmarole, it'd wear you out. And then if it's after a France or Italy game, you obviously have to sit through the translations as well. Eight speeches, more or less, and none of them getting better in any language. Drico would keep it short and sweet. And he'd throw in a nice touch of class too; he'd mention it if someone's wife had a baby or some player got his fiftieth cap that day, or whatever. He wouldn't leave anyone out; he'd remember a personal detail, and he'd have it all wrapped up in five minutes.

England reverted to their old-school ways that day in Croke Park. Two years before, we battered them, and they weren't going to put up with that again. This time they turned up with a massive pack to meet us head-on in the collisions, and it made for one long, hard grind. It was a punishing day's work. We beat them by thirty points in '07. We beat them by a single point in '09. But we had survived, and we were now three from three.

A fortnight later we were away to Scotland at Murrayfield. You wouldn't have thought that any manager, let alone Deccie, would've tampered much with a team that was in this vein of form. But Deccie threw a curve ball by dropping O'Leary, Flannery, Heaslip and Paddy Wallace. Or rather rotating them, to give it the politically correct term. In came Stringer, Rory Best, Leamy and D'Arcy. It's never easy reading Kidney's mind, but maybe he felt that if he kept saying to squad players, every time he had to tell them they weren't picked, that they were playing really well and they'd get their chance, sooner or later he'd have to back it up. He'd have to give them their chance at some stage. Going to Murrayfield makes people nervous at the best of times, and the changes probably didn't do much to relax our supporters. Scotland were fired up and hard to break down. It took a brilliant last-ditch tackle from O'Driscoll to keep them out late in the first half. Ten minutes into the second half Stringer reminded everyone why Kidney had recalled him. It was his break from the back of a line-out that finally opened up Scotland. Heaslip had come on for the injured Leamy, and he took the offload from Strings for the only try of the game. It was a dour, sticky old match, but we were four from four now, and talk of the Grand Slam couldn't be postponed any longer.

Everyone else had been talking about it for weeks, but as players we could only let it into our heads after we'd negotiated England and Scotland. Even then, we couldn't allow it to take over our preparations. We had Wales at the Millennium Stadium a week after Murrayfield, and we had to try and keep our heads clear for the actual match, not the prize at the end of it. At the same time, you couldn't ignore it either. You'd have this big elephant in the room with everyone afraid to mention it. So you had to accept it was there. If you ignored it, you were running away from it, and that's not healthy either. This was something we all wanted. It was a goal that the veterans in the team had shared for years. Mentally, it became a balancing act that week. You had to acknowledge we were going for a Grand Slam, but you had to keep a lid on it too and not look beyond the match itself.

We got a day off in the middle of the week. Róisín had been born ten days before the Scotland game, and I'd hardly spent any time with her. We'd built a new house on the family farm, and I was glad to get home, even if it was only for twenty-four hours. I was always glad of those midweek days off between Test matches. I'd shoot down to Limerick late on a Tuesday evening and head back up Wednesday. It'd break up the week; the game wouldn't take total control over you. Thursday was travelling day. I was lucky enough in that I was generally able to sleep well and eat well on the Thursday and Friday. The day of the Wales match, though, was hell on the nerves. On Saturday, 21 March 2009 they were as bad as they ever were, and maybe worse. The match wasn't until 5.30pm. I kept saying to myself, 'Will this match ever get going? Christ almighty, why can't this match just start?' We were still in the hotel at this stage. This was the Hilton, right in the middle of Cardiff. You could see the crowds gathering from your bedroom window. Thousands of fans in red and green jerseys. Some fellas would've pulled the curtains. I preferred to look out and take in some of the colour and atmosphere. Everyone was feeling the nerves, but they were good nerves. You can tell the difference.

Fellas were white in the face, but the nerves weren't nerves that were going to stop them from playing. Fellas were in a good place, despite the desperate tension. Everyone was fit and right. Everyone just wanted it. There was a feeling that, mentally and physically, everyone had arrived at the same place at the same time.

At half-time we were 0–6 down. It wasn't a worry in the dressing room. We were in the game, we were playing well, we had forty minutes to make it count on the scoreboard. Drico scored another of his specials from a close-in ruck. We'd been pounding the Welsh line, picking and driving, but none of us could go lower than O'Driscoll without actually hitting the ground. He grabbed the ball and reached for the line so close to the ground that they couldn't stop him planting it down. Two minutes later Rog chipped a lovely ball over the top, towards the right touchline. Gavin Henson and Shane Williams had a split second to deal with it, but Tommy Bowe was steaming onto it. The bounce sat up perfect for him, he caught it overhead and didn't have to break stride. After that it was a race to the line and under the posts. That score was pure confidence and form. Tommy was having a great season, and it showed in the way he attacked that ball. On another day a player with less confidence might have hesitated, worrying about the bounce or something. But he went after it with total conviction.

The only problem was that there were thirty-five minutes still to play. That's an eternity when you're only leading by eight points. Ten minutes later there were only two between us after a pair of Stephen Jones penalties. It was all in the balance. In the sixty-eighth minute I gave away a penalty for coming in from the side. It was on halfway and near the right touchline. Henson was their long-range kicker. He stepped up and missed. I believe that that was a very significant moment in the match.

Five minutes from time, Jones kicked the drop goal that put them in front. We were experienced enough to know we had time to engineer a score. And we we'd been around long enough to know how to do it too. Then we caught a big break. Mike Phillips threw a pass back from outside the Welsh twenty-two, to Jones who was inside the twenty-two. It wasn't like Jones to panic; he'd been around a long time too, but the noise and tension around the stadium was mind-bending anyway. He kicked the ball out on the full. It gave us a lineout well inside their twenty-two, an ideal platform. If Jones had walloped the ball straight down the field, we would've had to chase back and start from there. But he didn't, and it opened the door. Stringer was in for O'Leary at this stage, and he was an old hand in these situations too. We were going to go through phases off the lineout, and Strings would orchestrate it until he felt we were in the right position to set up Rog for the drop goal. The Welsh knew well what was coming. They were going to come charging at O'Gara as soon as the scrum half released the ball. The extra zip on Stringer's pass would buy Rog a split-second more time. The forwards had to be careful not to make a mistake: a stupid fumble, or someone flopping in, falling off their feet and getting pinged for sealing off the ball. Jesus, if you made a mistake like that, at a time like this, it would've haunted you for the rest of your life. But we went through the phases okay, gained ground, and crabbed infield until we were in the right position. Stringer flashed out the ball from the bottom of a ruck. O'Gara in one movement caught it, struck it and got it up, over, and between the posts.

There were still two and a half minutes on the clock. Then Paddy Wallace gave the country a heart attack. He got pinged for trying to poach the ball. They had a penalty from the halfway line to win it and destroy us. Stephen Jones decided that he would take it. That's why I think the earlier missed penalty by Henson was significant. If he'd landed it, there's no doubt in my mind that he'd have taken the final one. He would've had the distance; it was well within his range. And being the sort of character Henson is, he'd have had the bottle too. He'd have loved it. But Jones instead said he would take it. I was facing him when he stepped up; I wasn't that far away. I wouldn't often concentrate on a penalty kick, for or against us, but I was paying attention to this one. I watched him strike it, and turned around to follow the flight of the ball. And as it took off I knew it was good for accuracy. But the ball wasn't sailing through the air. About halfway into its trajectory I knew it was dying. It was touch and go; it still might flop a foot over the bar. But it was dying instead of sailing. It dropped below the crossbar. Geordan Murphy caught it, touched it down, and booted it into the crowd.

You felt relief before you felt any joy. Relief just flooding through you. Then it was all the happiness that only sport can give you when you've won something special. Complete and total happiness and contentment. Ireland had won the Grand Slam for the first time since 1948. People talked about us feeling the weight of the sixty-one years pressing down on us. I didn't feel that. I felt the weight of the ten years I'd been at it myself. I'd got my first cap in 2000. The Wales game was my ninety-fourth cap. The 2009 tournament was my tenth Six Nations. I was thirty-five years of age. You were starting to think at that stage that the ship might have sailed; that you were never going to do it. We'd won Triple Crowns, we'd been pipped for the championship, and had been hammered by England in the 2003 Grand Slam game. And now we'd finally done it. The fifty-one years before that, it didn't really impinge on me. It wasn't your era or your responsibility. We could only do something about it in our time. It was up to us to win it and leave a legacy. It was our time and our era, and I'm glad to think that we did leave something behind.

There's a sense of accomplishment there now. The relief I feel now is not that Stephen Jones missed that late penalty. It's the relief of knowing that, after ten years of trying, the likes of O'Driscoll and O'Gara and O'Connell and Stringer accomplished what they deserved and earned.

Cardiff and the Millennium Stadium have been good to us; we've won European Cups there and we won the Grand Slam there. The official dinner was fairly easy to get through that night. No problem at all. We heard there was going to be a civic reception in Dublin the next evening. I was humming and hawing about going. But getting off the plane in Dublin I had my mind up. I asked Deccie if I could slip away. He gave me the green light, and I appreciated that. There was a taxi organised at the airport to bring some of the travelling players who hadn't togged out back to the hotel in Killiney. I hopped into the taxi, packed my gear at the hotel, and headed for my car. It was a Sunday afternoon and there was no traffic on the road. I was back in Limerick in two hours. RTE showed the open air reception for the players live on television that evening. While Tommy Bowe was belting out *The Black Velvet Band* up on the stage in Dublin, I was sitting at home on the couch with my feet up, laughing my head off and drinking a mug of tea.

15

Six weeks later it was a different story. There was no one laughing, not in the Munster dressing room anyway. The emptiness was back again, the silence and numbness. We were in a state of shock. Leinster had dumped us out of the Heineken Cup and we hadn't fired a shot in anger.

That's what the game does to you, I suppose. It gives you a high in the Millennium Stadium the like of which you couldn't imagine. And then the pendulum swings back to the other extreme, and it gives you an injection of pure, raw hurt. Just to keep you honest, in case you're ever in danger of losing the run of yourself.

It's worse when you don't see it coming. We didn't see it coming that day. Everything looked on track, everything was on target. Tony McGahan had taken over from Deccie as head coach in the summer of 2008. He'd been with us for the previous three years as backs and defence coach, so the transition had gone smoothly. Munster were having a good season. We were looking good to defend our title. We'd even beaten Leinster, and fairly comprehensively too, in a Magners League match at the start of April. We then demolished a star-studded Ospreys side in the Heineken Cup quarter-final a week later. Two further wins in the Magners meant we were coming into the semi-final with near enough maximum momentum. The buzz, the confidence, the atmosphere in the squad – it was all top-notch. While we were beating the Ospreys 43–9 in Thomond Park, Leinster were surviving a siege at the Stoop to beat Harlequins 6–5. They fairly dug their way out of the trenches that day, and in hindsight I'd say it stood to them more than our cushy win over the Ospreys did to us.

But at the time Munster were hot favourites. A lot of people were still questioning Leinster's bottle, despite the way they'd toughed it out at the Stoop. They'd had to put up with a lot of questioning and doubting since we'd beaten them in the '06 semi-final at Lansdowne Road. We had won the Heineken Cup twice in the meantime. Leinster had a lot of proud players, and they weren't going to put up with it forever. I'd imagine they were sick of people doubting them. They came in a bit under the radar that day in Croke Park, and they had obviously decided that this was going to be their day. They weren't going to take no for an answer. We were hungry for more success. Once you've experienced the feeling of winning something like a European Cup, you want more of it. But Leinster were hungrier. It's the last thing you want to admit, but you have to accept it. If you are beaten by a team with more skill or whatever, it's easier to accept. We were outplayed by Leinster, but first of all we were out-wanted, if you can call it that. They wanted it more than we did. They turned up and we didn't. And that was very hard to swallow. We were beaten lots of times over the years, but we always turned up. We always played. A crowd of over 82,000 was in Croke Park that day, then a world record for a rugby club game. At least half of them were Munster supporters, and maybe more. And we gave them almost nothing to cheer about. It was a miserable way to go out as champions.

Leinster went on to win the Heineken Cup, and there was talk now of a power shift in Irish rugby. Basically, that Munster were on the slide and Leinster had taken over. Over the next few years it turned out to be true, but you didn't want to be listening to that kind of talk at the time. But it was harder to argue with after they put thirty points on us at the RDS the following season, in October '09. It was a dark night and it wasn't as if the floodlights weren't working. We were sent home with a duck beside our name: Leinster 30 Munster 0. And I was sent off after fifty-five minutes. It was the worst moment of my career, for club or country. Worse than the worst defeats. I felt embarrassed, maybe even ashamed. It was the one and only time I ever got a red card. In fact, I only ever got two or three yellow cards in my whole career. And for me to do this at the age of thirty-five, almost thirty-six, made it worse in my eyes.

We were already twenty points down. We had a second lineout near our own 5-metre line. There'd already been a bit of argy-bargy at the first. We won the ball and formed a maul. Cian Healy got into the middle of it and was trying to pull it down. Nothing wrong with that, nothing I hadn't done myself. Cian ended up on the floor, as often happens when you're trying to pull down a maul. If you end up on the ground in a situation like that, you're going to get a shoeing. If you don't succeed in pulling it down, you go under and the maul tramples over you. And they won't be picking and choosing their steps either. Pulling down a maul is illegal, and you pay the price for it if you end up on the deck. For me, and I think for most rugby players, shoeing is an accepted part of the game. Legs, arms, upper body – it's all fair game. But the head is off limits; it's out of bounds.

I could feel a body at my feet in this maul. Whoever it was, he was pulling at my leg. I was shoeing him, and so were a few other Munster players. But I caught him on the head. I didn't know who it was until he got up. Healy was roaring at me that I'd kicked him on the head. I told him I didn't know I'd caught him on the head. But the blood was flowing, and the touch judge had his flag up, and I knew there was trouble coming. The referee, Simon McDowell, consulted with the touch judge. Then he called me over and flashed the red card.

I sought out Cian straight after the match. He came over to me and we shook hands. He was a very young player at the time. I barely knew him at that stage. I apologised to him and told him I hadn't meant it. And fair play to him, he accepted that straight-away. A few other Leinster lads came over too and said they knew I hadn't meant it. I appreciated Cian's response and the other lads' too. Drico as well. As I was taking the long walk after the red card, Drico came over to me and gave me a pat on the shoulder. You mightn't think a small thing like that would make much difference to you. But at a time like that it would. It meant a lot to me, in fact.

Three days later I was facing an IRFU disciplinary hearing in Ravenhill. They brought me into a boardroom. Shaun Payne accompanied me as the Munster team manager, along with Donal Spring, my legal advisor. The committee played the incident on television and asked me to give my side of the story. I explained the circumstances. I admitted I was shoeing him. I admitted I was reckless and should have been more careful. I stated that it wasn't intentional. Thankfully, the video evidence backed me up. They could see I wasn't looking down at the time. I was being driven up in the maul and backwards, and my head was up. I wasn't looking down, trying to find out exactly where he was. The footage exon-erated me on that score. They accepted it wasn't intentional. That was important, because I'd never shoed anyone in the head, or near the head, in my career. There are boundaries you don't cross, and that's one of them. They sent me out of the room and did their deliberations and called me back in. They suspended me for nine weeks and mitigated it to six weeks, they said, because of my exemplary record over the years. Munster appealed, and the IRFU reduced it by another week. I beat myself up over that incident for a long time afterwards. I felt it damaged my reputation. If it had been against another team in another country, the publicity around it wouldn't have been as widespread. I wasn't comfortable even with positive publicity, so I found the whole episode very embarrassing. I wish to hell it had never happened.

The game had become a lot more sanitised by the end of my career. An awful lot of the Wild West stuff was gone. An older generation of players would probably say it was well cleaned up by the time I started in the mid-nineties. But it had changed a lot even during my time. You still got plenty of shoeings, and you still dished out plenty of them. But often they're not as bad as they look on television. A lot of the time you wouldn't even feel it when you were getting it; you'd have the marks on you after and you wouldn't even remember getting them. In the old days, if a fella ended up on the wrong side of a ruck, he'd get a good ripping. But that's gone out of the game too, to a great degree, because the referee will blow his whistle straightaway for a penalty if the fella in question is deliberately killing the ball. And if it's not intentional, the ref will still blow and award a scrum. So you don't see it as much on television these days, and I'd say television itself is a big reason why the culture has changed. It doesn't promote a good image of the game.

Ironically enough, my first game back after suspension was the November international against Australia at Croke Park. It happened to be the day Healy made his Ireland debut. We were both in the front row together, packing down against the Aussies. Cian was joking and laughing about it that week. He had moved on; it took me a bit longer to get over it.

In December Munster came up with one of their greatest ever performances in Europe. We went down to Perpignan's bear pit and beat them by twenty-three points. Dougie Howlett rounded off a brilliant day with a late try to get us the bonus point. The previous week we'd just scraped over them by a point in Thomond Park. We did it back to front this time: struggled at home and put the hammer on them away. The intensity came back that day, the work rate and appetite for the battle. It seemed like we were back firing on all cylinders. But in January our levels dropped again, this time against Northampton in the final pool match at Thomond Park. We won a scrappy match 12–9, but it was enough to top the group and get us a home quarter-final, against Northampton again, as it happened. We started well, scored two early tries, then dipped in the second quarter and a Northampton try in the last minute left them leading at the break. We got on top again in the second half, and eventually closed it out without too much stress. Northampton came with a powerful front row in Soane Tonga'uiha, Dylan Hartley and Euan Murray. They fancied themselves to do a bit of damage in the scrum. They were supposed to drive us back at a rate of knots. But it didn't happen. Tonga'uiha is a monster of a man, but his height and build suited me, and I did well against him on the day. It was the nuggety little fellas who could get under me that usually gave me more bother.

And I was in a whole heap of bother against Biarritz in the semi-final in San Sebastian. I was up against a South African by the name of Eduard Coetzee. I'd never played against him before. He'd never played international rugby, but he had my number on the day. I started out okay but he figured me out better than I figured him. He was getting in under me and driving me onto the back foot. Eventually, our scrum was decimated, and I was whipped off with less than an hour played. The team in general struggled badly in the second half. We'd done well in the first and led 7–3 at the break. The next forty minutes was one of the worst we ever put in. We were totally flat. It was typical of our season. We were able to hit top gear in spurts and spasms, but we weren't able to sustain it. I wasn't to know it then, but it was the last time I would play in the knock-out stages of the Heineken Cup. I suppose the writing was on the wall.

Naturally enough, people would've focused in on my scrummaging that day. I'm sure I got plenty of criticism for it. And, in fairness, I think I got proper recognition on the good days. This time I'd experienced the two sides of it within the space of three weeks. A fairly impressive display against a big unit like Tonga'uiha, and a fair old drilling against Coetzee. A lot of my ups and downs in the scrum were to do with the opponents I faced. Some suited my physique and some didn't. If you were going to be facing an opponent with a big reputation, you'd be on high alert for him, and more often than not you'd do fine against him. Other times you could be facing someone who didn't have the same reputation, and you'd struggle against him. So some of it was down to concentration issues too. It used to frustrate me an awful lot because you should have had the same intensity for all opponents.

Scrummaging was my primary function, and I worked harder on it than any other aspect of the game. The other parts came easier to me. Some days you met a fella who was just better than me at scrummaging, and there was no shame in that. The shame would be if you didn't improve the next time you met him. Generally I dealt with him better the next time we met. The reality is that I only started playing in the front row at the age of twenty-two, twenty-three. I didn't have the foundation. I missed out on the teenage years when ideally I'd have been learning the ropes and putting in that foundation. So I was always playing catch up. But I never wanted to use it as an excuse. I wouldn't allow it to hold me back. I didn't allow it to hold me back. Your bad days probably get highlighted more than your good days, in any walk of life I suppose. I think I had a lot more good days than bad.

We finished the '09/10 season empty-handed. Leinster had the upper hand on us again when we clashed in May, in the Magners League semi-final. We'd finished 08/09 with the Magners League trophy, which was some bit of consolation to take with us into the summer. At the end of '09/10 I signed one final contract with the IRFU. It would take me up to October 2011. The World Cup was happening in New Zealand in September 2011, and they wanted me for cover. Tony Buckley had been getting more and more game time at Munster over the previous few seasons, and he was starting to replace me regularly late on in international games. Tom Court and Mike Ross were also starting to come through for Ireland. I would turn thirty-seven in November 2010. By the time the World Cup came round I'd be closing in on thirty-eight. I had hummed and hawed about signing a new deal. We had two young kids at home and I wasn't responsible only for myself anymore. Full-time rugby meant being away from home a lot of the time. But it's hard to let go of something you love doing. I knew the end was approaching. I knew I wouldn't be first-choice anymore, for Munster or Ireland. But it was better than going cold turkey on it; a sudden stop would've been a bit of a shock to the system. I suppose I wasn't ready to let go.

By the middle of January 2011 Munster were out of Europe. Toulon beat us comprehensively in the second-last pool game at their place. For twelve years running we had made the quarter-finals of the Heineken Cup. Now we weren't even good enough to do that. It was a depressing place to be, after all the glory years. It was obvious to everyone else that we weren't the team we were. But we as players couldn't accept that. You have to deny to yourself that it's happening because you have to keep going. It's no good folding the tent once you can't win the big prizes. You have to keep fighting on the way down as well as the way up. A fortnight later we had London Irish at home in the final pool game. With twelve minutes to go we were 7–14 behind and staring down the barrel of a defeat at Thomond Park, only our second ever in the Heineken Cup. That was enough to get alarm bells ringing loud and clear. We ran in three late tries to turn the match on its head. It meant we finished second in the group and qualified for the Amlin Challenge Cup quarter-final. Our opponents were Brive on a scorching hot April day in southern France. It was a humdinger of a match, an absolute belter. It couldn't have been further away from a dogfight in the muck and rain of a winter's night in Limerick. Both sides were playing champagne rugby, which wasn't like us at all. Some brilliant tries were scored. I came on for the last twenty. We ended up winning on a ridiculous score-line of 37–42.

Three weeks later we had Harlequins at home in the semi-final. We were well below par and paid the price for a mediocre performance. We couldn't follow up on the Brive performance. We'd been playing in spurts and spasms all season. We couldn't sustain our form. The malaise had set in, and it wasn't going away. We couldn't raise a gallop on the day, not even at Thomond Park.

It was a Saturday afternoon, 30 April, and the club had organised an end-of-season barbecue for players and staff and their families afterwards at Adare Manor. It was a beautiful summer's evening but the mood was subdued. The result had left everyone down in the dumps. Fellas weren't on the lash, trying to drown their sorrows. We were just quietly sitting around, chatting and sipping at a beer. In hindsight, maybe it was more an end-of-an-era atmosphere than end-of-season. Quinny was retiring. Ian Dowling and Barry Murphy were retiring early because of injuries. Tony Buckley, known to everyone as Mushy, was moving on to England. Paul Warwick was moving on. And the team was in a bad place, worse than we'd ever known before. I'd be leaving the following October, so my days were numbered too. There was this general gloom in the air.

But Paul Darbyshire happened to be sitting at the table next to me. Darbs was a former rugby league player and coach in England. He'd joined Munster in 2007 as our strength and conditioning coach. He was a strong, powerfully-built lad himself. But he was in a wheelchair by now. He'd been suffering from motor neurone disease, and the poor fella was deteriorating rapidly. He was there in Adare Manor that night with his wife Lyndsay and their four young children. It was the saddest thing you could see. Seven weeks later Darbs passed away at the age of forty-one.

This was life, this was reality. Fiona and our two kids were at the barbecue too. I remember thinking at the time that there was no way I was going to get upset over my retirement. I was looking at Darbs and his family. There was no comparison in the two situations. I was lucky, I was blessed. What was I getting upset about? And I felt the Munster players that night, we needed to get a hold of ourselves and stop moping around, feeling sorry for ourselves. The club wanted to make a presentation to me that night. I didn't want it, but they said I was going in October, so they wanted to make this gesture on the night. I had nothing prepared to say, but I stood up and basically said we should get a grip on ourselves. There was an awful end-of-season vibe here, but the season wasn't over yet. If we beat Connacht the following weekend, we'd have a home semi-final in the Magners League. We still had something to play for if we didn't drop the heads.

We beat Connacht. Quinny scored a try. It was his last game for Munster, his last game at Thomond Park. He was substituted inside the last ten minutes, and the crowd gave him a massive reception as he made his way off. We'd been friends for a long time. We'd started out together on opposite sides in junior club rugby all those years earlier. He was a warrior on the field and a character off it. Actually, he was a character on the field too, come to think of it. You were never too far from a laugh when Quinny was around.

I started the game against Connacht, and I was mad for action. It was probably because I knew I hadn't too many games left in me either, but I really had the dander up. I wanted to stay in the team. I'd accepted my role as a sub that season a bit too passively. But maybe it wasn't all over yet. I did well enough against Connacht and stayed in the team for the semi-final against Ospreys at home. It was a weird feeling going out onto Thomond Park that day with the stadium only half full. Both ends of the ground were empty and closed up. Ospreys arrived with all of their big guns, but we were in the mood for a win. The blood was pumping, there was still a kick left in us. We controlled most of that match and were deserving winners.

There was a full house for the final. We were at home to Leinster, and our supporters weren't going to miss that one. The previous weekend Leinster had won their second Heineken Cup. They turned the game around with a tremendous second half performance against Northampton. In fairness to them, they only had seven days to recover physically and mentally, not just from the match but the euphoria and all the celebrations that went with it. It would've been hard for them to come down and get their heads around another big game a week later. But they were coming to Thomond Park looking to do the double that season, and if that wasn't going to get us wound up, nothing was. It was a brilliant match, full of intensity. They had us under the cosh in the third quarter, but we stayed in it and turned it round. Keith Earls's try gave us a narrow lead going into the last ten minutes. The icing on the cake was a penalty try after we drove their scrum back nearly under their posts in the final minute. It was a very nice win. Leinster had won the big one that season, but we needed something to give us a lift and restore our pride. It was great to get that special feeling back again, when you've won a big match at Thomond Park and the crowd is cheering you all the way.

We did a lap of honour that day. The thought went through my mind that this could be my last time ever to experience that atmosphere among our supporters. People were asking me, but I didn't know. If I made the World Cup squad, it would definitely be my last game. And I would have been more than happy with that, because I couldn't think of a better way to go: winning three games on the bounce in a place that had been such a happy hunting ground – and finishing it off with a trophy. You couldn't ask for more. As it turned out, and more or less by accident, I got a send-off that topped even this.

16

Having won the Grand Slam a month earlier, a lot of us in the Ireland team had high hopes of making the Lions squad when it was announced in April 2009.

As it turned out, a record fourteen Irish players were selected by the head coach, Ian McGeechan, to tour South Africa. But I wasn't one of them. They told me to remain on standby and keep myself fit in case any of the chosen prop forwards got injured. But, in all honesty, I didn't do a tap. I was thirty-five and needed a rest. Between Munster and Ireland it had been a draining season, and I was looking to recharge the batteries before pre-season began all over again.

By the middle of June there was no sign of any emergency anyway. The Lions had played five games and the props had all come through unscathed. The sixth was against the Southern Kings in Port Elizabeth. I was watching it live on television when Euan Murray, the Scottish tight-head, was taken off after only seven minutes with an ankle injury. I remember thinking at the time, 'Jeez I could be getting a phone call here.' Sure enough, it came the following morning. McGeechan was on the line. Murray was out for the rest of the tour. Could I travel straightaway? I could. I didn't tell him that I'd been idle since the season ended, but all of a sudden I was a bit worried.

The Southern Kings match was on a Tuesday. The first Test against the Springboks was the following Saturday in Durban. I landed in Durban the morning of the match. The next day we moved onto Cape Town for the midweek game against the Emerging Springboks. These were uncapped at senior level, but a lot of them were top provincial players with international potential. McGeechan billed it as the tour's 'fourth Test'. I was picked to start. I had two things in my favour: Cape Town is at sea level, as opposed to some South African venues which are at high altitude and usually have a bone-dry pitch in summer; and it was pissing rain on the night. If the sun had been beating down on me, I'd have blown a few head gaskets from the lack of training. But actually I felt fresh from the lay-off and played as well as I ever did in South Africa. My opposite number was Wian du Preez, who ended up at Munster a few months later.

This was a scaled-down operation from the tour of New Zealand four years earlier. Everyone travelled together; there was a better effort made to keep the midweek and Test sides united; it was a happier camp all round. The second Test in Pretoria was a tremendous game of rugby. Poor old Rog took a battering late in the game and ended up conceding the long-distance penalty in injury time that Morne Steyn converted. South Africa won the Test and the series with that kick. I wasn't involved, I watched it from the stands. But Adam Jones came off injured early in the second half and was out for the third and final Test in Johannesburg. I felt I was in with a good shout of getting a start in that game. Phil Vickery had got a rough old time of it in the first Test, and had been dropped for the second. But he was brought back to start the third. I got a place on the bench. McGeechan had coached Vickery at Wasps, and I suppose they had a bit of history together. He said he wanted to give Phil a chance to prove himself again. That pissed me off a bit. I felt he was entitled to give me a chance. Anyway, I did get on with twenty-five minutes left, which was a decent stretch of time, and I ended up thoroughly enjoying it. It was brilliant to get involved in a proper Lions Test match.

And it was brilliant to be part of a historic result too. The Springboks are rarely beaten at Ellis Park, but it happened this day, and it happened in style. Our lads played some fantastic rugby. O'Connell was Lions captain. It was a huge responsibility, and I thought the leadership he showed was very impressive. This game was played on 4 July. Most of the players were heading into their thirteenth month of rugby without a break. With the series lost, fellas could very easily have switched off in the final week. But Paulie made sure it didn't happen. He led by example; he wanted everyone to keep their standards up until the last minute of the last game. The squad had deserved to win the series, and certainly not to lose it in a 3–0 whitewash. Everyone kept going, and we got our reward in Jo'burg.

For me it was a really enjoyable three weeks. In the week between the second and third Tests the squad took off on safari for a couple of days. That was some experience. We headed out from Pretoria; it took us four or five hours to reach our destination in this vast national park. We were staying in this compound that had loads of little chalets for sleeping; dinner was barbecued on big fires out in the open air. We did a night tour in jeeps to see the wildlife. You had to get up in the middle of the night and drive around for a couple of hours to see what you could find. We came across this herd of elephants, maybe twenty of them, and seeing them up close made you realise how massive they are. Television doesn't do them justice. The adults must've been twelve, fifteen feet high. They are magnificent animals. Eventually we came across a pair of lions, but the day was getting hotter and they were heading for cover. The staff took us then to a park where the lions were kept in cages. We might've been Lions, but these were the real deal. They brought out a one-year-old cub for us to put our hands on and pet. He was already fairly formidable-looking. I had seen a couple of lions in the wild on the Irish tour of South Africa in '98. They are incredibly strong, powerful athletes. We went to another safari park that time, and the rangers had a good idea where the lions would be hanging around. There was a full-sized carcass in the back of our jeep; it looked like an antelope or one of those breeds. This thing must've weighed about 250 kilos. We finally came across a family of lions. The ranger opened the rear door of the jeep and hung the carcass out the back. Then this big adult male trotted over, sank his jaws into the antelope, and dragged it away. We were going, 'Holy shit! Did you see that?!' He could've picked any of us up like a doll.

During the '09 safari a troupe of dancers put on a show for us after dinner one night. It was traditional singing and dancing, but it wasn't what you'd get in Bunratty Castle. It was in this big open-air hut that had a straw roof on it. The dancers were all in traditional costume. There was no artificial lighting; it was lit by a big bonfire in the middle, and you couldn't really see clearly. Then this fella joined them on stage and he was dancing away. But he didn't look right. He wasn't in sync, he didn't have the moves. Then we noticed he was wearing a pair of white sports socks and white runners. The local dancers were barefoot. It turned out to be Ugo Monye! He'd gone away and stripped off and turned up dancing on the side of the stage. Well, we collapsed with the laughing. It was absolutely hilarious. I had tears coming down my face; it was one of the funniest things I ever saw.

The whole tour had a relaxed vibe about it. Fellas were allowed off the leash a bit between games and to have a few beers. No one went mad, but nights like that were great for bonding together a squad of fellas who were essentially strangers. We headed onto Johannesburg after our safari refreshed and ready for the final Test.

I had gotten one Lions cap for the match against Argentina in '05. But the one against the Springboks felt more like the genuine

article. I was delighted to sign off my Lions experience with a cap
and a Test victory. Over the course of two Lions tours I just about
did myself justice performance-wise. I could've played a lot better
in New Zealand, but the two games I played in South Africa
meant that I finished my Lions experience on a high note.

I got my 100th cap for Ireland, against England in Twickenham,
during the 2010 Six Nations. I beat Drico to the ton by a single
game. Not that it was a race between us or anything. Drico was
thirty-one, I was thirty-six. He was going to win dozens more
caps. Rog too was getting close to the century. For me it was more
a race against time. Once I got into the nineties I wanted to make
the ton. I had a dread, for some reason, of finishing on ninety-
nine. As it happened, I became the first Irish player to reach the
landmark. I had to do a bit of media in the days before the game.
I never did much of it over the years, but Kidney told me I'd
have to. When Deccie announced the team to play England at a
meeting that week he threw in a line about Hayes making his
hundred. The players all stood up and started clapping. I was
going red in the face and cringing in my seat. They all knew it, so
they kept going, just to make me more embarrassed. Then the
slagging started about how I was loving all the media attention
and all that stuff. It was their Neanderthal way of congratulating
me, I suppose. In fairness, I have to admit I was delighted to reach
the century. I'm not inclined to give myself too many pats on the
back, but I feel it was a huge achievement to clock up so many
games. Just for the staying power it required.

Anyway, the lads sent me out onto the field in Twickenham
on my own. It was only for about ten seconds but it felt like an
eternity. I felt like a proper tool out there on my own with 80,000
people looking at me. Like, what were you supposed to do? I
threw the ball up in the air and turned around to see if the lads
were coming but they were still hanging back, to let me dangle out
there for another while on my own. My mother was there, along

with Fiona and my sister Rosemary and Uncle Denis. I'm sure it was a proud moment for her. She and Dad had some great days out supporting Munster and Ireland; they'd travelled far and wide; I think it gave them some good memories. No more than myself, they never dreamed it would go so far or last so long. To cap it off, we came from behind to beat England with a Tommy Bowe try five minutes from time. The day couldn't have gone any better.

We beat Wales a fortnight later, the day of Drico's century, and that set us up for a Triple Crown game against Scotland in Dublin. It would be our last game in Croke Park. The new Lansdowne Road was nearing completion, and it'd be ready for the November series of internationals. A win over Scotland would give us our fifth Triple Crown in seven years. They were in a poor vein of form and we were hot favourites to beat them. But who better to turn up and spoil the party than the Scots? I don't know whether we were complacent, or whether we got sidetracked by it being our last game in Croke Park, but we didn't perform and they did. A seventy-ninth-minute penalty by Dan Parks closed it out for them. Scotland was my fifty-fourth consecutive Six Nations game. It turned out to be my last.

I signed my final contract around that time with the IRFU and strapped myself in for the last twelve months of my career. In June 2010 we headed for New Zealand. They gave us a frightful beating in New Plymouth, though we did salvage some pride in the second half. I was picked to start that match but pulled out a few days before with a virus. I'd been training hard and going well, but I just got run down and was suddenly wiped out by the virus. Tony Buckley came in and played out of his skin, despite the dominance of the All Blacks. I came on for the second half against New Zealand Maori a week later, and wasn't involved for the third game, against Australia in Brisbane. For me, it was a total washout of a tour, and I was finding the long-haul flights to that part of the world absolute hell at this stage. I never liked flying in the first place, but being confined to your seat on a plane for more or less thirty-six hours was torture. I couldn't wait to get home.

In November I was left out of a match-day squad for the first time since my international debut in 2000. The new Aviva stadium was being launched with a game against South Africa. Mushy was in at tight-head, Tom Court was backup. I was still in the extended squad for the autumn series, and started against Samoa a week later. I came on for the final twenty-five minutes against the All Blacks a week after that to get my 104th cap. By the time the 2011 Six Nations came round, Mike Ross had also moved up the pecking order, and I had slipped further down. I knew I wouldn't be involved, but it hit me hard enough at the same time. When something like that has been part of your life for eleven years it's difficult not to miss it when it's taken away. I suppose I was suffering from withdrawal symptoms, really. But I knuckled down with Munster for the final months of the season, got my starting place back, and was soon over the disappointment. In fact, I was loving it again. I made up my mind to give the World Cup a proper shot. It would be one last hurrah before the boots were hung up for good.

The Irish team management held a meeting in May in Carton House, Maynooth. There must've been between forty and fifty players there. Anyone with a chance of selection was there. We were told to keep ourselves fit over the summer, but I hadn't intended taking much of an off-season anyway. I wanted to do everything right, just in case an opening in the squad came along. I didn't take a break that summer; I trained continuously, and when we got back to Carton House for pre-season I was flying fit. I was actually setting personal bests in the power scores in the gym. My reflexes, jumping, lifting were all measured and were top notch. We went hard at it through June and July, and I was leaving no stone unturned. I wanted to give myself every chance of making the cut.

The first friendly of the new season was against Scotland in Murrayfield in early August. I came off the bench for the last twenty minutes. A week later I was left out of the squad for the game away to France. Two days after that, back in Carton House, I got the phone call. It was a Monday morning; I was just back from the gym and in my room. My mobile phone rang, Deccie's number was showing. I knew straightaway what was coming. He wasn't ringing for a general chat about hurling or the economy or silage. He asked if I could go down to his room. Okay. He was standing looking out the window when I came in. When he turned round I could tell by his face he had bad news. He didn't enjoy giving anyone bad news. He told me straight up there was no room for me in the squad. They were going with four props. If it was five, I'd have had a good chance. But they'd decided to go with four. I said fine. I didn't argue; I didn't say much at all. The day Warren Gatland told me I'd be getting my first cap, it was a brief conversation. The day I was told I'd played my last was the same. The Scotland game had been my 105th and final cap.

Before I left his room Deccie said he needed me for the game against Connacht four days later. The match had been arranged for one last look at the fringe players before the squad would be announced the following Monday. I asked him if there was much point in me playing. But he said I'd be on standby for the duration of the World Cup and I needed more game time. That match against Connacht was the first and only time I did not want to be on a rugby field. It was a nothing game. We were a scratch team. I had no interest, no motivation. The only reason I'd stayed play-ing was to try and make the World Cup. That was gone, but now I'd have to drag myself out onto the field for a match that meant nothing. I sat in the dressing room in Donnybrook that evening without even a spark of life in me. It was a weird feeling. I thought

I might find something once I got togged out and warmed up. But I was empty inside. I played; my body was on the pitch, but that was about it. I was taken off after fifty minutes, replaced by Marcus Horan. I couldn't wait to get out of there.

In theory, my international career wasn't over at this stage. But the lid was on the coffin and all the nails were buried in it, bar one. It was standing alone; the tip was in the timber, waiting for a few blows of the hammer. I went back to Limerick the night of the Connacht game and phoned up Tony McGahan the next day to go back training with Munster. I remained on standby through September, early October, but no one got injured and the call never came. Someone drove the last nail down and that was it.

In hindsight, it was a blessing in disguise. I wouldn't have been much use to anyone in New Zealand anyway. I'd have been hanging around knowing I was backup to the backup players, training and travelling and training and travelling with no sign of any game time. I'd have struggled. I'd have been bored out of my mind. As it turned out, I got a last little closing chapter with Munster instead, and it was a lovely way to finish the whole thing.

It's common practice to refer to players getting caps for their country, but you don't receive actual caps for most of the games you play. I got a cap for my debut, for my fiftieth game and for my 100th game. The first game I played for Ireland is my all-time favourite memory in rugby. It tops the lot, even the Heineken Cups and the Grand Slam. You won those with your teammates. But this was a personal achievement for yourself, your family and the people who helped you along the way. It was just such a major milestone for me in my life. A fella from Cappamore playing for Ireland. You could call it a dream come true, but I'd never even dreamt it. The nineteenth of February in the year 2000 was a special day.

Since I retired I've had strangers coming up to me in all sorts of places. They shake your hand and say 'Thanks for everything' and 'Enjoy your retirement.' Not just Munster supporters, but people from other provinces who cheered me on in the green of Ireland. I can't thank them enough for all the support they gave me over the years. Representing your country brought with it a big responsibility. You were duty-bound to give your best every time you put on the jersey. More than anything, though, it was an honour and a privilege. To do it more than a hundred times is an achievement I will always cherish.

17

A few weeks before the last game of my career, Tony McGahan asked me if I fancied finishing out the season. Munster were prepared to extend my contract one more time, to the end of May 2012.

It was nice of him to ask, but my mind was made up. I was ready to let go now. It was settled in my head. My career was over. It had reached its natural, organic end. There wasn't a tiny part of me that was tempted to hang on.

I had just turned thirty-eight. I couldn't summon up the same sort of hunger anymore. I was finding stuff like the travelling and the video analysis a chore. The physical training I still enjoyed. I still relished the action on the training ground. But we were spending more and more time doing analysis: reviewing games, previewing games, going over your stats, scrums, lineouts, the works. The level of preparation was increasing every year. Times were changing; the game doesn't stand still, and I was starting to struggle to keep up.

When I left Limerick or Cork after a day of weights and meetings and training, I wanted to leave it behind me. But I was bringing work home with me now. You were supposed to spend time on your laptop looking at footage and throwing in your tuppence worth on what went wrong last week and what we could do better next week. We were getting more and more computerised data; you'd have video footage edited and tailored for each player within hours of a game being over. It was the way to go; new ideas were coming in all the time, and Munster, like every club, had to keep moving forward. The young players were soaking it all up. They were immersed in it. They loved going through the analysis, doing the extras, driving it onto the next level. With some of it I was just going through the motions. I was the old dog, and I wasn't great at learning the new tricks. Put me out on the field and I'd train as hard as anyone. The rest of it, I could take it or leave it.

I suppose the fire in the belly was fading. A big match in Thomond, a big match anywhere, would get me revved up and rearing to go. But various league games in later years, I was finding it harder to light the fire for them. It was taking more of a mental effort to get into the right frame of mind. So if I'd taken up Tony on his offer, I'd only have been fooling the two of us.

I was a lot more enthusiastic about his next proposal. Out of the blue he suggested that Munster could do a training session in Bruff during my last week on the job. I said I'd love it, if it didn't become a sideshow or a distraction for the rest of the squad. But they liked the idea too, so three days before Christmas they did me the honour of turning up at the rugby club that had started me on my way nineteen years earlier. I hadn't trained there myself in over sixteen years. I was finishing back where I started. The wheel had come full circle.

It was a great occasion. A huge crowd turned up. Loads of children were there because they were on their Christmas holidays. There were TV crews and photographers and reporters, so the club ended up getting great exposure. All the players signed autographs and stood in for photos; it was just a happy, festive occasion. And to cap it all, I actually made a line break during the training session. It wasn't even choreographed by the lads to give me a bit of a boost in front of my home crowd. It was a full contact session. But Tomás O'Leary hit me with a super pass; it took out a defender and I was through the gap. I had twenty yards to the try line and I'd say Usain Bolt wouldn't have caught me. The crowd let out an almighty cheer when I went over. There must've been a bit of luck in the air that day because I could've done a hundred training sessions before this one and never got a line break like that. It was all good.

Coming out of the tunnel in Thomond Park four nights later for my final game I saw they had the banner draped across it. The one that says, GO ON BULL TIS YOUR FIELD. It's fairly well known at this stage, I suppose. I have no idea who came up with that nickname. Some people address me as John. Some use the full handle when they're greeting me: 'John Hayes'. The English and Welsh lads on a Lions tour would call me 'Hayesie'. But an awful lot of people call me 'Bull'. Friends, strangers, teammates. 'Howya, Bull.' I never minded. I actually liked it, and it became second nature a long time ago now. I didn't have the nickname when I was at Bruff or Shannon. It only started when I moved onto the Munster scene. But I can't for the life of me remember how it started or who started it. It caught on fairly quick anyway, and took on a life of its own. I presume it's farming-related in some way or other. It might have had something to do with my build too. I suppose, realistically, no one was ever going to nickname me 'Greyhound' anyway.

The week after I retired I received the regular group text that goes out to all the players from the Munster office. It would have our itinerary for the week laid out. Monday morning, a weights session with the Limerick-based lads in UL, about ninety minutes in total. The Cork-based players would do their weights session in Cork Institute of Technology. Lunch and then off to Mitchelstown for a full meeting of the squad. Mitchelstown was more or less a halfway house between Limerick and Cork, and in recent years a local hotel there was being used as a venue for squad meetings. The Monday meeting would be a review of the match at the weekend. Forwards would look at the performance of the set piece, backs would look at various moves and patterns. Problems would be analysed, and we'd plan to address them in training that week. Tuesdays the Cork boys would travel up to UL for a full day's work. We'd spend the morning indoors. The upcoming match would be previewed; we'd have information on the opposition. Forwards would have a lineout meeting and a scrum meeting; backs would have a meeting on the specific parts of their game. Lunch then, and out onto the pitch in the afternoon. The heavy work would be done Tuesday afternoons, practising defence and attack against live opposition; scrums, line-outs, tackling drills, defensive drills, breakdown drills. Wednesday was a recovery day; you'd have a swimming pool session to allevi-ate the usual soreness, stiffness and bruising. Thursday mornings the Limerick lads would travel to Cork. The forwards would finalise their lineout moves for that weekend and make sure every-one was up to speed on the calls. The backs would be wrapping up their stuff at a meeting too. Then a light session on the field for an hour or so, followed by lunch, and that would be it for the day. Friday was travelling day if we had an away game, with a chartered flight from Shannon Airport to Cork Airport to pick up the lads there, or vice versa. Then on to England, France or wherever. Otherwise Friday was a full day off. Complete rest and plenty of water. Saturday you went into match mode. On Monday morn-ing, repeat the process.

That was your working life, more or less, as a pro rugby player. The game itself only took up one day. The rest was your daily real-ity and took up most of your career. People would say it was a life of leisure, and I suppose it'd be hard to argue, compared to a lot of other jobs. You couldn't but say it was a nice way to make a living. But it was a serious business too, and it got more serious as the years went on. And if you had to face into those weights sessions every week, you mightn't consider it too leisurely. They were fairly gruelling. The games themselves, you were getting a fair old hammering any time you took to the field. You were guaranteed to be hurt and sore. But the truth is, I'd have done it all for free. We all would, or most of us anyway. When I started out I was looking at a career hopefully as a serious amateur, like the GAA players nowadays. I never dreamed I would one day make it my livelihood. But then almost overnight the game turned professional, and I happened to be around when it started. It was the luck of being in the right place at the right time. I jumped on board just as the train was pulling out of the station.

The first week I got the group text I read it, more or less out of habit. A week later I got the next one and glanced down through it. The third week I didn't even open it. I had moved on. I wasn't missing the daily grind, not even a small bit. Then they stopped sending them. At the start of February the Ireland squad was getting ready for their first game of the 2012 Six Nations campaign. It was always a hugely exciting time of the year. I loved the buzz and the energy coming into the Six Nations. And standing in line for the national anthem was a thrill and an honour that never diminished. I got the shivers and the emotions every single time the music started. The first match was against Wales. I watched it at home and felt a few pangs as the lads stood in line for the anthems. It was a slight feeling of loss, I suppose, and regret that I'd never get to do it again. But at the same time, a few days earlier I'd watched the sports news on television one evening and they were doing a report on the build-up to the match. They showed pictures of the lads going through their drills in training, hitting the tackle bags and rehearsing their moves. And I thought to myself, 'Oh, Jesus, no. Couldn't go through that again. Couldn't face that again.' I was gone from rugby, in body and soul.

*

Sally was born in May 2006, and Róisín in March 2009. It changes a man, a lot more than winning a Grand Slam does. Fiona and the kids are the best things that ever happened me. And it got even better in August 2012 when our son was born. We've named him Bill. We're thrilled to have him and his sisters are already doting on him.

We built a house on the land at home in Cappamore, and we hope to give our kids the good childhood experiences that we had growing up. They have their grandparents beside them. They'll have the space and freedom that comes with living in the countryside. Hopefully, they'll grow up well-grounded and happy here. If they want to play some sports, that'll be great too.

Between the farm and the family I'm looking forward to a long and contented life. I was steeped to get out of the game without any of the injuries that could affect the quality of your life in later years. Lots of fellas who played my position ended up needing operations on their shoulders or neck or back. The worst I can complain of is a bit of stiffness. I never needed an operation, I never missed more than a couple of weeks with injury. I'm convinced it was because I came late to the game. I hadn't suffered wear and tear while I was still developing. I had physically matured before I started taking the hits and the impacts. It helped me last longer in the game, and I was better able to absorb the punishment.

I don't think I'll go coaching rugby teams. If either of us is going to be a coach, it'll more likely be Fiona. She did three years as coach to the Munster women's team before the kids came along.

But I still would like to give something back, probably on an individual basis. I could definitely see myself doing something like that. If Bruff were to come to me with a promising young prop forward, I would like to help him in his development. A lot of people helped me. He wouldn't have to be a local lad either. If a player from a non-rugby background wanted advice on the game, I'd be happy to pass on whatever I know. Because I know from personal experience that it's harder when you're coming to it from the outside. I'd like to tell him that it doesn't matter if he didn't go to the right school, or didn't grow up in the tradition. It's a big reason why I wrote this book. Rugby is a great game to play, and it can open up a new world for you too. You can live it and enjoy it. It doesn't matter where you come from or who you are.

Before that first Six Nations game in 2012 I got a text from Donncha O'Callaghan. He was checking in, seeing how I was doing. In fairness, it was very nice of Donners, I suppose, very thoughtful, quite sensitive. I texted him back: 'Sorry, don't recognise the number, who is this? When I retired I deleted a lot of numbers I wouldn't need again. Yours is obviously one of them!' I got a fair mouthful back from him.

I decided to make a clean break once I packed it in. Part of that was making a conscious decision not to wear a tracksuit. I haven't worn a tracksuit since I retired. I'm a civilian now, I suppose you could call it. I'll probably wear one around the house at some stage, because they're comfortable to relax in of an evening. But I won't be caught dead in a Munster or Ireland tracksuit in public. I never would've done it much anyway. I have a stack of them at home but they won't see the light of day. Being a Munster or an Ireland player isn't my identity anymore.

I will meet my former teammates many times I'm sure in the years to come. I'm more likely to meet the Munster lads, but I'll steer clear of them while they're in Munster mode. I've a fair idea where they'll be most days and there's no danger of me running into them. There's a restaurant in Castletroy where we used to go for lunch most days. I like to go there myself any time I'm in Limerick, but if I know there's a chance that ten or twelve of them will be in there, I'll go somewhere else. The first thing they'd do is slag the arse off me anyway. They'll have finished a weights session that morning or a video review or an afternoon pitch session. That's their world now, not mine. Some of those lads, I played with them through thick and thin. I'll watch their games on television and wish them well. For the moment though, I'd prefer to meet them in a different setting, just socially, without any of the rugby baggage. It's a clean break from the environment, not from the individuals.

And when we do meet up in the years to come, I suppose we'll still be taking the mick and slagging each other and having plenty of laughs. Between us all we've a fair few yarns and stories and comical moments stacked up at this stage. That should keep us going for a while. We'll be talking about our kids and life in general, like ordinary friends do. I certainly won't be talking about the '06 Heineken final or the Grand Slam or some famous night when we did great things in Thomond Park. I won't be hanging onto that. It's done, it's over. It's up to others to assess whatever legacy we managed to leave behind us, for Munster and Ireland.

But I suppose I can talk about the legacy the game left me personally. It changed my life. It challenged me mentally and physically. You had a feeling always that you were out on the edge. There was no security, no safety net. Every Saturday or Sunday you played you were tested on the pitch and judged off it. You were on show, you were exposed. And if you weren't right and ready you'd be found out. It was great to be tested like that week in week out. It pushed you out of your comfort zone. I had never been challenged like that before. School didn't do it to me, and, with all due respect, I doubt it if farming or welding would have either.

I don't know if playing serious rugby, or any sport, changes your character. But maybe it brings out of you what's in there. Stuff that you didn't know was there. It forces you to find out things about yourself. What kind of mental strength do you have? How far can you push yourself? Is there more in you? I found out that there was always a bit more in you than you thought. You could find another few per cent of willpower if it was dragged out of you. And you learned to deal with adversity and success. You got your gut sickened with defeats and disappointments. And you experienced some amazing moments of pure joy. It was all there, it all went into the mix. And along the way you had a barrel of laughs too, with fellas who became your best friends.

I couldn't have asked for more. I didn't expect the half of it. It was for me the journey of a lifetime.

Statistics

LIONS

- Toured New Zealand in 2005 and sent out to South Africa as a replacement in 2009.
- 7 appearances as a Lion including 2 Tests (1 win and 1 draw).

LIONS TEST APPEARANCES CAP BY CAP

CAP	DATE	OPPONENTS	VENUE	RESULT
1	23.05.2005	Argentina	Cardiff	D 25–25
2	04.07.2009	South Africa	Johannesburg	W 28–9

IRELAND

- Toured South Africa in 1998 before making Test debut during the 2000 Six Nations Championship against Scotland.
- Member of Ireland Grand Slam side 2009 and four Triple Crown sides (2004, 2006, 2007 and 2009).
- First Irishman to win 100 Test caps for his country (when he played against England in 2010).
- Won 105 caps for Ireland (won 66, drew two and lost 37)

scoring one Test try (against Scotland in 2005). Insists he did NOT score against Romania in Limerick in 2002.

- Ireland's oldest player to win a cap when he appeared against Scotland aged 37 years, 277 days in August 2011, his last match.
- Retired as the second most-capped prop in the world behind Jason Leonard of England.

IRELAND TEST APPEARANCES CAP BY CAP

CAP	DATE	OPPONENTS	VENUE	RESULT
1	19.02.2000	Scotland	Dublin	W 44–22
2	04.03.2000	Italy	Dublin	W 60–13
3	19.03.2000	France	Paris	W 27–25
4	01.04.2000	Wales	Dublin	L 19–23
5	03.06.2000	Argentina	Buenos Aires	L 23–34
6	17.06.2000	Canada	Markham	D 27–27
7	11.11.2000	Japan	Dublin	W 78–9
8	19.11.2000	South Africa	Dublin	L 18–28
9	03.02.2001	Italy	Rome	W 41–22
10	17.02.2001	France	Dublin	W 22–15
11	02.06.2001	Romania	Bucharest	W 37–3
12	22.09.2001	Scotland	Murrayfield	L 10–32
13	13.10.2001	Wales	Cardiff	W 36–6
14	20.10.2001	England	Dublin	W 20–14
15	11.11.2001	Samoa	Dublin	W 35–8
16	17.11.2001	New Zealand	Dublin	L 29–40
17	03.02.2002	Wales	Dublin	W 54–10
18	16.02.2002	England	Twickenham	L 11–45
19	02.03.2002	Scotland	Dublin	W 43–22
20	23.03.2002	Italy	Dublin	W 32–17
21	06.04.2002	France	Paris	L 5–44
22	15.06.2002	New Zealand	Dunedin	L 6–15

CAP	DATE	OPPONENTS	VENUE	RESULT
23	22.06.2002	New Zealand	Auckland	L 8–40
24	07.09.2002	Romania	Limerick	W 39–8
25	21.09.2002	Russia	Krasnoyarsk	W 35–3
26	28.09.2002	Georgia	Dublin	W 63–14
27	09.11.2002	Australia	Dublin	W 18–9
28	17.11.2002	Fiji	Dublin	W 64–17
29	23.11.2002	Argentina	Dublin	W 16–7
30	16.02.2003	Scotland	Murrayfield	W 36–6
31	22.02.2003	Italy	Rome	W 37–13
32	08.03.2003	France	Dublin	W 15–12
33	22.03.2003	Wales	Cardiff	W 25–24
34	30.03.2003	England	Dublin	L 6–42
35	11.10.2003	Romania	Gosford	W 45–17
36	19.10.2003	Namibia	Sydney	W 64–7
37	26.10.2003	Argentina	Adelaide	W 16–15
38	01.11.2003	Australia	Melbourne	L 16–17
39	09.11.2003	France	Melbourne	L 21–43
40	14.02.2004	France	Paris	L 17–35
41	22.02.2004	Wales	Dublin	W 36–15
42	06.03.2004	England	Twickenham	W 19–13
43	20.03.2004	Italy	Dublin	W 19–3
44	27.03.2004	Scotland	Dublin	W 37–16
45	12.06.2004	South Africa	Bloemfontein	L 17–31
46	19.06.2004	South Africa	Cape Town	L 17–26
47	13.11.2004	South Africa	Dublin	W 17–12
48	20.11.2004	United States	Dublin	W 55–6
49	27.11.2004	Argentina	Dublin	W 21–19
50	06.02.2005	Italy	Rome	W 28–17
51	12.02.2005	Scotland	Murrayfield	W 40–13
52	27.02.2005	England	Dublin	W 19–13
53	12.03.2005	France	Dublin	L 19–26
54	19.03.2005	Wales	Cardiff	L 20–32

John Hayes

CAP	DATE	OPPONENTS	VENUE	RESULT
55	12.11.2005	New Zealand	Dublin	L 7–45
56	19.11.2005	Australia	Dublin	L 14–30
57	26.11.2005	Romania	Dublin	W 43–12
58	04.02.2006	Italy	Dublin	W 26–16
59	11.02.2006	France	Paris	L 31–43
60	26.02.2006	Wales	Dublin	W 31–5
61	11.03.2006	Scotland	Dublin	W 15–9
62	18.03.2006	England	Twickenham	W 28–24
63	10.06.2006	New Zealand	Hamilton	L 23–34
64	17.06.2006	New Zealand	Auckland	L 17–27
65	24.06.2006	Australia	Perth	L 15–37
66	11.11.2006	South Africa	Dublin	W 32–15
67	19.11.2006	Australia	Dublin	W 21–6
68	26.11.2006	Pacific Islands	Dublin	W 61–17
69	04.02.2007	Wales	Cardiff	W 19–9
70	11.02.2007	France	Dublin	L 17–20
71	24.02.2007	England	Dublin	W 43–13
72	10.03.2007	Scotland	Murrayfield	W 19–18
73	17.03.2007	Italy	Rome	W 51–24
74	11.08.2007	Scotland	Murrayfield	L 21–31
75	24.08.2007	Italy	Belfast	W 23–20
76	09.09.2007	Namibia	Bordeaux	W 32–17
77	15.09.2007	Georgia	Bordeaux	W 14–10
78	21.09.2007	France	Paris	L 3–25
79	30.09.2007	Argentina	Paris	L 15–30
80	02.02.2008	Italy	Dublin	W 16–11
81	09.02.2008	France	Paris	L 21–26
82	23.02.2008	Scotland	Dublin	W 34–13
83	08.03.2008	Wales	Dublin	L 12–16
84	15.03.2008	England	Twickenham	L 10–33
85	07.06.2008	New Zealand	Wellington	L 11–21
86	14.06.2008	Australia	Melbourne	L 12–18

CAP	DATE	OPPONENTS	VENUE	RESULT
87	08.11.2008	Canada	Limerick	W 55–0
88	15.11.2008	New Zealand	Dublin	L 3–22
89	22.11.2008	Argentina	Dublin	W 17–3
90	07.02.2009	France	Dublin	W 30–21
91	15.02.2009	Italy	Rome	W 38–9
92	28.02.2009	England	Dublin	W 14–13
93	14.03.2009	Scotland	Murrayfield	W 22–15
94	21.03.2009	Wales	Cardiff	W 17–15
95	15.11.2009	Australia	Dublin	D 20–20
96	21.11.2009	Fiji	Dublin	W 41–6
97	28.11.2009	South Africa	Dublin	W 15–10
98	06.02.2010	Italy	Dublin	W 29–11
99	13.02.2010	France	Paris	L 10–33
100	27.02.2010	England	Twickenham	W 20–16
101	13.03.2010	Wales	Dublin	W 27–12
102	20.03.2010	Scotland	Dublin	L 20–23
103	13.11.2010	Samoa	Dublin	W 20–10
104	20.11.2010	New Zealand	Dublin	L 18–38
105	06.08.2011	Scotland	Murrayfield	L 6–10

MUNSTER

- Senior debut August 1997 against Edinburgh.
- 212 competitive appearances scoring four tries (20 points).
- Competition honours: one Celtic League (2003), one Celtic Cup (2005), two Magners League (2009 and 2011) and two Heineken Cup (2006 and 2008) titles.
- First player to make 100 Heineken Cup appearances (when he played against Northampton in November 2011).
- Last match December 2011 against Connacht in the Rabo/Direct League.

MUNSTER APPEARANCES SEASON BY SEASON

SEASON	Heineken Cup	Amlin	Rabo/ Direct	Magners League	Celtic League	Celtic Cup	Irish Inter/ Pro	Friendlies	TOTAL
1998/99	7	0	0	0	0	0	3	1	11
1999/00	9	0	0	0	0	0	6	1	16
2000/01	8	0	0	0	0	0	6	0	14
2001/02	7	0	0	0	6	0	2	0	15
2002/03	8	0	0	0	7	0	0	0	15
2003/04	8	0	0	0	2	0	0	0	10
2004/05	7	0	0	0	8	3	0	0	18
2005/06	9	0	0	0	10	0	0	0	19
2006/07	7	0	0	6	0	0	0	0	13
2007/08	9	0	0	8	0	0	0	0	17
2008/09	8	0	0	8	0	0	0	0	16
2009/10	6	0	0	7	0	0	0	0	13
2010/11	6	2	0	16	0	0	0	0	24
2011/12	2	0	9	0	0	0	0	0	11
OVERALL	101	2	9	45	33	3	17	2	212

Acknowledgements

It started with Bruff RFC. I owe a big thanks to the team mates who showed me the ropes, and to the supporters and volunteers who kept the club going in those years. Willie Conway was a mentor to me when I needed one. He believed in me and never stopped encouraging me.

I had a brilliant time at Shannon. I'd like to thank all the players, supporters and coaches who helped me on my way there.

When I landed in New Zealand, the Nally family took me in. Vin and Jan: I will never forget your hospitality and generosity. A sincere thanks also to everyone at the Marist rugby club in Invercargill for two great years.

The Munster team I played on gave me a lifetime's memories. But I started out with a lot of great long-serving veterans and finished up with the new, young generation coming through. It was a pleasure sharing the dressing room with all those players. My thanks also to the management and backroom staff for making it a great working environment.

Playing for Ireland gave me the proudest moments of my life. The support I got from team mates, coaches and back-up staff was outstanding. A big thanks to everyone who made it possible.

*

Mam and Dad followed me everywhere and supported me through thick and thin. They were there for me long before I ever picked up a rugby ball and are there for me still.

The same goes for my sisters and brothers. Rosemary, Carmel, Mike and Tom managed to follow my career without passing much remarks one way or the other, which was exactly how I preferred it.

To my agent John Baker, sincere thanks for all your advice and guidance over the years.

Thanks also to Rhea Halford and the staff at Simon & Schuster who worked on this book. Tommy Conlon had a job on his hands, putting my thoughts into words. I'm grateful to Tommy for his help.

Special mention to Drico for his Foreword. I wouldn't believe the half of it, but I appreciate it all the same.

Finally, to Fiona: your love and help and support over the last eleven years has meant the world to me.

(Tommy Conlon thanks Jane and Finbar Conlon for their unstinting support. Thanks also to Anna Barrett for her sterling work on transcription.)

For Fiona. And for Sally, Róisín and Bill.

Index

Note: 'JH' denotes John Hayes. The names of countries, regions, etc., refer to rugby teams unless otherwise indicated. Page numbers in *italic* denote entries in the Statistics section.

Ahane GAA Club 59